FORBIDDEN NATION

A History of Taiwan

FORBIDDEN NATION

A History of Taiwan

Jonathan Manthorpe

palgrave
macmillan

FORBIDDEN NATION

First published 2002 by
PALGRAVE MACMILLAN™
175 Fifth Avenue, New York, N.Y. 10010 and
Houndmills, Basingstoke, Hampshire, England RG21 6XS.
Companies and representatives throughout the world.

PALGRAVE MACMILLAN IS THE GLOBAL ACADEMIC IMPRINT OF THE PALGRAVE MACMILLAN division of St. Martin's Press, LLC and of Palgrave Macmillan Ltd. Macmillan® is a registered trademark in the United States, United Kingdom and other countries. Palgrave is a registered trademark in the European Union and other countries.

ISBN 1-4039-6981-7 hardback

Library of Congress Cataloging-in-Publication Data
Forbidden nation: the history of Taiwan/ Jonathan Manthorpe.
p. cm.
Includes index.
ISBN 1-4039-6981-7
1. Taiwan—History—2000– I. Title: History of Taiwan. II. Title.

DS799.844.M36 2005
951.24'9—dc22

2005047413

A catalogue record for this book is available from the British Library.

Design by Letra Libre, Inc.

First edition: October 2005
10 9 8 7 6 5 4 3 2 1
Printed in the United States of America

CONTENTS

ACKNOWLEDGMENTS

My first visit to Taiwan was in the mid-1970s. Chiang Kai-shek had died a few months before and the government was a colonial military dictatorship thinly glossed with some trappings of democracy. The authorities regarded visiting foreign journalists with only marginally less suspicion than did the mainland government in Beijing. My impression was of a forbidding and unhappy place.

That visit was part of my first tour of Asia and the beginning of my career as a foreign correspondent. I went on to postings in Europe and Africa before returning to Asia and a base in Hong Kong in 1993. I visited Taiwan soon after my return to Asia. It was a different place from the one I remembered. Taipei was vibrant and cosmopolitan, already showing the signs of renewal that have made it one of the most attractive cities in Asia. The general mood was optimistic and life seemed to offer a wealth of possibilities. In Africa I had reported on many countries attempting to make the transition from colonial rule to democracy. Taiwan, in contrast, was clearly making the same transition with many more hopes of success than I had seen in places like Zimbabwe, Zambia, Angola, Namibia, Ethiopia, Nigeria, and South Africa. It was clear too that political and social changes were more soundly based in Taiwan than in some other Asian countries where similar transitions were underway at the same period. I wondered what had given Taiwan its advantage. I started exploring the island's history even as I reported on the final stages of democratic transition in the 1990s. This book is the product of that exploration and my response to what I found.

Writing in English about societies that use variations of the Chinese language and written characters poses a very basic problem. How should one spell Chinese names using the Roman alphabet? This problem goes beyond accuracy; it is a highly political issue. Many sounds used in the Chinese language and dialects have no easy equivalent in English. Several systems have been developed over the years and under different political regimes. Thus the system that a writer in English uses is frequently seen as a political statement of his or her approach to the subject. There are two main systems for the Romanization of Chinese names. There is the Wade-Giles system, first developed in the mid-nineteenth century and which is used on Taiwan, and there is pinyin, a simplified form which was instituted by the Communists after they came to power on the mainland in 1949. I have had long discussions with both Taiwanese and Chinese about which system I should use. My main debt on these questions of English spelling is to Dr. Charles Yang, former president of the Taiwan Cultural Association in Vancouver, and Mark Yang. They gave thoughtful advice not only on the question of names, but on several other aspects of the manuscript.

While I tend to regard the Wade-Giles system as giving a better rendering of Chinese in the Roman alphabet than does pinyin, I have decided to compromise in favor of the reader. Most readers will now be familiar with mainland names rendered in pinyin. For example, Beijing is now established as the English spelling of the name of the Chinese capital rather than the older Wade-Giles version, Peking. Similarly, Mao Zedong is now the more common spelling of the name of the Communist revolutionary leader in place of Mao Tse-tung under the Wade-Giles system. So I have used pinyin spelling for mainland names and Wade-Giles for those on Taiwan. Where older names, such as the Fujian provincial port city of Amoy, appear in quotations I have put the modern name, in this case Xiamen, in brackets.

There are similar questions about how to render Japanese characters into English. There are, for example, several ways of expressing the long "o" which occurs at the end of many Japanese names such as Tokyo and Kyoto. After much discussion I have decided to follow the stance of most English-language Japanese publications, which is not to include any accent at all.

The gestation period of this book has been so long that the list of those whose help and guidance I should recognize is massive. I must therefore confine myself to people most directly involved or consulted in the production of this book. I cannot neglect to mention, however, my editors at the Southam News Service—Nick Hills, Jim Travers, and Aileen McCabe—without whose support my career as a foreign correspondent would not have followed the same path.

Robert Mackwood of the Seventh Avenue Literary Agency understood the idea of the book from the start and championed it through thick and thin. Toby Wahl of Palgrave Macmillan has been an essential link, tempering and bending the author's inclination to explore the story's side streams toward what's best for the reader. Alan Bradshaw of Palgrave Macmillan has done a splendid job of editing the manuscript as well as engaging in an interesting exploration of those English words and phrases that need translation when they cross the Canada-United States border. I am indebted to many members of

Vancouver's community of immigrants from Taiwan, especially Dr. Charles Yang and James Chou, for their encouragement and readiness to spend hours drinking tea and chatting in order to help me understand aspects of Taiwan's story. On Taiwan I am grateful to Kang Tien-wang and the staff of the Taipei Artist Village, where much of this book was written; my stay there would have been a more emotionally exhausting experience without the delightful company of that community. Dr. Thomas Chen, Taiwan's representative in Canada, and several members of the staff of the Government Information Office in Taipei were of essential help in arranging interviews for me with a broad range of people on the island. I am grateful for the assistance of Peter Chen, Wendy Lin Ching-wen, Carmen Tsai, James Yu, Jason Yuan, and Liu Wei-ling. Several rotations of diplomats at Canada's unofficial embassy in Taipei, the Canadian Trade Office, have been of unstinting assistance during my many visits to Taiwan over the years. Office directors David Mulroney, Ted Lipman, and Gordon Holden have all offered advice and analysis from their bountiful experience in the region. Many staff members have been equally helpful. In the context of this book I must mention James Mitchell, Weldon Epp, Sylvia Yan, and Sumeeta Chandavarkar.

Among those who talked to me about their visions of Taiwan's past, present, and future were Mayaw Biho, convener of the Amis Tribe Film Festival, Dr. Bien Chiang of the Institute of Ethnology at Academica Sinica, and Ku Lin-lin of the Graduate School of Journalism at the National Taiwan University. There was Voyu Yakumangana of the Association for Taiwan Indigenous People's Policies; Wei Ti, professor of mass communications at Tamkang University and a member of Taiwan Media Watch; and Dr. Chao Chien-min of the Sun Yat-sen Graduate Institute for Social Science and Humanities at Chengchi University. Yao Chia-wen, president of the Examination Yuan, was generous with his time recalling his experiences of the 1979 Kaohsiung Incident, and as a political prisoner afterward, and discussing his current plans for Taiwan's constitutional reform. Dr. Ho Szu-yin, the director of International Affairs for the Kuomintang and professor at the Department of Political Science of Chengchi University, was a valuable source of views on Taiwan's political present and future. Dr. Hung Chien-chao of the Kuomintang-linked National Policy Foundation was a pleasure to meet and talk to after having enjoyed and benefited from his writing for so many years. Peng Ming-min, senior advisor to President Chen Shui-bian, and the father of the modern movement for Taiwan nationhood, was as welcoming and eager to exchange views as he has always been. Dr. Leng Tse-kang of the Institute of International relations at Chengchi University was most helpful in giving regional context to the Taiwan issue. Lin Sheng-yi of the Taiwan Indigenous Culture Alliance showed me aspects of aboriginal history and modern influences I had not discovered elsewhere, as did Dr. Tong Chun-fa of the College of Indigenous Studies at Donghua University. Dr. Wu Shuh-min, the President of the Foundation of Medical Professionals Alliance in Taiwan, gave me fresh insights into the passion and logic that drives many of the islanders' desire for internationally recognized nationhood. Chao Yu-ling, professor of choreography at the National Taiwan University of Arts, was a patient tutor on the emergence and expression of a distinct Taiwanese cultural identity. I am indebted to Joann Yu, who made the index with care and imagination in the face of a seemingly impossible deadline.

Needless to say, this book does not reflect the views of these and many other people with whom I have spoken. It is my distillation of all that I have garnered from words and print, and represents my views alone.

I must also thank my wife Petrina and sons Nicholas, Tobyn, and Thomas for their support and forbearance during a period when I was only a bit-player in family life. Tobyn gets extra thanks for preparing the two maps that accompany this book.

Jonathan Manthorpe
Vancouver, June 2005

PREFACE

Taiwan is entering an era when the four-hundred-year-old dream of the island's 23 million people to be internationally recognized as sovereign masters of their own house will be won or lost. Since the early 1600s the efforts of the Taiwanese settlers and pioneers, mostly from China, to create their own nation on the island have been suppressed or smothered by a succession of colonial administrations. The voice of Taiwanese aspirations began to gain volume and power in the late 1980s with the transition to democracy. The affirmation of Taiwan as a distinct society—predominantly ethnic Chinese but not of China—has blossomed since then. It has been nurtured by the election of successive administrations dedicated to severing the remaining links of Taiwan's colonial past and establishing nationhood.

The question for Taiwanese is how to achieve that end. The growth of democracy has unleashed its own dynamic on the island. Taiwanese are celebrating their distinctiveness and exploring their cultural potential as never before now that colonialism by outsiders has been largely removed. The last interlopers, the mainland nationalist Kuomintang government, whose remnants fled to Taiwan in 1949 and established there a 50-year regime of reasonably benevolent despotism, have been largely absorbed. What is rapidly emerging is a unique country fashioned from its own distinct history and geography. It is also a composite society with not always friendly internal relations between the aborigines, the close-knit Hakka, the majority Hoklo, and the recently arrived mainlanders. Taiwan's aborigines are ethnic Malays from Southeast Asia whose ancestors migrated to the island over thousands of years before recorded history. Intermarriage with Chinese over the past five hundred years means that about 70 percent of modern Taiwanese have aboriginal blood. The Hakka are ethnically mainstream Han Chinese, but their distinct culture and language has made them outcasts within Chinese society. Hakka origins are in northern China, but over hundreds of years they were pushed down into the mountainous border country between Guangdong and Fujian provinces. Many Hakka became sea nomads and were among the first Chinese to establish outposts on Taiwan. Hoklo is the name given to natives of Fujian province. They make up the majority of modern Taiwanese. The mainlanders who came to Taiwan after 1945 are of mixed origins, but many came from the two last outposts of Generalissimo Chiang Kai-shek's Kuomintang administration: Shanghai on China's east coast and Guangdong province north and west of Hong Kong.

About half of Taiwan's people applaud President Chen Shui-bian's policy of asserting at every opportunity the island's independence and cultural individuality. Most of the other half quietly support the aim, but not Chen's means. They think Chen's style unnecessarily goads China and is an abuse of American friendship. They think the Chen administration is putting at risk the extraordinary economic success and social development Taiwan has achieved in recent decades.

Most countries emerging from colonial rule have faced similar internal stresses and strains. But Taiwan languishes in a muddy legal quagmire without historical precedent. China claims to own the island, which is just 100 miles (160 kilometers) off the mainland's coast. The case for China's sovereignty over the island, especially by the communist one-party government currently in power in Beijing, is frail. The new generation of leaders in Beijing, however, is steeped in old propaganda of imperial hubris and new pride in their country's growing economic power and regional political influence. For them Taiwan's de facto independence is unfinished business from China's civil war in 1949 that brought the Communists to power in Beijing and the ousted Kuomintang government to exile on Taiwan. Reclaiming Taiwan would also, in Beijing's eyes, finally end the "humiliation" that began in the 1840s when industrialized powers grabbed chunks of China as colonies and trading enclaves.

Since the 1970s China has used the lure of its vast market to blackmail most governments into consigning Taiwan and its people to an opaque international status. Governments the world over have been seduced by the lure of China's market of 1.3 billion people for goods and services. That lure has become ever more enticing as China's economy has developed. The hypocrisy of this deal is especially stark in the capitals of Europe and North America, where it would normally be an easy choice between a repressive one-party state in Beijing and Taiwan's vibrant democracy. Taiwan has been betrayed by greed and the age-old Western missionary zeal to transform China. Taiwan is a de facto independent nation upholding all the Western political values of freely elected and open government, and the rule of law by an independent judiciary. Yet Taiwan is denied membership in the United Nations and remains in legal limbo because of Beijing's persistent diplomatic pressure on the international stage. Even the island's main ally, the United States, refuses to give Taiwan formal diplomatic recognition or support its membership in international organizations.

Beijing has made some half-hearted efforts to persuade Taiwan to agree to unification with the mainland. It has proposed some variation of the "one country, two systems" formula used to frame the return to Chinese sovereignty of Hong Kong in 1997 and Macau in 2000 after centuries of British and Portuguese colonial rule. China's leaders, however, have shown no understanding or sympathy for the workings of free and open societies, especially in Hong Kong. Taiwanese have been repulsed by those examples. Beijing's passion for the dominance of one country constantly overrides respect for the promised autonomy of the peoples gathered into the embrace of the Chinese motherland. The deciding, unacceptable issue for most Taiwanese, however, is Beijing's unwavering insistence that the islanders must acknowledge they are subjects of the Communist Party, that they submit to Beijing's view that there is only "one China" and Taiwan is part of it, before negotiations begin.

The alternative to Taiwan's submission, Beijing warns, is war and invasion of the island by mainland forces. China's legal pretext for military intervention is that Taiwan is merely a "rebel province." Therefore an invasion would be only an internal police action; an entirely domestic affair. Taiwan, however, is well armed and has powerful friends. It will be some years before China could launch an attack on Taiwan with any certainty of success. Beijing must calculate too what the effect of an invasion would be on its sustained efforts in Asia and beyond to present modern China as a reliable business partner and diplomatic player on the international stage.

Sustained economic growth in China is vital to the maintenance of internal civic order and the unchallenged authority of the Communist Party. The country has quite massive social problems stemming from a wandering population of over 200 million unemployed people and popular outrage at the corruption of Communist Party officials. There are daily outbreaks of unrest on a large scale requiring the use of force by the police or army to contain them. Beijing has managed to prevent a national uprising by ensuring that no organization is allowed to emerge that could provide a coordinating focus for dissent. So Beijing's leaders must ask themselves whether the loss of international reputation and perhaps even domestic political power is worth the gamble of invading Taiwan.

Sentiments are strong on the island and particularly among Taiwanese nationalists that China has too much to lose by invading and will not do so. This often leads to China's threats being quickly dismissed as mere bluster, an attitude that makes Taiwan's allies angry and anxious. The island sits on the strategically critical meeting place between the Far East and Southeast Asia, an accident of geography that has made Taiwan such an attractive target for colonial occupation throughout its history. If Taiwan were invaded by China the United States would be required to come to Taiwan's aid because of these regional strategic considerations as well as American public opinion and domestic legislation. The realization in the Taiwanese capital Taipei, in Washington, and in Beijing that missteps or mistakes in handling the Taiwan file could lead to armed confrontation between the United States and China looms behind the daily drive on the island to assert its nationhood.

Often forgotten is that Japan, whose southern Ryukyu Islands are closer to Taiwan than is the mainland, also has a keen interest in the future of the island. Perhaps surprisingly, warm bonds of friendship and mutual regard persist between Japan and Taiwan despite Japan's 50-year colonial occupation of the island. And Japan views with deep concern the idea that the Taiwan Strait, a seaway that carries much of Japan's exports and essential imported commodities, might become an internal Chinese waterway.

Successive administrations in Washington have fudged the Taiwan question. What some see as Washington's betrayal of Taiwan began with President Richard Nixon's ground-breaking visit to Beijing in 1972 and his meeting with the Communist revolutionary leader Mao Zedong. That initiative culminated in 1978 with President Jimmy Carter's "acknowledgement" of the "one China principle" and his shifting of America's diplomatic relations from Taipei to Beijing. Washington's strategic ambiguity in courting Beijing while remaining Taiwan's principal ally has been reasonably utilitarian. It is now becoming a farce, however, under pressure from China's growing national confidence as an economic and political power and the uncorking of Taiwan's bottled-up nationalism with the advent of democracy. These are fiercely competing tides of history. It may be there is an elegant solution that can satisfy with a minimum of compromise all the hotly contending positions. If so, that happy median line is not immediately apparent. And there is no reason to imagine that Taiwan's future will be any neater, tidier, or more orderly than has been its tumultuous, factious, and often chaotic past.

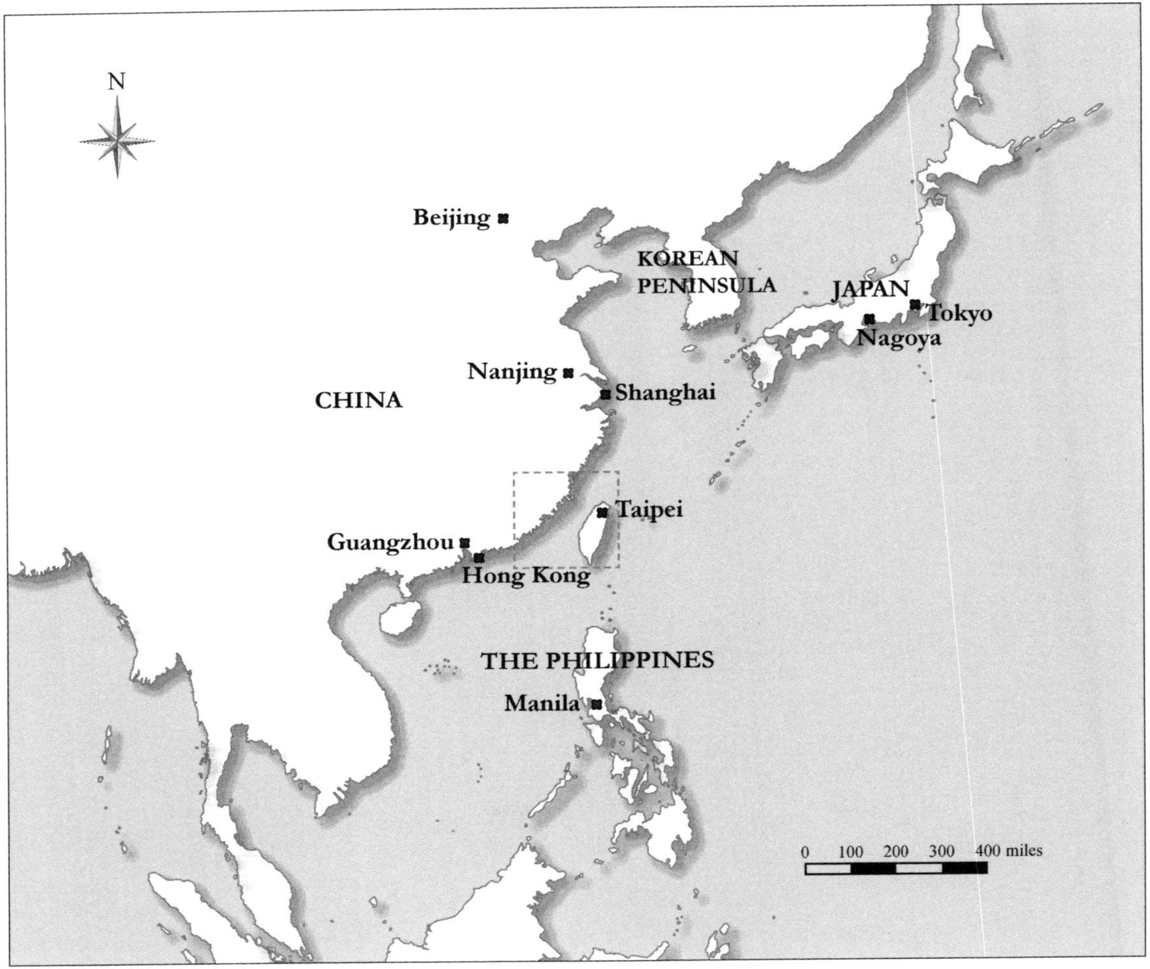
N
Beijing
KOREAN
PENINSULA
JAPAN
Tokyo
Nagoya
Nanjing
Shanghai
CHINA
Taipei
Guangzhou
Hong Kong
THE PHILIPPINES
Manila
0 100 200 300 400 miles

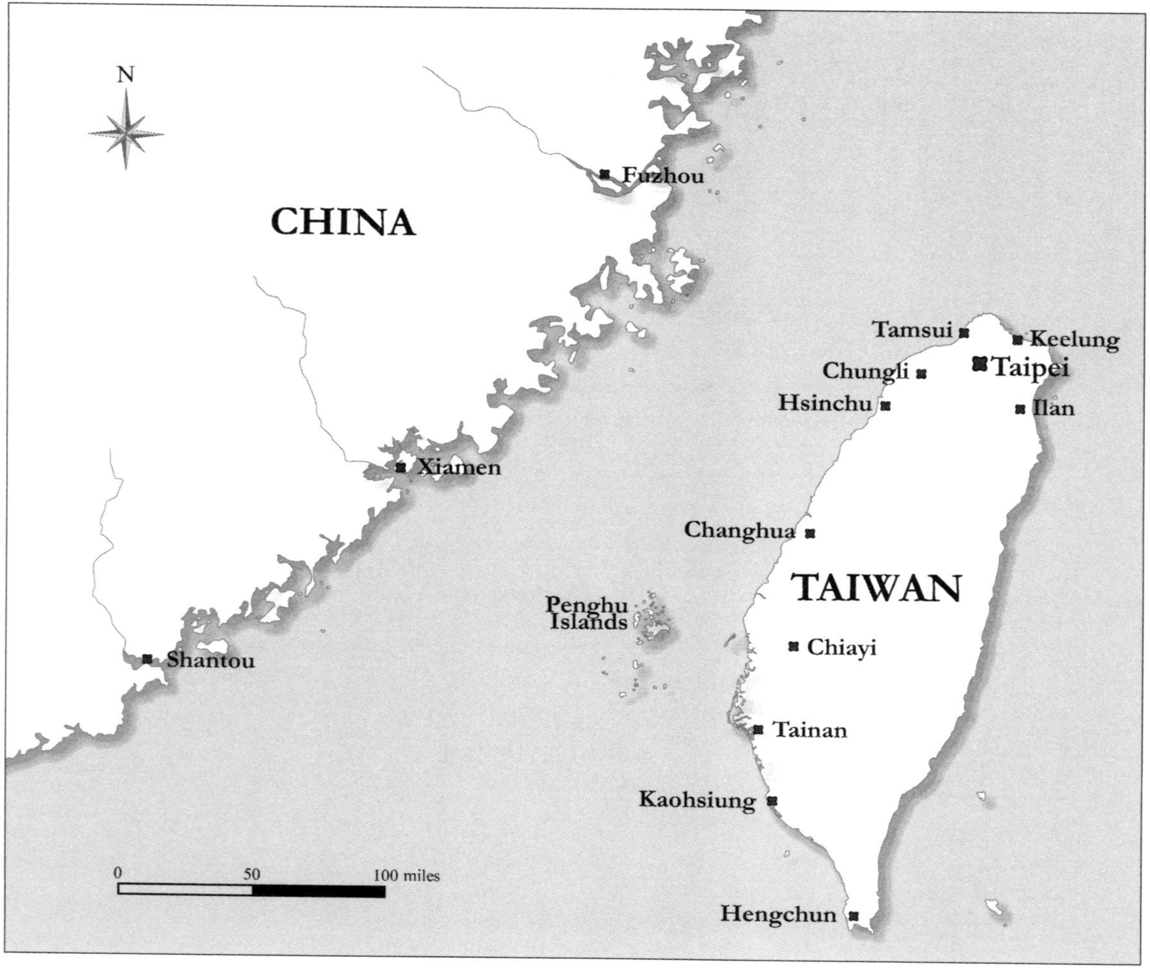
N
CHINA
Fuzhou
Xiamen
Shantou
Tamsui
Keelung
Chungli
Taipei
Hsinchu
Ilan
Changhua
TAIWAN
Penghu
Islands
Chiayi
Tainan
Kaohsiung
Hengchun
0
50
100 miles

Chapter One

TWO SHOTS ON CHINHUA ROAD

No one heard the two pistol shots or saw the gunman amid the continuous, overwhelming rattling roar and billowing smoke of the strings of exploding firecrackers. Remembering the scene three weeks later, Vice President Annette Lu was sure she heard the cracks of the two shots above the staccato noise of the fireworks. At the time, though, the sharper sound of the gun did not register in her mind. Yet it was Lu who first thought something was wrong. She felt a strong "impact" on her right knee.[1] Recalling the incident in a statement issued a few days later, Lu described the force of the bullet hitting her as strangely heavy and painful, enough to make her cry out. Her immediate conclusion was the logical one: Lu imagined she had been hit by the empty cardboard casing of one of the firecrackers that were exploding everywhere and are a common feature of Chinese festive occasions. It wasn't until she looked down and saw a rip in her slacks seeping blood that she knew it was something more. She turned to Taiwan's president, Chen Shui-bian, standing next to her in the back of an open-topped Jeep Wrangler in a motorcade parading slowly through the island's southern city of Tainan. Chen, she noticed, was holding his stomach with one hand and waving to the crowd with the other. It was then that she noticed the bullet hole in the windscreen, just above the head of the president's chief bodyguard, Lt. Gen. Chen Tsai-fu, who was sitting in the front passenger seat. Lu pointed out the bullet hole to the president who, shouting to be heard above the din of the fireworks, said: "I kept thinking we were hit by firecrackers. Why didn't you tell me earlier?"

It was March 19, 2004, the last day of campaigning in a passionate, fierce, and sometimes verbally vitriolic contest for the Taiwanese presidency. Chen and Lu were seeking to return to office in only the third open presidential elections since the island's ponderous, two-decade transition from one-party military rule. They had won a three-cornered contest in the 2000 election with only 39 percent of the vote and ousted the Kuomintang, the old national party of China, which had ruled Taiwan since 1945. That had been a signal moment in Chinese history. For the first time in any predominantly ethnic Chinese society there was a peaceful and legal democratic change of administration. The coming to power of Chen's Democratic Progressive Party (DPP) with its emphasis on asserting the distinct cultural identity and independence of Taiwan and its 23 million people, was also a blow to China. Beijing claims sovereignty over the island, which is just one hundred miles (one hundred and sixty kilometers) off its southeastern coast. But the mainland Communists have never controlled the island, which has been a de facto independent state since the end of China's civil war in 1949. Taiwan then became the refuge for defeated Kuomintang leader Generalissimo Chiang Kai-shek and some two million of his followers. The long-term policy of Chen and the DPP is to affirm the country's independence and to edge Beijing into giving up its claim to Taiwan. Beijing responded to the election of Chen and Lu in 2000 by deploying hundreds of missiles aimed at the island and constantly repeating its threat to invade Taiwan if there were moves toward internationally recognized independence. Undaunted by Beijing's threats, in their first four years in office Chen and Lu pursued policies boosting "Taiwan consciousness" and a sense of island nationalism, often to the neglect of more immediate economic and social problems.

The neglect of bread-and-butter issues meant their reelection was anything but certain. Samples of public opinion before the 2004 campaign indicated Kuomintang presidential candidate Lien Chan and his running mate James Soong had a lead of about 10 percentage points. They should have been able to win handily. But they presented a lackluster campaign and their advantage dwindled. Polls taken in the last days of the campaign showed a very close race, but with the challengers Lien and Soong having a marginal advantage. However, Chen and Lu skillfully controlled the agenda of election issues and insisted that the central questions revolved around Taiwanese identity and nationhood. A vote for Lien and Soong, the DPP campaign strategists implied, was a vote for Taiwan's submission to China. A victory for Chen and Lu in 2004 would, therefore, be a political watershed just as profound as the change of administration in 2000. For the first time a majority of the island's people would be giving open support to Taiwan's independence movement. Such an outcome would mark the failure of China's attempts to lure Taiwan by peaceful means into unification with the mainland. It would present Beijing with few options but to focus even more fixedly on a military solution.

A Chen and Lu victory would be just as destabilizing for Taiwan's chief ally, the United States. A return to power with a majority vote by the DPP presidential and vice presidential candidates would make it near impossible for Washington to continue with its purposefully ambiguous "one China" policy. (For nearly 30 years successive U.S. administrations have managed to maintain good relations with both Beijing and Taipei by asserting that there is only "one China" but refusing to say what that means. Does it mean Washington accepts there is one China and Taiwan is part of it? That is Beijing's position. Or does it mean there is one China, but Taiwan is a separate country?) The utility of this piece of diplomatic obfuscation began to collapse with Taiwan's transition to democracy, which started with the lifting of martial law in 1987. The reelection of Chen and Lu, with their clear intention of finally severing any pretence that Taiwan is or will ever be a willing part of China, would force Washington to confront the conflicts and paradoxes in its policy. That risked putting the United States on a collision course with China. So it was easy to imagine many motives for attempting to affect the outcome of the election by shooting Chen and Lu.

The assassination attempt was in the early afternoon as Chen and Lu were leading a last, morale-boosting parade through Tainan city, Chen's hometown and the heartland of support for their Democratic Progressive Party. They were due to return to Taipei later to prepare for a final, highly choreographed rally that night.

The gunman's plan was simple and effective. The lone assassin is always the most difficult and unpredictable assailant for security staff to prepare against. And police security was muddled and ineffectual, as a subsequent investigation showed. It was later found that police had received intelligence reports that an attempt might be made on Chen's life, but they disregarded the information. That dismissal was remarkable. Taiwan has a long record of violent repression during four hundred years of control by various colonial masters. And in recent years there had been several politically sponsored murders, most engineered by the old ruling party, the Kuomintang. The memory of these killings quickly fuelled rampant rumor mongering after the shooting. But on the bright and cheerful afternoon of March 19 the police apparently chose not to recall those dark incidents, and security was lax. Neither Chen nor Lu was wearing a bulletproof vest and bodyguards were not stationed close enough to the couple to block the line of sight of any would-be assassins.

Police believe the gunman stood at the back of the crowd lining the route of the motorcade close to No. 2 Chinhua Road in Tainan. He waited until the Jeep carrying Chen and Lu was about 20 feet (seven meters) away and then fired twice. It was only the gunman's lack of skill that saved Chen's life. The Jeep was approaching the gunman at an angle and about 10 miles an hour (16 km/h). It is always a difficult shot to hit a moving target approaching at an angle. To do so with a pistol rather than a more accurate rifle is even more difficult. The gunman had to aim ahead of Chen, allowing for the speed of the Jeep and the time it would take after he pulled the trigger for the cartridge to detonate and the bullet to travel to the target. With both shots he overestimated and aimed too far ahead of his target. The first bullet punched through the windscreen of the Jeep well ahead of Chen, narrowly missed bodyguard Lt. Gen. Chen sitting in the front seat, and grazed Lu's knee before burying itself in the upholstery of the rear seat. When police retrieved the slug, microscopic examination showed fragments of glass, confirming its path through the windscreen.

The gunman fired a second time almost immediately after the first shot. By this time, the Jeep was almost parallel with him. The gunman judged the second shot better than the first, but again he aimed too far ahead of his target, the president. The bullet gashed the surface of Chen's stomach but did not penetrate below the surface fat. Doctors said later even a fractional difference in the assassin's aim could have been fatal for the president.

Chen was wearing a gray golf jacket with an elasticized waist. The bullet punched through the right side of the jacket and then the shirt and t-shirt the president was wearing underneath. Doctors later found a wound four and one-quarter inches long (11-cm) and three-quarters of an inch (2 cm) wide gouged across Chen's stomach just below the navel. The bullet then tore through the left side of Chen's t-shirt and his shirt. At this point the slug's energy was spent. It could not get through the thicker material of the president's coat and was found inside the elasticized waist.

After Annette Lu cried out to the security officers that she and president Chen had been shot, it took the bodyguards several minutes to work out what to do. They belatedly clustered around the Jeep while debating where to take Chen and Lu. It should not have been a difficult decision. Officials of Chen's DPP said later that in planning for the visit, the Chi-Mei Medical Center just outside the city in Tainan County had been designated the emergency center rather than the closer public hospital in the city center. The more distant Chi-Mei center was chosen because organizers anticipated that crowds of people waiting to see the cavalcade would block the route to the city hospital. On arrival at the medical center Chen walked in unaided while Lu, now hobbling from her knee wound, had to be helped in. Inside the clinic doctors quickly removed the president's top clothes to examine the wound while Chen starting making calls on his cell phone. Chen spoke first with his wife, Wu Shu-chen, to assure her he was not seriously injured. He then called his closest advisor, the secretary general to the presidential office, Chiou I-jen, to set the national security apparatus in motion.

Chiou called a meeting of the National Security Council, which ordered the immediate upgrading of the island's state of military and police readiness to face an invasion. Tens of thousands of troops were called to duty and many were unable to vote the following day as a result. This became grist to the conspiracy theory mill. It is usually reckoned that support for the Kuomintang in the military is higher than the national average, about 75 percent, because pre-democracy culture is still strong in armed forces training. The denying of votes to many thousands of soldiers who were required to stay on duty was seen as evidence of a conspiracy by the president to cut support for Lien and Soong.

The inevitable first thought for any Taiwanese administration after an attempted assassination is that Beijing might be behind it and that the "decapitation" of the island's government is a prelude to invasion. So one of the first people swept into action was the head of Taiwan's National Security Bureau, Tsai Tsao-ming. He flew immediately from Taipei to Tainan to take charge of security and the shooting investigation. While in transit Tsai telephoned the U.S. military's Pacific command center in Hawaii. He also called Washington. Tsai's calls were to inform the Americans of what had happened and to see if there were any indications that the attempt on Chen's life was the first move in an invasion by China. Tsai was given assurance that American satellites and spy planes in their regular monitoring of Chinese military communications and activities had seen no signs of any preparations for an invasion. Those calls and the ready responses Tsai received emphasizes the close functional alliance between Taiwan and the United States on regional security matters.

The information from the United States suggesting Taiwan was not under imminent threat of invasion from China was a relief to all those trying to assess the implications of the shooting. It didn't remove China entirely from the list of suspects, but it did shift attention toward the Kuomintang with its history of politically motivated assassinations. In the mid 1980s, when it was beginning to become obvious that military rule by the Kuomintang was becoming increasingly untenable, government security organizations became frantic and irrational in their attempts to halt the tide of history. One such organization, the Intelligence Bureau of the Ministry of National Defense (IBMND), hit on the idea of using gunmen from the island's triad gangs to remove or intimidate the government's political opponents. The triads began life many hundreds of years ago as nationalist organizations with a spiritual belief in the intertwined relationship of three elements of the Chinese nation—heaven, earth, and the people—hence the name triad. Over the centuries, however, the triads evolved into secret criminal gangs with elaborate initiation rites designed to instill life-long loyalty to the brotherhood. The then deputy director of the IBMND, Major General Hu Yi-min, pursued the idea of utilizing triads and developed a working relationship with Chen Ch'i-li, the boss of the Bamboo Union gang. In 1984 a Taiwanese journalist, Henry Liu, then living in exile in California and a naturalized American citizen, was close to finishing and publishing a book that was believed, with good reason, to be heavily critical of the island's then president, Chiang Ching-kuo. Major General Hu hoped Liu could be removed before he could complete the book. American police who investigated the killing came to think that Chiang Ching-kuo's dissolute son, Alex, was the necessary link with the "royal family" who approved the killing. Bamboo Union boss Chen was contracted to do the job. The management of the shooting of Henry Liu in the garage of his home just outside San Francisco in October 1984 illustrates the stupidity that can overtake such ventures. Before Chen set off on his assignment on September 14, senior IBMND officers threw a farewell banquet for him. And when Chen returned to Taiwan's Chiang Kai-shek International Airport on October 21, bringing with him the two gunmen who shot Liu, IBMND officers were there to greet him and applaud him for a job well done. What never seemed to have occurred to them was that American intelligence agencies might get wind of the operation. Washington's National Security Agency monitored several highly incriminating telephone calls from Chen in California to his IBMND managers back in Taiwan. The killing of Liu, an American, generated intense anger in the U.S. administration, which led to accelerated pressure from Washington on Taipei to speed up political reform. So, far from stalling political change in Taiwan, the killing of Liu had the reverse effect.

At about the same time, 1985, an attempt was made to kill Chen Shuibian's wife, Wu Shu-chen, that left her paralyzed from the waist down and confined to a wheelchair. Chen had sought election as commissioner of Tainan

County. He lost the election, but afterward both Chen and his wife traveled independently around the county to thank supporters. At one stop Wu was hit by a truck in a dead-end street. The truck driver made a concerted effort to kill Wu by backing up and running her over several times. It has never been established beyond doubt whether the truck driver acted on his own behalf or on instruction from a faction within the Kuomintang. But he never stood trial and his action enhanced greatly the popular view of Chen and his wife as victims of state terrorism and champions of Taiwanese aspirations.

Another more recent killing with official connections failed equally in its objectives. On December 9, 1993, the body of Taiwanese navy captain Yin Ching-feng was found on a beach. Military coroners delivered a quick verdict of death by drowning. But Yin's widow demanded an independent autopsy that concluded he had been bludgeoned to death. The case aroused interest because Captain Yin was one of the officers overseeing a U.S. $2.8 billion deal for Taiwan to buy six Lafayette-class frigates from France. Taiwan's diplomatic isolation makes arms purchases for the island's forces difficult. Arms sales to Taiwan always require strong political will in the selling countries, where there is bound to be pressure from China not to go through with the sale. There is therefore an obvious opportunity for corruption among both buyers and sellers. It quickly became known that Captain Yin was unhappy with the way the agreement was progressing, did not believe Taiwan was getting its money's worth, and further believed that massive bribery had been involved in France's acquisition of the contract. The shock waves from Captain Yin's death reverberated for years. In France the revelations led to the downfall of the foreign minister, Roland Dumas, and the imprisonment of several officials in companies that had laundered the bribes. In Taiwan several senior officers were sacked or imprisoned and the upper echelons of the military were scoured for evidence of affiliations to triad gangs. Investigators looked unsuccessfully for links to the Green Gang, the Shanghai triad in which Generalissimo Chiang Kai-shek had begun his career as a gunman in the 1920s and that still has tentacles in Taiwan's military.

Politically motivated violence in Taiwan is not, however, exclusively a Kuomintang preserve. In 1966 a parcel bomb was sent to the office of then vice president Hsieh Tung-min. Hsieh suffered serious injuries to his hands when he opened the parcel. The package was sent by Wang Sing-nan, who, by 2004 had become a DPP member of the Taiwanese parliament. In 1970 an attempt was made to kill then Taiwanese president Chiang Ching-kuo while he was visiting New York. The assailant was Peter Huang, who later became president of the Taiwan Association for Human Rights and in 2004 was an advisor to President Chen Shui-bian.

Violence, politics, and crime have been essential ingredients of the bubbling brew of Taiwanese life since the 1500s. The first Chinese settlements on the island were safe havens established by pirate gangs that preyed on shipping routes off China's south and east coasts. Triad secret societies, which in their early years hovered somewhere between patriotic rebel conspiracies and criminal outlaws, were brought to Taiwan in the mid-1600s when the "pirate prince" Cheng Cheng-kong, known in the West as Koxinga, ousted the Dutch and established his own kingdom on the island. Triad-based patriotic uprisings and turf wars between rival gangs were behind much of the civil turmoil that was part of daily life on Taiwan during the eighteenth and nineteenth centuries. Even the Japanese, who acquired Taiwan as a colony in 1895 and introduced a meticulously organized system of authoritarian rule, were unable to totally eradicate what Japanese official accounts describe as "banditry."[2] It was evident, though, that one of the main hopes Taiwanese voters had for democracy was that it would finally break the link on the island between crime and politics, known in headline vernacular as "black gold." Popular demands that this hangover from Taiwan's one-party past be confronted were the main domestic issue in all the elections after the advent of democracy. When Chen Shui-bian was elected president in 2000, among his first acts was to establish a new, independent investigation and prosecution agency to attack "black gold." Thus the attempted assassination of the president was doubly shocking and troubling for many Taiwanese. It appeared to be a resurgence of a violent style of conduct of public affairs they hoped had been relegated by political reform to the island's past.

During the afternoon of March 19 at the Kuomintang headquarters in Taipei, presidential candidate Lien Chan and his running mate James Soong were quick to appreciate they were ripe for blame for the Tainan shooting. They issued a statement that afternoon condemning the violence, and Lien told local media reporters that the campaign had decided to postpone that night's rallies so as to maintain a sense of calm among the electorate. The "Pan Blue Alliance" of Lien's Kuomintang and Soong's People First Party had planned four simultaneous rallies in Taipei, Taoyuan, Taichung, and Kaohsiung. The rallies were expected to draw over a million people in all and give a final burst of momentum to their campaign.

Meanwhile, in Tainan investigators were beginning to gather scraps of evidence about the shooting. When doctors at the Chi-Mei clinic had removed Chen's clothes they had found in the folds of his golf jacket the bullet that had gashed his stomach but lost so much power it was unable to punch out through the coat material. Examination by ballistic experts showed that the bullet was made of lead, but, significantly, it was homemade. Other investigators examining the Jeep found imbedded in the upholstery the bullet that had grazed Vice President Lu's knee. This too was homemade, but fashioned out of bronze. Police scouring the area around No. 2 Chinhua Road, where the gunman was thought to have stood, found two spent cartridge cases from an automatic pistol. Like the bullets, the cartridge cases were clearly homemade.

The private ownership of pistols is not permitted in Taiwan. Gangsters, however, manage to get hold of weapons. One source is to adapt replica firearms. Replicas are made for collectors and gun buffs in jurisdictions with tight firearms ownership laws such as Taiwan. They look and function like the real thing, except they cannot fire a real cartridge and the steel used in their casting is not of the same high quality as a factory-made weapon. They can be made to work, however, by replacing key components such as barrels with ones made of higher-grade steel. Police believe there are about 2,000 small workshops in Taiwan where replica firearms are changed into working guns, mostly for mobsters. These guns are not very accurate or reliable and that probably helped save President Chen's life.

The type of gun used suggests the assassin was a lone disgruntled voter. A professional would have used a hard-hitting and accurate rifle. But from the moment of the official announcement that the president had been shot, nearly two hours after the event, speculation about the identity of the gunman and his motive dominated the election and its inconclusive outcome. Political opponents decided almost immediately the attempted assassination was an election stunt aimed at garnering support from undecided voters. The most cynical did not believe Chen and Lu had been shot at all. They were convinced the whole incident had been faked.

Even as Chen and Lu were being flown back to Taipei on the evening of the shooting, Taiwan's scandal- and rumor-obsessed media was in full cry. Sisy Chen, hostess of one of the most outrageous radio and television phone-in shows and a maverick member of Taiwan's parliament, the Legislative Yuan, told her audience with utter certainty the shooting had been faked and the entire incident fabricated to sway voters. She had received, the media maven said, information from a source at the clinic where the president and Lu were treated that the medical records had been falsified. Most of her audience would have been aware that Sisy Chen was a disgruntled former member of the president's Democratic Progressive Party and that she was then giving election campaign advice to the opposition Pan Blue Alliance. But such was the climate of mistrust and suspicion generated by the boiling emotions of the election campaign that many Taiwanese were prepared to believe any rumor without wanting verification or wondering about the motives of the source. The mistrust of President Chen and his DPP administration among political opponents was so deep that some opponents even speculated that in order to win the election the president had shot and wounded himself or that his chief bodyguard, Lt. Gen. Chen, had been assigned to do it.

Speculation on the influence of the shooting on the election might not have been so intense if the victory by Chen and Lu had not been so narrow. As the votes were counted and running totals announced on the night of March 20 the lead seesawed back and forth. It was only when the results started coming in from the DPP stronghold in the south that Chen and Lu began to hold a consistent, narrow lead. Their victory, however, could not have been much slimmer. Out of 12,914,422 votes cast—80.2 per cent of registered voters—Chen and Lu won by only 29,518 votes. This inevitably raised questions whether the shooting incident had excited a sympathy vote or encouraged DPP supporters who might otherwise have stayed at home to get out to cast their ballots. Over the following days and weeks the details of the incident were minutely dissected in the Taiwanese media, in cafés and tea houses, and in a cacophony of cell phone text message chatter. It sometimes seemed during those days that every new detail, every attempt by President Chen's officials to issue clarifying information, only solidified the conviction among half the Taiwanese population that officials were trying to fool them. The shooting happened shortly before two o'clock in the afternoon of March 19. In response to an instant media hue and cry, the president's office later that afternoon released medical photographs of a prosperously round tummy with a shallow, gouged wound across it just below the navel, and other pictures with the wound stitched up. More photos showed a gashed knee before and after treatment. Skeptics, however, sneered that this could be anybody's stomach and anyone's knee. Moreover, they said, who was to say if these were real injuries. They could just be the work of a skilled make-up artist.

A few days later Chen's office made another attempt to calm the clamor by releasing videotape of the president being treated in the Chi Mei Medical Center. The video was filmed from behind Chen's head while he lay on an operating table and showed the president talking on a cell phone while doctors cleaned and stitched the stomach wound using a local anaesthetic. Ha-ha, laughed the skeptics. This little tableau was clearly staged. The doctors were not wearing any head covering, as they should have done if this were a real medical operation. And, anyway, everyone knew a friend of the president owned the clinic. Why hadn't he and Lu been taken to the larger and better-equipped public hospital in Tainan, which was closer to the scene of the shooting? Obviously it was because Chen's doctor friend was in on the plot to garner a sympathy vote with the fake assassination attempt.

Then there was the mystery of the red patch. Out of focus and jittery videotape of Chen and Lu in the Jeep at the time of the shooting appeared to show a red mark on the president's waist-length golf jacket. But later video showed him walking unaided—in itself suspicious, said the skeptics—into the medical center and there was no red mark on the coat. The explanation that the red on the first video was the out-of-focus image of a safety belt, not a bloodstain, came too late to stop the story becoming embedded in popular imagination as part of the sheaf of evidence of duplicity.

To try to quell the seething and dangerous tide of rumor and speculation about the shooting, the Chen administration turned, as Taiwanese often do in times of trouble, to the United States. From the start opposition candidates Lien and Soong said there should be an independent investigation into the shooting. They did not trust police and prosecutors beholden to the Chen administration to investigate the case. The police may not have been biased, but their investigation certainly did not produce much in the way of results in the days and weeks after the shooting. There were no suspects and only a sketchy outline of what had happened during the shooting. Lien suggested calling in a well-known team of American forensic experts led by Henry Lee, a former Taipei police captain who immigrated to the United States in the 1960s. Lee gained an international reputation as a forensic expert and gave evidence for the defense in the O. J. Simpson murder trial.

The Chen administration agreed to invite Lee and his team to examine the evidence, the scene of the shooting, and even the president's stomach. Lee issued a report on April 11 saying the examination of the wound showed that the president had definitely been shot. The gash was not the work of a make-up artist. Lee also concluded the gunman had not been in the Jeep Wrangler, thus attempting to bury speculation that Chen had either shot himself or that his bodyguards had been commissioned to carefully fire a wounding bullet. But Lee was unable to say conclusively that the assassination attempt had not been staged.

Taiwanese police were just as unable to say much that was definitive about the shooting, even after months of investigation. They scrutinized 223 videotapes made by various people recording Chen and Lu's campaign parade and interviewed 260 people who were either at the scene or who might know something. Occasionally in the succeeding months the police would issue a notice with a description of someone seen near the parade whom they regarded as "a person of interest" to the inquiry and wished to talk to. None of these initiatives produced evidence against anyone. In June, three months after the shooting, the Criminal Investigation Bureau conducted an experiment that appeared to owe more to desperate theatrics than useful forensic science. Officers covered a model with the skin of a pig, including an appropriate layer of fat, and then dressed the dummy in clothes similar to those Chen had been wearing on March 19. Then police fired three bullets at the model with a homemade gun from the same angle and distance as the would-be assassin. To no one's surprise the recreation produced the same damage as the original. It did, however, produce some amusement with the imagery of the president's stomach being simulated by a thick layer of pig fat.

Finally in mid-December 2004, nearly ten months after the shooting, the police had a breakthrough. They discovered and arrested an arms maker in the Tainan area whom they identified only as "Tang." "We are very, very sure that this man is the one who manufactured the bullets used in the shooting of the president and vice president," the commissioner of the Criminal Investigation Bureau, Hou Yu-ih, told local reporters.[3] The investigators' certainty that they had found the right gun maker was based on distinctive tools found in Tang's workshop and on machine markings on the cartridge cases, Commissioner Hou said. "According to our understanding, he has no political colors. He is simply an arms maker in the Tainan area. We now have the upstream supplier, and we need to work our way downstream" to his customers.

The barrage of accusations and innuendo from the Pan Blue camp and its supporters neatly deflected attention from the very obvious answer to the questions of who was most likely to have taken the shots at president Chen and why. It is far more likely to have been a supporter of the Kuomintang or James Soong's People First Party than anyone else. The simple equation is that someone thought that the removal of Chen would aid an election victory by Lien and Soong. Would-be assassins are usually not very clever, or are motivated by intense anger or by misguided devotional loyalty. Most frequently they are spurred by a combination of all three impulses and fail to grasp that assassinations seldom achieve their intended outcomes. The homemade or adapted gun used also suggests no professionals or high-grade criminals were involved. Such people could be expected to use a weapon capable of efficiently doing the job. The most convincing explanation is that the shooting was done by a lone disgruntled man, someone perhaps on the fringes of the underworld. This was the conclusion police came to in March 2005, when they announced they were certain the shooting had been carried out by a middle-aged man who was depressed because he could not sell his house. The man blamed Chen for poor economic management and the depressed property market. Police certainty that they had found the culprit did not stop the conspiracy theories however. The man drowned himself ten days after the shooting and left a suicide note confessing to the attempted assassination, but, according to the police, his ashamed family burned the note.

Like most people in countries that have newly made the fraught transition from dictatorship to democracy, Taiwanese are passionate about their politics and the issues that face their society. There is little apathy, save among the young who have known only the good life Taiwanese have come to expect. The transition is still so fresh that the memories of the years under Kuomintang rule have not yet been erased or eroded by the passage of time. For many of the so-called native Taiwanese whose forebears escaped chaotic and repressive life in China from the sixteenth to the nineteenth centuries, the last 50 years was a bitter period of authoritarian rule by the Kuomintang. It must be acknowledged, however, that the leavening of economic and social development promoted by the Kuomintang in the later years of their exclusive rule made the party's style more akin to strict Chinese paternalism than pure totalitarianism.

Kuomintang rule was not so kind in its early years. Generalissimo Chiang Kai-shek, his army, and about two million Kuomintang followers fled to the island in 1949 after their defeat in China by the Communists of Mao Zedong. Chiang and the Kuomintang regarded Taiwan merely as a brief haven where they would rebuild their strength in preparation for an eventual return to the mainland to oust the Communists. The rule Chiang and his followers established over Taiwan was colonial in all but name. It was not totalitarian in the strict sense but limited the opportunities available to native Taiwanese to low- and middle-level positions in the hierarchy. Within those boundaries Chiang's government allowed some real reform. Land reform in the 1950s and early 1960s ended the power of the landlord class that had prospered during Qing and Japanese rule. Landlords were forced to sell much of their holdings to their tenants. Armed with the deeds to their land, many Taiwanese were able to go to the banks with collateral for loans. Their small plots became the sites of cottage industries which within a couple of decades evolved into Taiwan's high technology miracle. But behind this enlightened despotism real power and influence was kept firmly in the hands of mainlanders. Many native Taiwanese quickly realized the key to survival under this regime was acquiescence. A few years after the arrival of Chiang and his followers, half the members of the Kuomintang were native Taiwanese.

The Kuomintang had become a deeply corrupt political organization during the war with Japan on the mainland in the 1930s and 1940s. One of the many disdainful nicknames for Chiang Kai-shek adopted by American military advisers to the Kuomintang during those years was Generalissimo "Cash My Check." In exile on Taiwan the Kuomintang kept its old habits, and a spider's web of fraud and bribery quickly enmeshed the whole community. The party accumulated vast wealth and became, by some estimates, the richest political organization anywhere as the lines blurred between state-owned enterprises, Kuomintang companies, and supporters' corporations.

From the time of the Kuomintang's arrival Chiang allowed free democracy to operate only at local levels where political power was largely meaningless. A few non-Kuomintang parties were allowed to operate, but they were totally suborned operations, entirely dependent on ruling party patronage and money for their survival. Significant political reform and change at municipal and national levels only began in the 1980s, when the Kuomintang finally acknowledged that its dream of reconquering China was a fantasy. Washington's formal diplomatic recognition of Beijing at the beginning of 1979 and the parallel downgrading of relations with Taipei forced this change of attitude.

The demoralization of the Kuomintang gave heart to the underground and outlawed opposition of native Taiwanese dedicated to democracy and self-determination for the island. The opposition attempted to mount a rally on December 10, 1979, United Nations Human Rights Day, in Kaohsiung. State security forces were ready for them. With up to 30,000 demonstrators assembled, there were scuffles with riot squads, and the protest organizers, known as the Kaohsiung Eight, were arrested. The arrests did not come, however, until after the eight had spoken to the crowd. One of the organizers was a young woman, Annette Lu, who had abandoned her PhD law studies at Harvard a few months before to come home to Taiwan and take up the life of a reform activist. "That speech changed Lu, it changed everything," remarked her friend, Linda Arrigo, to journalist Ron Gluckman for a profile published in the magazine *Asiaweek* in August 2000.[4] "It was an amazing speech. I think it even surprised Lu." The speech also earned her a 12-year prison sentence. She was adopted by Amnesty International as a prisoner of conscience, and her arrest brought worldwide condemnation of the Kuomintang regime. She contracted thyroid cancer while in prison, and this gave the authorities a face-saving excuse to release her in 1985 so she could return to the United States for treatment. When martial law was lifted and political reform begun, Lu returned to Taiwan and was elected to the Legislative Yuan, the parliament, in 1992. Friends say she had hoped to be the DPP's presidential candidate in the first free elections in 1996. She was passed over in favor of the lion of Taiwanese political activism, Peng Ming-min. Lu retreated to her home town of Taoyuan, where she became the elected chief executive of the county. Her performance there was unremarkable, according to local journalists, but in 2000 Chen Shui-bian plucked Lu out of gathering obscurity to be his vice presidential running mate. Many of his close advisers had no idea they had loosed a political wildcat. Chen should have known what he was taking on, though some say he did not.

"Chen never realized how difficult she is," Antonio Chiang, newspaper publisher and friend of both Chen and Lu, said in the *Asiaweek* profile.[5] "He underestimated how difficult she can be. It's beyond most people's imagination. She's close to impossible. In the beginning, every time she opened her mouth, everyone held their breath. We had no idea what would come out."

If Beijing hates and mistrusts Chen Shui-bian, it loathes Lu with an even greater and shriller contempt. That is because she is the pure face of Taiwanese nationalism that China can never hope to charm or buy off. At various times Beijing's official media have called her a lunatic, "scum of the nation,"[6] and "betrayer of her ancestors."[7] Lu, born in June 1944, the youngest of four children of a poor shopkeeper in Taoyuan, delights in her notoriety. Every outburst from Beijing equals a badge of honor and votes in her pocket.

"I have no idea why Beijing is so angry with me," she told a local interviewer in 2000 with a coy twinkle in her eye. "I like China. But we're part of the Chinese. Not China."[8]

When Lu was tried for her involvement in the Kaohsiung Incident, among those on her legal team was a young expert in maritime law named Chen Shui-bian, who had no courtroom experience. Like Lu, Chen came from a poor Taiwanese family and had had to fight every step of the way to gain university degrees. Chen was born in February 1951 in His-chuang, a dirt-poor village of less than a hundred households in Tainan county. His mother was illiterate and his father had only a primary school education. Both worked as agricultural day laborers. Like many peasant families Chen's parents gave him a name, Shui-bian, that suggested poverty so that jealous spirits would not be tempted by pompous aspirations to play tricks on him. Shui-bian is the name for the split bamboo pole that many rural and poor Chinese use to carry two water buckets or other loads. Chen's nickname, A-bian, is used constantly and is a familiar diminutive in the way Robert is shortened to Bob or Bobby in English. What is sometimes off-putting about Chen to the uninitiated is the way he invariably refers to himself in the third person as A-bian. To outsiders this smacks of the royal "we," but it does not have the same connotation on Taiwan. What it does convey, though, is Chen's roots as a son of the Taiwanese soil and its people. It is also a highly successful piece of populist political brand marketing. In a region where politics, even in democracies, is carried out in measured tones by formal men in somber suits, Chen's rousing populist style is unusual and raises suspicions about his sagacity and dependability. This has led Chen to be labeled an "impetuous maniac" and a "clown," to quote his political opponent Lien Chan. For Chen the A-bian image is essential. While he can use formal and cultured Mandarin Chinese when required (though in his government's drive for Taiwanization these occasions are less and less frequent), Chen prefers to use the often earthy Taiwanese dialect, including, in the company of close friends, ribald curses and swear words.

Chen obtained an education the same way many poor Chinese children do: well-off relatives were persuaded to invest in what was clearly a talented child whose future advancement might benefit the entire family. Chen's critical experiences began at middle school, where his talents as an essayist and polemicist began to emerge. In 1963 he won a national prize for an essay on the death of U.S. president John F. Kennedy. He was also politicized by one of his teachers, Yang Hung-kai, a former student of Peng Ming-min, who in 1964 was imprisoned for circulating a manifesto calling for Taiwanese independence. Yang also instructed his favored students on recent Taiwanese political history, such as the Two-Two-Eight Incident, the White Terror, and the general oppression of the Taiwanese by the ruling mainland clique, discussion of which was forbidden by the Kuomintang government. In 1969 Chen was the top graduate in his high school class and won a place at the island's foremost college, National Taiwan University. He started on a business degree with the aim of being able to repay the debt to his family for providing for his education. At the end of his first year, however, Chen switched to commercial law, arguing to himself that this would still give him business skills while feeding his growing interest in politics. Chen was spurred in part to make this move by the arrest in 1969 of his middle school teacher Yang. Yang was detained for two months for, as the official explanation put it, "teaching subjects outside the curriculum" on Kuomintang oppression.[9] In 1971 Yang was arrested again for direct involvement in the Taiwan independence movement. This seems to have solidified Chen's growing contempt for the Kuomintang, though he kept most of his political views to himself as he completed his law degree. Chen graduated in 1974 and joined the Formosan International Marine and Commercial Law firm where he quickly gained a reputation for winning cases. That success made him very much a businessman-lawyer, accumulating a healthy personal fortune from fees and returning his family's investment. He stayed with the law firm for 13 years, until 1989, by which time he and his wife, Wu Shu-jen, whom he married in 1975, were financially secure, and he could move into a fulltime political career.

Chen began that formal move in 1979 when he helped defend the Kaohsiung Eight. He ran unsuccessfully for office in his native Tainan in 1985 but was victorious when the mayoralty of Taipei became a freely elected office in 1994. He won in the mainlanders' Taiwan heartland by downplaying the DPP's staunchly pro-independence, pro-self-determination positions and portraying himself as a man who could clean up the capital both physically and ethically. Chen's tenure as mayor of the capital was the beginning of a transformation that has made Taipei one of the most attractive cities in Asia. But his successes and populist style were not enough to beat off a determined campaign by the Kuomintang machine and its attractive candidate, Ma Ying-jeou, in 1998. Chen lost, but his term as mayor had given him a national profile that made him the logical DPP presidential candidate in 2000.

The period of Chen's political apprenticeship coincided with the progress of political reform on Taiwan. Having abandoned the hope of returning to the mainland and under pressure from Taiwanese dissenters and increasingly pointed advice from its allies, especially the United States, the Kuomintang began dismantling the one-party state in the late 1980s and allowed democratic development. But for many Kuomintang members, democracy has removed much of the privilege that went with being a colonial elite. Since Chen and his Democratic Progressive Party won power in the presidential elections of 2000 many Kuomintang stalwarts see themselves under the thumb of a government made up of people they consider an underclass. The policies of the Chen government have tended to rub salt in these wounds. The Chen administration has vigorously promoted, and not always wisely, notions of "Taiwanese consciousness." This includes the near eradication of Chinese history from the school syllabus and the almost exclusive use of the Taiwan dialect, Minnan—as different from the mainlanders' Mandarin as Portuguese is from English—in daily life.

China's claim to own Taiwan and its citizens is based on historically frail arguments and outdated legal concepts that have been overridden by new notions of the rights of peoples to self-determination that have developed since the inception of the United Nations. In contemporary terms, there can be no doubt that the 23 million Taiwanese have the right to choose their own future. The legal and moral imperatives should have led to the Taiwanese being asked to choose their own course after the end of Japanese colonial control of the island in 1945. That did not happen. Even so, the only people who have established sovereignty over Taiwan are the Taiwanese, no one else. Taiwan has been a de facto independent state for nearly 60 years and an administration outside Chinese rule for over a century. The island has never been ruled by the Chinese

Communist Party, currently in power in Beijing. Taiwan has had no significant administrative ties to mainland China since 1895. In the 200 years before that, when parts of Taiwan were ostensibly under Chinese administration, the island was beyond any effective governmental control that amounted to clear sovereignty. As late as the mid-1870s the Qing imperial court in Beijing denied having any responsibility for what happened in the island's aborigine territory in the mountainous eastern two-thirds of Taiwan. Public opinion polls over many years show consistently that the vast majority of Taiwanese would choose internationally recognized independence for their island if they were given an opportunity to do so free of menace from the mainland. Only the threats of invasion by China have kept Taiwanese from speaking out clearly about their desire for recognized independence. As the continued rise in popularity of the cause of Taiwanese consciousness shows, that hesitancy is fast disappearing as the islanders become increasingly confident in using the freedoms embedded by democracy.

China's great failure has been its inability to convince the Taiwanese they can engage with safety in any form of sovereignty association with the mainland. China set out its first substantial prescription for peaceful unification with Taiwan in 1979. This statement by the Standing Committee of the National People's Congress, China's rubber-stamp parliament, called for talks on peaceful unification by officials from both sides of the Taiwan Strait. To that end Beijing pledged to "respect the status quo on Taiwan and the views of people in all walks of life there and adopt reasonable policies and measures."[10] This approach was fleshed out in the early 1980s when the Chinese paramount leader Deng Xiaoping enunciated the concept of "one country, two systems" that was to govern Britain's return of Hong Kong to Beijing's sovereignty. Hong Kong was to keep its British institutions, such as the rule of law and an independent judiciary, for at least 50 years and be able to govern itself "with a high degree of autonomy." Taiwan watched with growing skepticism in the late 1990s and early 2000s as Beijing first intervened in ways that seemed to undermine Hong Kong's legal autonomy and then blocked a timetable for democratic reform, which had been promised in the hand-over package. When confronted with challenges to Communist Party authority, the power of "one country" always trumped the demands of "two systems." So even when Beijing tried to extend the concept and said Taiwan could even keep its own armed forces if it would agree to unify with the mainland, the islanders were not inclined to believe they would be allowed to remain autonomous.

For the same reasons, Taiwanese were not seduced when the then Chinese president and secretary general of the Communist Party, Jiang Zemin, offered on January 30, 1995, an eight-point proposal to frame talks on unification. Jiang's first point was that "the principle of 'One China' is a sine qua non for peaceful reunification."[11] Under that umbrella, Jiang continued, Taiwan would be allowed to maintain people-to-people, cultural, and economic relations with other countries. Negotiations must start to end the formal state of war still existing between the two sides of the Taiwan Strait, he said. Every effort should be made to resolve the dispute peacefully, but, he emphasized, "we do not renounce the use of force" especially if there is interference by "foreign powers" inspiring an independence plot. Efforts should be made to start direct mail, shipping, and trading services across the Taiwan Strait. And, finally, people on both sides of the strait should "bring into play" China's five thousand-year history.[12]

At the core of Beijing's failure to seduce the islanders is the insistence by the Communist Party leaders that Taiwan must acknowledge there is only "one China," and that the island is only "a rebel province." In the Communist Party's view, discussions about the island's future relationship with the capital and its degree of autonomy can only start after Taiwan has submitted to Beijing's authority. Taiwanese do not find this prospect at all attractive. They do not see why they should be expected to give up their current well-established independence, based on democracy and a vibrant market economy, as a precondition for talks with a despotic and repressive regime that has little evident political legitimacy beyond the use of force on its own people. Most Taiwanese come from families that immigrated to the island for the express purpose of escaping life on the mainland. They have developed their own distinct society and view of the world. They have only recently extricated themselves from the coils of the corrupt and dictatorial one-party Kuomintang state, and see no reason to jump into the arms of another one, the Communist Party of China.

The raw truth is that no government of China, neither the current Communist administration nor the previous Kuomintang regime, has a persuasive legal or moral claim to sovereignty over Taiwan. During the 300 years of Qing dynasty presence on the island, which ended in 1895 with Japanese annexation, China exercised a feeble and constantly challenged administration on only the western third of Taiwan. After Taiwan was handed to Chiang Kai-shek at the end of the Second World War in 1945—an illegal bequest as will be shown—the mainland Kuomintang government was already on the run from the Communists. Large areas of China were never under effective Kuomintang control and Chiang lost it all to Mao Zedong by the end of 1949. Thus there has never been a Chinese administration that exercised government over both the mainland and Taiwan at the same time. Beijing's lust to now possess Taiwan is excited by the same passions that have driven other empires over the last five centuries to gather the island under their imperial mantles. Taiwanese, for whom the island has simply been a refuge from the horrors of life elsewhere, are cursed for living on an outcrop of mountains and plains that sits on the strategic meeting place between the Far East and Southeast Asia. It is also a spot in the oceans that can give control over the south China coast. For that unhappy accident of geography Taiwanese have paid and continue to pay dearly.

Chapter Two

A LEAF ON THE WAVES

Taiwan has had a confused and confusing kaleidoscope of names across its colorful history. The names have been muddled because sometimes the people identifying the island were unsure where it was and how it related to other islands in the vicinity. The name Taiwan is both new and old. It has been adopted as the standard name for the island among westerners only within the last four decades or so. Chinese speakers have used it for a long time. The derivation of the name goes back at least four hundred years. Taoyuan was the name the Dutch used for their settlement, the area of modern Tainan on the island's southwest coast, when they established their trading colony in 1624. Chinese adopted it as the name for the whole island around the end of the seventeenth century, when Tainan was the capital of the Qing dynasty's administrative outpost on Taiwan's western lowlands. Where this word, with several spellings, came from is disputed. Some authorities say it is a word the local aborigines used when they found Chinese, Japanese, and Dutch voyagers on their shores. Taoyuan, Taian, or Taiyan is said to mean "foreigners" or "aliens" in the local aboriginal language, and the Dutch picked it up because it was the most discernible part of the natives' conversation. Others say it is a corruption of Chinese words meaning "terraced bay." Another opinion is that it may have been the name of the tribe living in the region where the Dutch established their forts and trading post. A further speculation is that Taiwan may be a corruption of the Chinese phrase *tung hwan,* meaning "eastern savages," thus encapsulating much of what the mainlanders knew and thought about the island. While Taiwan is the name mainland Chinese have used for the island in recent history, Yosaburo's theory gets some backing from an earlier Chinese name for the island. Chinese geographical records from the third century A.D. refer to the island as "I Chou," meaning "a barbarous region to the east," a phrase that acknowledges a degree of ignorance rather like the apocryphal European maps that filled in blank spaces with the all-purpose phrase "here be dragons." For a while, still confused about Taiwan's position, Chinese cartographers called the island "Liu Chiu," mistakenly believing it was what is now known as Okinawa in the Japanese Ryukyu chain. When the mistake became understood around 607 A.D. during the Sui dynasty, the Chinese changed the name to "Little Liu Chiu." To the Japanese the island has long been called "Takasago," though this is thought by some historians to have been adopted from the name of the first aboriginal tribe with which the Japanese came in contact. Other authorities report it simply as the name of a Japanese pirate and trading outpost established on the island's southwest coast in the late sixteenth century.

The name "Formosa" is an abbreviation of "Ilha Formosa," meaning "beautiful island," and was used for several hundred years among westerners until the recent domination of "Taiwan." The derivation of the name Formosa is a pleasant story, but it may be no more than that. In 1517 an early Portuguese expedition, led by the merchant Tome Pires, was dispatched by the viceroy of Malacca to open trade with China. Pires got at least as far as Guangzhou and is believed by some to have sailed further up the south China coast to Fujian and Taiwan. Other authorities are more certain that a group of Portuguese traders, sailing with a Chinese pirate in 1542, stumbled upon the island. On its way north, the party, led by Fernao Mendes Pinto, was blown off course by a typhoon and, much to their joy, ended up at Japan, which they had been trying to find for some years. On the way back the ship traveled down Taiwan's lush west coast. The problem with this story is that the only authority is Pinto in his book *Peregrinacao,* and he was notoriously extravagant with the truth. As one writer put it, reflecting widespread skepticism about Pinto's tales: "Politely stated, the book has not enjoyed universal credibility with historians."[1] Among the problems with believing Pinto is that there is at least one other European account of the existence of Taiwan before the Portuguese got into print with his 60-year-old reminiscences in 1614.

Some erroneous accounts claim there was a Dutchman, Jan Huygen van Linschoten, with Pinto on the pirate ship, who exclaimed in Portuguese, "Ilha Formosa" (beautiful island), on seeing Taiwan's dramatic eastern coast. Van

Linschoten has gotten enormous mileage out of this one moment of epiphany, and he deserves it, but for other reasons. His name for the island has survived over four hundred years and is still preferred over the name "Taiwan" by many. Not least of the objections to the story of van Linschoten naming the island Formosa is that he was not born until 1563, more than 20 years after Pinto's expedition to Japan. While van Linschoten's exclamation was his only direct contribution to Taiwanese history, he is an essential figure in the age of exploration in the sixteenth and seventeenth centuries. Van Linschoten was actually a spy, a mole who infiltrated the Portuguese maritime establishment—the most successful explorers and navigators of the age—to learn the secrets of their technological advantage. While van Linschoten probably did not give the name Formosa to Taiwan, there is no doubt he popularized it. In 1596 he published a book called *Itineratio,* exposing the secrets of Portugal's routes to Asia. The book included references to Taiwan as "Ilha Formosa." *Itinerartio* was translated into several languages and quickly became a handbook and guide for the Europeans lusting to trade with China and Japan. Within five years Portugal's supremacy in Asia vanished as Dutch and English traders, with van Linschoten's handbook as their guide, swarmed all over the East. It was a signal moment in Europe's relationship with Asia and changed the entire balance of power in as profound a way as the acquisition of the secrets of the atom bomb by agents of the Soviet Union in the mid-twentieth century.

When the Spanish briefly established a fortified trading enclave in northern Taiwan in the early seventeenth century, they used van Linschoten's name. They simply translated it into Spanish and called the island "Hermosa."

There is one other significant name for the island, and that is "Pekan." This name is still used by the aborigines of southern Taiwan, whose ancestors came to the island from Southeast Asia when the expansion of the Indian empire forced local peoples to flee eastward in search of land. These peoples of proto-Malayan or Austronesian heritage arrived by raft and canoe and named their new home "Pekan," meaning, "a haven gained after long wandering."

These names in the context of their times hold great political significance. Islanders over the ages have consistently adopted the usage of a name for their state that in their minds establishes their communal distinctiveness. Among themselves they purposefully use in a small act of defiance a name that is not used by their colonial rulers. There are many instances of this persistent drive to enforce recognition of the island as a separate and special place. A good example is that of a man who might be called the intellectual father of the modern Taiwanese independence movement, Peng Ming-min. In his account of his emotional and pragmatic journey from Japanese colonial subject to Taiwanese patriot, *A Taste of Freedom,* Peng consistently refers to himself as "Formosan."[2] Peng does this because his torment, imprisonment, escape, and exile were during the Stalinist rule of Chiang Kai-shek and the Kuomintang, mainlanders who saw the islanders as a lesser breed and the island "Taiwan Province" as a brief sanctuary from which they would strike out to regain rule of China. Peng now happily describes himself as "Taiwanese," but a lot has changed since he wrote his book as a "Formosan" in 1972. For Peng to now label himself a "Taiwanese" is just as much a political statement as to call himself "Formosan" 30 years ago. Mainland China's rulers like to consider their "Taiwan compatriots," as they are usually called in the Beijing-controlled official media, as merely wayward sons and daughters of China, cast into the wilderness by a quirk of history and now misguided and deceived by nefarious, self-seeking rulers. There is therefore no such thing as a "Taiwanese" in Beijing's view. There are Chinese who live on Taiwan island and who, in Beijing's view, are yearning to rush to the arms of the motherland once they perceive the destructive foolishness of the jumped-up petty politicians controlling their lives. But Beijing just does not understand Taiwan and its people. The statement "I am Taiwanese" that the island's people make every day in how they live, their communal and political values, their relationship with authority, and their view of their part in Asia and the world, is beyond Beijing's current comprehension. Beijing may one day understand that there are people of primarily Chinese stock who relish the culture, love the history, glory in the poetry of the language, but who do not wish to be considered Chinese in the way it is currently defined by mainland China. Taiwan is a repository of those reservations about what "one China" currently entails, but there is much more to the mix of peoples and experiences on Taiwan than that.

It is not only Taiwan's various names that have made it an ambiguous and deceptive place. Even its geography presents an island of differing contexts and characters depending on the viewpoint. A map looked at from close up presents the conventional picture of Taiwan as an offshore island of China, shaped like a leaf and separated from the mainland by only one hundred miles (one hundred and sixty kilometers) of sea across the Taiwan Strait. Moreover, towards the southern end of that strait are the 64 islands of the Pescadores group, in Chinese the Penghu Islands, which dot the seas like a string of stepping stones linking island with mainland. On many occasions in history that has been the function of the Penghu Islands, and most of the invasions and tides of immigrants to Taiwan have first established themselves on this archipelago.

With a close-up view of the map of Taiwan, however, the eye is drawn to another context for the island. Poking into the north-east, top right corner of the map is Yonaguni Island, the most easterly in Japan's southern Ryukyu chain. Yonaguni is actually only sixty miles (one hundred kilometers) from Taiwan, considerably closer than mainland China. Draw back a little further from the map and Taiwan appears to be not exclusively a Chinese offshore island, but also what has been described as the period dot at the base of the question mark formed by Japan's island chain.

That broader view then brings in another perspective in the southeast, bottom-left corner of the map. There, about one hundred miles (one hundred sixty kilometers) off Taiwan and a mere sixty miles (one hundred kilometers) from Taiwan's Lan Yu group of south-eastern outer islands, is the Philippines' northern outpost of Batan. Draw the eye back a little further and Taiwan takes on another geographic character. It is the northern end of the Philippine archipelago and clearly linked to the whole network of islands, including Indonesia, that make up much of Southeast Asia.

Thus, in the full panoramic view, Taiwan's geographic position presents three different realities at once. It is an offshore extension of China, the southernmost reach of the Japanese chain, and the northernmost stretch of Southeast Asia. In its tumultuous story Taiwan has played all three roles. But it also has a fourth part in its own drama: as a link and crossroads where the three geographic pressures on Taiwan, and thus where the human cultures they have spawned, meet and collide. Sometimes these collisions have been peaceful and to the advantage of all involved. Far more frequently they have not. The peoples of the island have usually found themselves buffeted and torn by pressures from elsewhere over which they have had little or no control. That is true to this day.

It was entirely natural pressures that made Taiwan the leaf-shaped island of today. Until the end of the Pleistocene era, about ten thousand years ago, Taiwan was with the Japanese islands and most of archipelagic Southeast Asia, part of a larger Eurasian land mass, much of it covered by Ice Age glaciers. What are now islands were then mountain ranges on the southern fringe of the Asian continent. It is easy to imagine that the southern and eastern coast of China at that time looked much like the western regions and coast of North America today with the coastal mountains forming a barrier between the ocean and the great plains behind. The slow ending of the Ice Age and melting and retreat of the glaciers, however, caused a rise in sea levels, flooding the plains and creating the Sea of Japan, the Yellow Sea, the East China Sea and the South China Sea. The Taiwan Strait was fashioned at the same time. The strait is relatively shallow, only one hundred fathoms, while off Taiwan's east coast the ocean floor of the Pacific falls sharply to one thousand fathoms.

Above the tide line this drama continues. The east coast of Taiwan has cliffs rising up to six thousand feet (two thousand meters), some of the highest seacoast cliffs in the world.

Other natural forces were at work shaping Taiwan both before and since the retreat of the last Ice Age. Volcanic activity and shifts in the continental tectonic plates under the Pacific Ocean exerted massive pressures on Taiwan, continuing to thrust up a series of mountain ranges with the highest, Mount Morrison, rising over thirteen thousand feet or almost four thousand meters. Between these folded mountain ranges is a series of high valleys running roughly north and south the length of the island. Lushly forested mountains and hill country now cover almost 70 percent of the island. These forces are still at work and the island continues to suffer irregular but persistent earthquakes.

As the mountains rose from the Pacific floor they carried up with them vast amounts of seabed coral, which became the raw material of Taiwan's exceptional agricultural fertility. Having established Taiwan's basic form, nature now started sculpting its creation. Taiwan straddles the Tropic of Cancer and is in the direct path of monsoon rain storms and typhoons - Asian hurricanes—that sweep in from the Pacific every year. The island's average annual rainfall is 98.5 inches, but it does not fall evenly. Most falls on the east coast and the mountains. The west coast receives only about 50 inches of rain a year. Millennia of torrential rain have done much to shape modern Taiwan. Wind and water have worked away at the mountains. Toward the east the torrents of water have created sharply etched river valleys that rush into the sea. To the west, however, similar rivers have annually deposited masses of eroded tailings from the mountains into the much shallower seas between the island and mainland China. The deposits from these rivers have created a large and fertile plain down the western side of the island. This natural construction project continues. Sites and geographic features such as the coastline mapped or settled by the first European explorers, traders, and colonists four hundred years ago are now well inland. Physically, at least, Taiwan continues to progress toward China.

The stories of Taiwan's early inhabitants are epic sagas in themselves. People have lived on the island for tens of thousands of years. But identifying with scientific certainty who they were and how they came there is an ongoing process. It is inevitable that as more becomes known about these peoples, more questions will appear. What is evident from the continuing exploration of the origins of Taiwan's aborigines, as they have come to be known, is that tribal peoples were arriving on the island from several points of the compass and over many more thousands of years than has been acknowledged until recently.

Partial knowledge and the natural desire to tell a clear-cut story has led some writers to dramatically oversimplify the immigrations. A common analysis is that there were prehistoric people living on Taiwan as long ago as the last Ice Age, when there was still a land link with the mainland. This part is true and well established. But, the writers continue, these people died out and were replaced by other, non-Han Chinese tribes from the mainland about one thousand years B.C., within the time of Chinese recorded history. This assertion is far more problematic and unproven. An alternative view is that the original inhabitants may have been assimilated by new arrivals or their cultures and habits may have evolved into a different social order. Then, the clear-cut version continues, sometime around five hundred A.D., Austronesian tribes from the Philippines, Indonesia, and perhaps mainland Southeast Asia began arriving and eventually clashed with the tribes originally from the mainland.

While this handy outline contains a core of truth, it is no more than a handy outline. A more probable scenario is a continuous and fluid movement of people to the island. Some new arrivals would indeed have been ethnically distinct from those already on the island. Others were from the same heritage as previous settlers, except that their adaptation to living conditions over the generations created substantially different cultures. This formless pattern of migration has, like much else on Taiwan, often become confused by politics. Schools of thought about the origins of Taiwan's aboriginal peoples have frequently been influenced by contemporary considerations. Too often scholarship is based on claims to the island's ownership rather than the evidence of science. Japanese scholars, for example, while doing some of the first academically stringent work on Taiwan's prehistory, have tended to emphasize the speculation that there was a significant influx of peoples from Japan's nearby Ryukyu Islands. Japanese analysts also often acknowledge the dominant component of Austronesians of Southeast Asia while minimizing prehistoric influxes of mainland Chinese groups. Contemporary independentist or "nativist" Taiwanese anthropologists enthusiastically acknowledge the Southeast Asian origin of most of the island's aboriginal peoples. But they frequently stress as well the intermarriage of aborigines with later Chinese pioneer settlers, who were predominantly men. This view carries the political message that modern Taiwanese are a hybrid, distinct people who have evolved from many heritages and who should not be considered Chinese in the way, say, that people from Shanghai or Beijing are Chinese.

During the period of oppressive military rule by the Kuomintang mainlanders, from 1945 until martial law was lifted in 1987, the island's aboriginal peoples, who now number about 350,000 and two percent of the population, were largely ignored and their languages and culture suppressed. Chiang Kai-shek saw Taiwan's natives as just one of the over 50 minority ethnic groups in China proper—groups to be tolerated but not encouraged. It was when Lee Teng-hui, a Taiwanese-born ethnic Chinese of the Hakka minority, was selected president in 1990 that a profound cultural and political transformation began on the island. Political freedom gave a voice to Taiwanese of all ethnic backgrounds with a long heritage on the island who had been kept silent by the ruling minority of Chiang's mainlanders. They latched on to the aboriginal component of their heritage as one of the distinctive elements in the island's multicultural ethnic identity. Modern Taiwanese aborigines frequently view this new attention as a mixed blessing. On the one hand it offers the opportunity for them to rise out of the third-class citizen status of the last several hundred years. (The Hakka have claimed the dubious right to second-class position after the dominant Hoklo.) At the same time, the majority view of the aborigines has not progressed much beyond stereotypical images of an exotic minority with colorful costumes, songs, and dances. Political freedom, as well as the international networks made possible by modern means of communication, has also brought a new assertiveness among Taiwan's 13 recognized indigenous groups. This is evident not only in pressure for official recognition and support but also in academic exploration of the place of Taiwan's aboriginal peoples in the wider world of indigenous races living in the Pacific Ocean region.

There is a radical theory of Taiwan's place in regional migration that was first propounded in the late 1970s by Peter Bellwood of Australia's National University.[3] Bellwood contends that as well as being the target of immigration, Taiwan was the base from which early migrants to Southeast Asia, Polynesia and other Pacific islands, and even the Indian Ocean spread between 6,000 and 3,600 years ago. Work by scientists in New Zealand, Canada, the United States, and Taiwan has produced supporting evidence of cultural, linguistic, and ethnic links between the Polynesian peoples of the island of the Pacific Ocean and the Austronesians of Taiwan. New Zealand's Geoffrey Chambers, for example, has identified clear similarity in mitochondrial DNA samples from Maoris in New Zealand and the Yami people of Taiwan's Lan Yu Island.[4] This is not conclusive proof of Taiwan as the fount of Polynesian migration, however, because the Yami was one of the later tribal groups to arrive on Taiwan. They migrated to Lan Yu from the islands of the Batan archipelago of the northern Philippines around 500 A.D. More recently, David Burley of Canada's Simon Fraser University and William Dickinson of the University of Arizona have found pottery evidence in the South Pacific from about 850 B.C. suggesting links back to Austronesian pioneer voyagers from Southeast Asia.[5] The work by Burley and Dickinson indicates the Pacific islands were settled over an extended period and through a complex pattern of voyages of which Taiwanese migration from as early as 3000 B.C. may have been a part.

There is a long history of radical scientific theories exciting great passions, and Bellwood's thesis is no different. Professor Martin Nakata of Australia's University of Technology in Sydney, Australia, was abruptly dismissive in comments made at the end of 2003: "Bellwood's model is bunk. The idea of a relatively rapid dispersal of proto-Austronesian people based on Taiwan does not tally with the data from DNA and medical studies," he wrote in an article for the magazine *Taiwan News*.[6]

Others are prepared to keep an open mind. In an interview for this book in February 2004, Dr. Bien Chiang, deputy director of the Institute of Ethnology at Taiwan's Academica Sinica, said:

> From my point of view, Bellwood's is the most economical theory. If you place Taiwan as the base [for regional population] you can come up with many reasons why that should be so. Otherwise you have to look at the mainland and Southeast Asia as the base. There are problems with that, especially the timing of migrations. But if you place the fount in Taiwan, then the timing works better. Taiwan, for example, has one of the earliest datings for Austronesian people, though there are at the moment earlier examples known in Malaysia and Sarawak. So there is some irregular evidence to be ironed out. But I think Bellwood's theory is the most economical and gives the least difficulties. One must also keep in mind, though, that for ideological reasons the idea of making Taiwan the homeland for the Polynesian people is very acceptable politically at the moment.[7]

Indeed it is. Taiwanese cultural self-awareness has been heavily promoted since the transition to an open society. Within a fairly narrow corridor of differences both main political parties on the island, the Kuomintang and the Democratic Progressive Party, have sought to emphasize for audiences both at home and abroad Taiwan's cultural individuality and diversity. At home, this involves much greater governmental support and recognition than in the past for aborigines and their organizations. Abroad, it includes the government funding for the creation of nongovernmental organizations like the Taipei-based Austronesian Co-operation and Exchange. China has managed to force the exclusion of Taiwan from most international organizations. So successive Taiwanese governments have taken every opportunity to create their own bodies that operate on the international stage outside China's sphere of influence.

Archaeologists and anthropologists are still discovering the clues left by the first inhabitants of Taiwan. From remains that have been found it seems certain that what is now Taiwan was first inhabited when the island was joined to the mainland at the time of lower sea levels during the last Ice Age. In the 1960s human remains, pottery, and stone tools were found in caves in southern Taiwan at Changpin in the far southeast and at Tsochen near Tainan on the southern west coast. This Paleolithic, Stone Age culture existed until about 15,000 B.C. and several of the relics found on Taiwan are similar to those discovered from the same period on the mainland. There have also been several discoveries in northern and southwestern Taiwan of evidence of later prehistoric Neolithic tribes. Finds have included polished stone arrowheads and axes as well as cord-patterned and painted pottery with similarities to northern China's Yang-shao culture. Evidence of another painted pottery culture has been found at Fengpitou near Kaohsiung in southern Taiwan. These people were farmers, and not the hunter-gatherers of the previous cultures. Many of their artifacts show common ancestry with the tools used by people on the mainland side of the strait between 1,500 and 1,200 B.C. The picture that emerges from the more intense archaeological investigations of recent years is of a continuous trickle of tribes and communities migrating to and, if one accepts Bellwood's theory, from the island over many thousands of years.

The aspect of Taiwan's character that made the island a haven for peoples seeking refuge from troubles or pressures elsewhere was established early. Of the groups identifiable today as distinct, some of the earliest arrivals were the people now known as the Atayal. They established themselves over large areas of northern Taiwan from about one thousand B.C. Atayal men practiced facial tattooing, primarily to display their status as successful headhunters. Women were also adorned with facial tattoos, suggesting that the patterns were also intended to ward off evil spirits. Where the Atayal came from is debated, and the argument is an early example of the continuing habit of outsiders to impose their own national and nationalist imperatives on the island. The nineteenth-century German anthropologist Ludwig Riess contended that the Atayal arrived on Taiwan from the Ryukyus to the east of the island. Riess drew on Japanese research available at the time, 1895, when Tokyo had assumed colonial control of Taiwan.[8] There was undoubtedly a subliminal Japanese desire to establish historic links with their new possession, though that need not have affected academic scientific rigor. Riess suggests the Atayal were a branch of the people called Lonkius who originally came from the northern Japanese Kurile Islands, but who retreated south before the advancing Ice Age. Their descendants are the Ainu of Japan's Hokkaido Island. Japanese anthropologists identified the story of the "Cutting of the Sun" as told by tribesmen of the Taruko, a subclan of the Atayal, as evidence of a historic journey to escape the cold of the north.

Chinese anthropologists and historians, in contrast and in line with their own national inclinations, make the case that the early aboriginal tribes of Taiwan came not from Japan but from the mainland. As Taiwan was to become, as we will see, a sanctuary for a mélange of peoples over the centuries, it is most probable that both the Chinese and Japanese analysts are right.

The Chinese version of the early aboriginal colonization of Taiwan begins in the forested, mountainous region of central China about 2200 B.C. during the Xia dynasty. Emperor Yu oversaw the implementation of agricultural development among his people, the Han Chinese. Among the emperor's innovations was a project to construct many thousands of irrigation and drainage channels both to control flood waters and to bring land into effective agricultural production. The area under Emperor Yu's control was, however, relatively small and the success of his revolution soon led to land hunger and pressure to expand the borders of his territory. This brought the Han farmers into conflict with primitive Guizhou tribesmen; an ethnically distinct community of hunter-gatherers living in the forests to the south of the Xia empire. The emperor's armies made several attempts to dislodge the Guizhou from their hill forests and mountains, but without success. The Guizhou fought fiercely to protect their territory and for several hundred years an uneasy standoff was maintained along the Han empire's southern border. That changed with the coming to power of the Shang dynasty founded by Ch'eng Tang. In 1740 B.C. he launched a national campaign to conquer the Guizhou "barbarians." The land lust among the Han was so strong that Ch'eng mustered a massive volunteer army that was able, after much bloody fighting over some 60 years, to take possession of the southern forests, hills, and mountains. But the Han did not conquer the Guizhou. The tribesmen decided to migrate rather than submit. The Guizhou fled primarily to the south and west. Some Chinese historians believe that in their flight to the west the Guizhou established themselves in what are now the Chinese provinces of Sichuan and Yunnan as well as the northern reaches of modern Burma, Cambodia, Laos, and Vietnam. The migrants are, these historians believe, the ancestors of the people now known as the Yueh and still significant minorities in the same regions. The Guizhou who moved south readily adapted to their new coastal environment and became renowned navigators and traders. In the late 1950s the Chinese historian Chang Chi-yun wrote that there are indications the Guizhou/Yueh migrated to Taiwan around 770–469 B.C., the period of the "Spring and Autumn Annals."[9] Chang cites common customs among the Guizhou and the Atayal of northern Taiwan. One is the custom of a husband pretending illness when his wife is about to give birth. Until the late twentieth century this habit was still followed among the Yueh peoples of Southeast Asia. There is also the combination of headhunting and tattooing. While each of these practices was followed separately by peoples of China and Southeast Asia, only among the Guizhou, Yueh, and Atayal are they known within one culture and pursued in uniquely similar ways.

It is unlikely that the Atayal and associated tribes had Taiwan to themselves. About one thousand years after their emergence, upheavals in another part of Asia, the Indian subcontinent, in the early centuries of the Christian period, set another chain reaction of migrations in motion. Indeed, beyond India it was the expansion and economic might of the Roman Empire in far off Europe that led eventually to fleets of canoes with their crews of pioneers riding the surf to land on Taiwan's southern shores.

Rome's conquest of Egypt in 30 B.C. accelerated a passion for eastern goods and artifacts. Until it acquired Egypt and control of ports on the sea routes to Asia, Rome's access to eastern trade had been hampered by the long, arduous, and dangerous overland trails through Central Asia. But within 50 years of bringing Egypt into its empire, Rome had well-established maritime trade links with India. The development of this commerce had a profound effect on the subcontinent. India became not only a trading partner with Rome but also a clearing house for goods from further east: Southeast Asia and China. For centuries the ebb and flow of Indian empires and dynasties had been in the north of the subcontinent. The south had been largely ignored. The development of the southern ports such as Muziris (Cranganore) and Arikamedu (Pondicherry) brought not only new wealth but also commercial and cultural contact with the principalities in Southeast Asia and what is now Indonesia. The first four centuries A.D. saw a sustained spreading of Indian trade, culture, Hindu-Buddhist religion, and colonizers through Southeast Asia. Kingdoms dominated by Indian culture and military strength were established over much of the region and as far south as the island of Java, now the hub of Indonesia. Early Chinese texts recorded by John Keay in his book *India: A History*, published in 2000, describe several of these "petty Indian states."[10] One Malay peninsular state, which the Chinese called Tun-Sun, was ruled by five Indian families and a thousand high-caste religious Brahmans.

The local Malays took to giving their daughters in marriage to the Brahmans in order to ensure family security. "Consequently," wrote the Chinese, "many of the Brahmans do not go away. They do nothing but study the sacred canon, bathe themselves with scents and flowers, and practice piety ceaselessly by day and by night." The ultimate expression of this transplanted Indian idyll is the huge palace and temple complex of the Indianized kingdom of the Khmers at Angkor in what is now Cambodia.

Ethnic Malays lived throughout Southeast Asia and many of the islands of what are now Indonesia and the Philippines. They resented the imposition of the alien Indian monarchies and religions over them and the accompanying demands for land. The military dominance of the Indians, however, made Malay resistance ineffective. People began moving to find new land away from the power and influence of the Indian princes. Some merely ousted their neighbors, who then did the same and set off an ever-widening ripple of pressure for land. Some Malays inevitably had to take to their canoes and rafts and seek land beyond the seas. It was on these pioneering voyages that the Malays discovered and settled southern Taiwan.

There is general agreement among anthropologists and ethnologists that the Yami people of the Lan Yu islands came from the northern islands of the Philippines. The Yami are probably the most recent arrivals, the last wave of the ripple effect set off by the pressure for land in Southeast Asia. When and how the earlier tides of immigration reached Taiwan remains a matter of academic investigation. There is well-founded speculation that migrants did not just island hop to Taiwan. Some immigrants probably made longer sea journeys from Borneo and used favorable currents in the South China Sea that carried them to Taiwan's southwest coast. Another current from the Celebes Sea sweeps up the eastern coast of the Philippines and reaches the east coast of Taiwan. A common race memory among many of the aboriginal peoples of southern Taiwan is of the tribal ancestor who arrived by canoe or raft from the south. Until relatively recently many of these peoples conducted annual reenactments of the arrival as a prelude to days of feasting in which the gathering of food and planting of crops were a central feature. The lifting of martial law on the island in 1987 helped sideline the negative attitude toward aborigines of the mainlanders who arrived with Chiang Kai-shek in 1945, and official sympathy and encouragement has allowed the revival of many of the aboriginal people's customs.

Although the new arrivals on Taiwan were all ethnic Malays, they came in family, tribal, and cultural groups from various parts of Southeast Asia with their own specific cultural traditions and languages. Once they arrived, the geography of Taiwan tended to promote the maintenance of these differences and the evolution of even greater distinctions. Those who colonized the west coast flatlands were separated by the island's spinal mountain ranges from those who settled on the narrower plains and steep river valleys of the east coast. The ridge formation of the central mountains tended to form isolated pockets of habitation for those who worked their way up into the high country. These solitudes created over time groups that have become distinct in language and other aspects of their cultures. The Paiwan in the far south, Puyuma in the southeast, the central Bunun, the Ami of the eastern central region, and Yami on Lan Yu Islands, with the Tsou in central Taiwan are all of Malay heritage, but their languages, religious ideas, manners of livelihood, and communal structures vary widely.

Geography and ferocious warrior cultures sustained aboriginal independence on Taiwan for a remarkably long time. Neither the Dutch nor early Chinese administrations ever controlled much more than the western third of the island. It was not until the 1930s that the Japanese administration, with the help of machine guns and poison gas, brought Taiwan as a whole under central control.

Chapter Three

BARBARIAN TERRITORY

The first written record of contact with Taiwan is in 230 A.D. Sun Chuan, the first emperor of the Wu "Three Kingdoms" dynasty, sent an expedition to explore for islands said to be in the seas off China's east and southern coasts. The explorers found Taiwan and returned with several thousand captives and enough information to conclude that the island was "barbarian territory" unworthy of China's attention. No official interest in Taiwan is recorded for nearly four more hundred years. Then, the second emperor of the short-lived Sui dynasty, Yang Ti, received in about 605 A.D. intriguing reports from Fujian province that in spring and autumn when the weather was calm and clear a smoky haze could be seen out at sea stretching several hundred miles along the horizon. The emperor sent Captain Chu K'uan to investigate the phenomenon. Chu and his fleet reached Taiwan, but because of the language barrier could not communicate with the natives, a peaceful group according to the captain's report. He nonetheless captured at least one of the natives—some accounts say he took several prisoners—and returned to the mainland. Two years later, in 607 A.D., another expedition of one thousand soldiers led by General Chen Ling was dispatched with orders to "explore the new land."[1] The general was given a very different reception from the welcoming greetings offered to Chu K'uan two years before. General Chen had with him one of the natives captured by the previous expedition who had learned enough Chinese to be able to translate. It appeared that the peaceful natives of Taiwan's northwestern plains encountered by Captain Chu had been ousted by a far more bellicose group pushing up from the south. Chen demanded tribute from the Taiwanese and recognition of the sovereignty of Emperor Yang Ti. The island's natives not only refused but challenged the Chinese to combat. General Chen's forces fought three battles with the Taiwanese and triumphed on each occasion, but the cost of victory was high. He returned to China convinced that taking possession of Taiwan would not be worth the necessary investment in blood. His judgment was confirmed at the court of Emperor Tang Yi, who had other more pressing military problems. Three of the emperor's other armies had just received their third crushing defeat in attempts to subjugate Korea.

General Chen believed he had been to what the Chinese then called "Liu Ch'iu," meaning "Precious Round Stone." This was what the Chinese called the southern Japan Ryukyu Island now known as Okinawa. During the centuries of the Tang dynasty, following the Sui, little attention was paid to Taiwan as the emperors and their armies concentrated on pacifying the northeastern and northwestern reaches of the empire. There was, however, private Chinese movement toward Taiwan. There are indications of a significant migration of mainland people to the Penghu groups of islands midway between Taiwan and the mainland. A poet from Zhejiang province, Shi Jianwu, moved to Penghu with his family around 806 A.D. Shih kept up a regular correspondence with friends and relatives at home and composed several poems while living on the islands. Migration to the Penghu group, mostly by fishermen and their families, continued over the next three hundred years, and the official history of the Sung dynasty mentions Penghu as being under the administration of Fujian province. This outpost was far from secure. An official, Wang Ta-yu, mentions in his records of 1171 that the Penghu colonies were regularly attacked by "island barbarians" from Taiwan. Wang recounts one such invasion in which four hundred of the Taiwanese were captured and their chief killed. Some accounts say the Taiwanese raids were spurred by the hunt for iron, which was used to fashion arrowheads, spears, and knives. Others say the raids were a response to migration and incursions on Taiwan by the Hakka people, a Han Chinese offshoot minority of sea nomads who have played a central role in the island's history. Whatever the cause or combination of reasons for the seaborne raids by the Taiwanese natives, their attacks were not confined to Penghu. They had the skill and confidence to make lightening assaults on the mainland too. The records of the Sung Dynasty note that on many occasions between 1174–89, "Hundreds of natives of Liu Ch'iu, led by their chiefs, suddenly appeared at Shui-ao, Wei-t'ao and other villages on the coast of Fujian, robbing them of all the iron and armor."[2]

The Hakka, whose name means "guests" and who were treated as an untouchable caste, came originally from northern Henan province. They were driven south in a pogrom around 419 A.D. and sought a temporary sanctuary in the mountains of Fujian and Guangdong provinces. But they were forbidden to own land and their sons were prohibited from taking the imperial examinations that were the route to advancement for other Chinese families. It is understandable, then, that the Hakka were in the forefront of the substantial overseas Chinese migration into Southeast Asia during the period of civil chaos and famine in the twelfth century. The Hakka's second-class status—evident on Taiwan and in China to this day—has created a fiercely independent and ambitious community. Some mainstream Han Chinese note ruefully that in the early 1990s the three predominantly ethnic Chinese states—China, Taiwan, and Singapore—were all led by Hakka. There was Deng Xiaoping, the paramount leader of China; Lee K'uan Yew, the founding father and in retirement the hidden guiding hand of Singapore; and Lee Teng-hui, the president of Taiwan. Some accounts place Hakka migration to southwestern Taiwan as early as 1000 A.D. and state that the Hakka established pioneer farms on land wrested from the aboriginal Taiwanese. Defending their homesteads from attacks by the aborigines was a constant battle for the Hakka, whose heads were considered prime trophies by the native Taiwanese. Yet the Hakka survived and thrived. There are reports from this period of tea, dyes, sugar, and rice being exported to China through the Penghu islands by the Hakka frontiersmen.

Interest in Taiwan revived in China with the conquest of the empire by the great Mongol leader Chinggis Khan. In 1281 his grandson and successor in China, Kublai Khan, was determined to extend the empire to Japan. But his fleet was battered and scattered by a typhoon that the Japanese called *Kamikaze,* "the divine wind," a word that was to resound into the future. A decade later, in 1291, Kublai Khan decided to make another effort to conquer Japan. This time, however, he decided on the more cautious approach of first capturing the Liu Ch'iu islands as a stepping stone. Admiral Yang Tsiang, still believing Liu Ch'iu and Taiwan were one and the same, set off across the Taiwan Strait. He quickly discovered his mistake and named Taiwan "Little Liu Ch'iu." When he did eventually make landfall further north on what is now Okinawa he met with no greater success than the ill-fated 1281 armada. His forces encountered such stiff resistance from the islanders that he decided to return to China.

Meanwhile the raids on the Penghu Islands and even on the mainland by the Taiwanese natives continued and intensified. In 1297 the governor of

Fujian, Kao Hsing, sent an anguished memorial to the emperor saying that there was a need to immediately pacify Taiwan and requested authority to undertake the task. Permission was given and the commander of the provincial army, Chang Hao, soon set off. The expedition was no more able to subjugate the island than its predecessors had been. But it did return with 130 captured Taiwanese and, to official surprise, news that some 1,300 Chinese were living on Penghu and that their "several tens" of oceangoing ships, called "junks," were engaged in regular trade with the Taiwanese aborigines and the Hakka colonists. China's Mongol emperors formally gathered the Penghu Islands into the empire and a garrison was stationed there. This military presence was ineffectual, especially against the Japanese Wakou, "dwarf pirate" sea raiders who infested the Taiwan Strait and East China Sea at this time. In 1387, 19 years after the native Chinese Ming dynasty took over from the Mongols, the military garrison was withdrawn from Penghu and was replaced by a naval base with the intention of combating the pirates. At the same time the settlers on Penghu, many of them Hakka, were ordered to return to the mainland. Some did, but others decided to defy the order and go on to Taiwan.

Over the next century the Hakka pioneers extended their domains on Taiwan's western plains, but the settler families were never dominant and lived under a permanent state of siege. Even this tenuous Hakka hold in the west was soon challenged by a new wave of migrants, the Hoklo from Fujian, where 95 percent of the province is hills and mountains unsuitable for agriculture. The Hoklo were driven across the treacherous seas of the Taiwan Strait by famine, land hunger, and civil upheaval in China. These Hoklo were the vanguard of a prolonged migration from which the great majority of modern Taiwanese trace their ancestry. Their sheer weight of numbers drove the Hakka ever deeper into aboriginal territory and reaffirmed the traditional animosity and suspicion between the two Chinese peoples that remain significant elements in Taiwanese society and politics even now.

The increasing seaborne activity in the oceans around Taiwan by fishermen, traders, pirates, and imperial naval ships was a natural result of China's remarkable developments in ship design and technology. Until the eighth century A.D., China's boat design accomplishments were largely focused on river craft. Foreign commerce was of minor importance and what trade there was was conducted by Arab, Persian, and Singhalese merchants. That began to change in the ninth century, when under imperial patronage China started to develop a blue ocean navy and trading fleet. In 1161 A.D., a Chinese naval fleet defeated a larger Korean fleet and gained control of the East China Sea. There are carvings dating from 1185 on the Bayon temple at Angkor Thom in Cambodia showing two-masted Chinese trading junks, indicating the size and range of the merchant ships. The Mongols, who came to power in 1279, continued the policy of maritime development. They produced the massive four-masted ocean-going junks with holds divided into compartments by watertight bulkheads—a protection against the hull being breached by submarine rocks not adopted by Europeans until the nineteenth century—that so impressed the Venetian explorer Marco Polo.

When the Ming dynasty began in 1368 there was a natural inclination to reestablish nativist Chinese culture after a century of Mongol rule. Within the imperial court Confucian scholars became increasingly ascendant as the fount of policy. But they were in almost constant conflict with the emperor's eunuchs in charge of daily administration. It was, perhaps surprisingly, on the back of this tussle for power that China's great age as a naval force grew and then died. Naval power grew because the early Ming emperors saw the payment of regular tribute from neighboring "vassal states" as an essential affirmation of China as the Middle Kingdom between lesser peoples and Heaven. The projection of naval power was a necessary element in enforcing that relationship and, ultimately, in embellishing the legitimacy of the Ming emperors, the sons of Heaven, themselves. This hubris reached its zenith in the person of Emperor Cheng Tsu, usually referred to as the Yung Lo emperor.

Some historians argue that the vassal state system was profoundly different from the aggressive imperialism then beginning to reach out from Europe. Rather, it was an expression of Chinese cultural certainty. In order to benefit from the patronage of the Middle Kingdom, foreign potentates had to accept and acknowledge the universal supremacy of the emperor of China. Vassals were required to pay tribute and perform the "kowtow"—kneeling three times and prostrating themselves nine times before the emperor or his empty throne—in order to receive the blessings of trade and diplomatic relations. Today, Communist Party cadres in tailored suits have superceded mandarins in costumes of imperial silk, and the ceremonies of supplication have moved from the Forbidden City across the road to Mao Zedong's Great Hall of the People, but little else has changed. The foreign diplomats, investors, merchants, bankers, and opportunist carpetbaggers who now flock to Beijing are presented with the same choice: Accept China's terms or be frozen out of its market and future potential. Now, of course, an essential tribute Beijing exacts concerns Taiwan. Diplomatic relations with Beijing, and all they promise, will not be accepted from any nation that maintains formal ties with Taiwan. Over the last half-century few nations and no internationally significant ones have balked at making that kowtow.

In the fourteenth century the eunuchs, with their control over the palace and all its grandeur, were prime promoters of gathering more vassal states under the imperial domain. Yung Lo agreed and in the dying years of the century he ordered the construction and fitting out of a great fleet of treasure ships, warships, and supply vessels to bring known and unknown lands under China's influence.

The fleet was put under the command of a Muslim eunuch, Zheng He, who set off in 1405 with 62 vessels (some probably exaggerated accounts say 317 ships) carrying 28,000 men. The treasure ships have been calculated by authorities such as maritime historian Louise Levathes to have been about four hundred feet long, among the largest sailing vessels ever built. Others carried cavalry horses, some were fighting ships, and there were even bulk water carriers.[3] Admiral Zheng's first three voyages were through Southeast Asia to India. The fourth and fifth voyages also showed the flag in Southeast Asia and India before going on to Aden. The sixth voyage in 1421 has achieved recent celebrity with the claim by British writer and former submarine commander Gavin Menzies, supported by much speculative evidence, that elements of Admiral Zheng's fleet not only found the American continent 70 years before Christopher Columbus, but also circumnavigated the world.[4] Menzies tells a riveting story, but he has at least as many expert detractors as he does supporters.

After the sixth voyage the massive expenditure of energy and investment prompted a hiatus, a few years of seeming exhaustion. When the young Zhanji, Yong Lo's grandson, became emperor in 1426 he quickly noticed a falling off of the tribute from vassal states and a corresponding loss of the dynasty's prestige and influence. In 1430 the emperor ordered a seventh voyage by the treasure fleet. Preparations took time because the fleet needed restoration. Admiral Zheng, now in his sixties, finally left Nanjing on January 19, 1431, but it was a year later that he finally left the south China coast of Fujian, bound again for India. At the eastern Indian port of Calicut the fleet divided into flotillas and one of the eunuch commanders, Hong Bao, sailed down the east coast of Africa to what is now Malindi in Kenya. The fleet returned to China and the mouth of the Chang Jiang River, better known outside of China as the Yangtze River, in July 1433, laden with the exotica of India, Africa, and the Middle East, including giraffes and elephants. Zheng He also brought with him ambassadors from Ceylon, Sumatra, Cochin (Vietnam), Calicut, Hormuz, Aden, and Dhufar to pay tribute and homage to the Son of Heaven.

Taiwan figures little in the story of Admiral Zheng's voyages, but the implications of the aftermath of this great age of Chinese naval power were profound. By some accounts one or two of Zheng's ships visited Taiwan during the first voyage and, finding it inhabited largely by headhunting savages and a haven of tropical diseases, decided it was a worthless place. It is also believed that one of the fleet's ships was wrecked on the island during the return on the seventh voyage. What was important for the island's history, however, was the tremendous growth of private regional maritime trade inspired by the example and technological advances of Admiral Zheng's fleet. Of even more immediate importance for the island was what happened when the emperor abruptly abandoned China's maritime prowess.

Even as Zheng He conducted his last triumph the political climate in Beijing was changing. The ascendancy of the eunuchs and their promotion of the grandiose overseas missions were being successfully undermined by the Confucian scholars. There is much debate among modern historians about why imperial China so decisively turned its back on the sea. Four central reasons are put forward. One is that there was a growing focus in the court on development of the administration within China. Another is that there was an intense philosophical debate within the court on the benefits of international commerce and technological gain versus the more spiritual gain of cultural purity and isolationism. Third was the enormous cost of the navy and the belief, based on historical experience, that all threats to China's territorial integrity and sovereignty came overland. And fourth, all these debates pitted the Confucians against the eunuchs in a contest for power and influence within the palace. The eunuchs lost the argument and power.

At its pinnacle of power in the early 1400s, the Ming navy had over 3,500 vessels. Some 2,700 of these were warships stationed at dozens of naval bases along the China coast, keeping the seas safe for merchantmen. By the mid-1400s that fleet possessed only a fraction of its former strength. Then, in an act that may seem like overkill but is typical of the single-mindedness of Chinese authority, the building of ocean-going ships was made a capital offense by 1500. That ruling was strengthened in 1525 by an imperial edict authorizing coastal officials to destroy all ocean-going ships and to arrest merchants who used them. But the principle and benefits of foreign trade had been seen and established. And as they always do, Chinese people found countless ways to defy authority. Into the vacuum left by the shriveled Chinese navy flowed a new sea power of private maritime entrepreneurs: merchants or pirates depending on the fortunes and opportunities of the day. For some of them, looking at the now established trade routes between China, Japan, and Southeast Asia, one place leapt out as the key to domination of the rich traffic. That place was the easily dismissed island of savages and sickness, Taiwan.

Chapter Four

PIRATE HAVEN

There has always been a fine line between commerce and piracy. Profit, after all, is simply recompense for risk. Whether an entrepreneur is willing to put only monetary investment at risk or if he is prepared to venture life, limb, and liberty is largely a matter of desperation or other circumstance. As the fulsome writer on Taiwan James W. Davidson said in 1903 of the Wakou Japanese pirates who flourished after the decline of the Ming navy, "They combined piracy with legitimate trade, resorting to the former when opportunities for the latter were not at hand."[1]

By the late 1500s trade among China, Japan, and Southeast Asia was well established. It flourished despite the decision of the Ming court in Beijing, influenced by the cultural superiority of the Confucian literati, to adopt a policy of splendid isolation, *tsung chu chuan.* With the first buccaneer merchants from Europe beginning to make their appearance in Asian waters, China's decision to cease exercising power beyond its borders created an anarchic marketplace. Even by the mid-1500s formidable pirate confederacies had been formed, and they not only preyed mercilessly on shipping in the East China Sea and Taiwan Strait but even attacked coastal villages and towns. For these sea rovers the island of Taiwan, astride the trade routes but beyond the rule of any law and with its dark reputation as a dangerous and forbidding place, was the perfect refuge.

The identity of the Wakou pirates has been decorated with as much politically inspired interpretation as other aspects of history involving Taiwan. Chinese texts refer to them as Japanese and there is a clear propaganda benefit in blaming foreigners for China's ills. But historians such as Hung Chien-chao say that what records there are on the Wakou suggest that while there was undoubtedly a Japanese component, sometimes even leadership, in the pirate bands, the rank-and-file cut-throats were usually Chinese.[2] Hung says that among the Wakou, Chinese outnumbered Japanese by ten to three and sometimes ten to one. Certainly when the major pirate chieftains and princes begin to appear in the 1550s they were Chinese. The first was Lin Tao-chen, who commanded a large pirate fleet based on the Penghu Islands, which were at the time abandoned by the Chinese officialdom and military. Lin and his crews became such a scourge to shipping in the Taiwan Strait and to villages on the mainland that Beijing was stirred from its isolationism. In 1562 (some authorities say 1564), Admiral Yu Ta-yu was dispatched to deal with Lin.[3] The admiral and his fleet encountered the pirates in the open sea. It is a measure of Lin's confidence in his military power that instead of running, his ships turned to face Yu's armada and, in Davidson's words, "with full sail charged straight for the intruders and assailed them briskly."[4] Yu apparently made a disciplined defense and the battle raged for five hours before Lin and his ships broke off the action and made a run for the safety of their havens in the Penghu Islands. Admiral Yu, however, was able to outsail Lin and got to the islands ahead of the much-battered pirate fleet. Lin found his way blocked and rather than risk a further engagement, he sailed for Taiwan, landing at Luerhman near present-day Anping and the site of later invasions of the island. Yu decided not to follow the pirates into the treacherous and unfamiliar shoals and islets guarding the harbor and returned to Penghu. There the admiral captured Lin's followers stationed on Penghu and left a garrison. The court in Beijing was delighted with Yu's exploits and, it may be said in some conflict with its isolationist ideals, drew the Penghu chain further into the empire by sending a governor. The arrival of a semblance of law and order on the Penghu Islands attracted colonists and for the first time the chain became a recognized entrepot for trade with the mainland, a status that assumed considerable significance a few years later when European traders began arriving in force.

Meanwhile Lin and his several hundred followers on Taiwan were not having an easy time of it. The island proved to be a far cry from the mythical land of milk, honey, and an indolent old age that pirates of all cultures are said to seek. Lin and his men found the land of Taiwan inhospitable and the natives even more so. The pirate outpost suffered near constant raids and attacks by aborigines, who valued Chinese heads above all in their measure of tribal hierarchical status. Lin eventually decided on a preemptive strike. His men attacked several surrounding villages and slaughtered scores of the aborigines.

There is a story, perhaps a folkloric embellishment, that Lin and his men then caulked their ships with the blood of their victims before sailing off and abandoning Taiwan. The survivors of the pirate fleet made their way to the Pearl River delta in China's Guangdong province where Lin is said by Davidson to have retired and later "died a miserable death, richly deserved."[5]

Although Chinese pirates made up the majority of those plundering shipping and mainland coastal villages in the fifteenth and sixteenth centuries, the Japanese were far from inactive. On several occasions in the 1500s Beijing emperors sent outraged messages to the Japanese shoguns, then completing their unification of the archipelago, demanding that the pirates be brought to heel. There is little evidence the Japanese made any strenuous efforts to comply, or that what they did attempt was at all effective. In frustration Beijing eventually forbade all contact between Chinese and Japanese and ordered that any Japanese caught in China and any Chinese apprehended returning from Japan be immediately decapitated.

The shoguns and the Japanese trader/pirates did clearly see Taiwan's dominant position on regional trade routes. The establishment of the Japanese merchant buccaneer outpost at Takasago on Taiwan's southwest coast in the 1590s has already been mentioned. At around the same time Japanese established a small colony at Keelung on the northeastern coast, a short voyage from Japan's Ryukyu Islands, only recently brought under the shogun control. There was a clear belief among the Japanese rulers that Taiwan was a logical and useful southern extension of their island empire, which created a lust that would take another three hundred years to fulfill. In 1591 Harada Magoshichiro was sent on an armed diplomatic mission to Manila, the capital of the Spanish colony in the Philippines. On his return Harada stopped at Takasago on Taiwan to deliver a letter from the shogun demanding that the Japanese outpost submit to their home country's rule and send tribute under threat of invasion. This piece of bombast ended lamely. Harada was unable to find a leader or any group in authority at the outpost to which he could deliver the ultimatum and felt compelled to carry the letter back home with him. In 1603 the new shogun, Ieyasu, first of the Tokugawa shogunate, continued Japan's interest in acquiring Taiwan. In 1609 he sent a senior lord, Arima Harunobu, to Taiwan to examine the island's potential for seizure and colonization. Arima toured Taiwan and made some attempts to fashion the Japanese trader/pirate outposts into a coherent colonial network, but without success.

Ieyasu was not dissuaded from his Taiwan ambitions by Arima's failure. In 1615 the shogun ordered the governor of the port city of Nagasaki, Murayama

Toan, to invade and capture Taiwan. Murayama set off in May 1616 with a fleet of thirteen ships and about three thousand troops. The enterprise was ill-starred from the start. The small fleet ran into a typhoon during the crossing and only one ship reached the Japanese outpost at Keelung. Aborigines attacked the survivors of the voyage and many of the Japanese were killed. For the abject failure of his mission, Murayama and his family were all executed on the shogun's orders. Had Arima been more forceful or Murayama luckier with the weather the story of Taiwan and its position today might have been very different, but history is replete with such twists of chance.

In August 1604, while shogun Ieyasu was contemplating seizing Taiwan, ships arrived at Penghu, beginning a chain of events that shaped the island's future for over half a century and that have faint echoes to this day. Wybrand van Warwyk, a captain of the Dutch East India Company, anchored at Penghu after one of many unsuccessful attempts by the company to capture the Portuguese enclave at Macau on China's Guangdong coast. Van Warwyk's mission was to open up a still-isolationist China to trade with the Dutch. As Macau was unobtainable, van Warwyk looked to Penghu to be a reasonable second choice for a base from which to establish commercial links with China. The captain sent messages to Xiamen requesting official permission to travel to the mainland to negotiate a trade treaty. Then he waited. When, by the middle of December and after four months of kicking his heels in mounting frustration, there had been no reply from Xiamen, van Warwyk upped anchor and returned to the company's regional headquarters at Bantam in West Java, now central Indonesia.

The Dutch did not forget about Penghu, however. In 1623 the East India Company directors, now established in their new Indonesian capital of Batavia, dispatched Cornelius Reijersen to again try to capture Macau. If that proved impossible, as it did, Reijersen was to go on to Penghu, which he did. Reijersen was a good deal more persistent in trying to force the Chinese authorities to allow trade with Penghu as a base. But he was no more successful and in the summer of 1624 was replaced as commander of the expedition by Martinus Sonck. To negotiate a settlement with the persistent and brutal Dutch, the governor of Fujian province, Nan Juyi, nominated an unlikely candidate, Li Tan, the head of the Chinese traders based illegally on Taiwan.

Li Tan wore many guises in his life, and it sometimes seems that he adopted a new name for every role he played in the history of Taiwan, South China, and Japan. This has confused posterity, though doubtless Li's objective was to befuddle his contemporaries rather than those who would later try to track the footprints of his extraordinary career. For when all the false trails and deceptive roles are put aside, Li Tan emerges as the greatest pirate prince of his place and age. And Li's heirs built an even greater corporate enterprise of robbery and plunder, culminating in the capture of Taiwan and the creation of a kingdom on the island. Just as significant, though less dramatic, Li can be seen as the prototype of the compradores, those later shadowy middlemen marshalling business between China and the West. They often amassed great but discreet personal fortunes in the process and, in places like Hong Kong and Macau, spawned huge corporate empires that still dominate commerce in southern China and beyond.

Li Tan was, so far as is known, born in a Fujian province, and as a young man he joined the steady migration of Chinese to Manila, where the Spanish colony offered great opportunities. Some accounts say Li fled to Manila after killing the servant of a local official in Li's home village. On arriving in Manila young Li became a Christian and took a new name, Andrea Dittis, one of his first deceptive guises employed to further his ambitions. There is little in Li's subsequent life story to suggest his conversion to Christianity was anything but a convenience for doing business with the Europeans, who were then beginning to appear in significant numbers in Asia. Even early on his piety clearly did not run deep. He was soon convicted of a serious offense—what, exactly, is unclear—and was sentenced to slavery in the galleys. Somehow Li managed to escape and to stow away on a ship bound for Japan. Some say Li was a tailor by trade and first worked in this business before establishing himself as a merchant in Hirado. If this record is accurate it makes an elegant link to Li's future choice of successor. In 1616 he received a license from the shogun to engage in foreign trade.

It was a time of opportunity in Japan as the major European sea powers—Portugal, Spain, Britain, and Holland—all vied with each other for Japanese and Chinese goods and markets. Li became very rich very quickly. More than that, he became the recognized leader of the Chinese merchant community in Hirado. From this recognition came one of the names that stayed with him all his life, Captain China. That nickname has an English ring to it that is not surprising. Li had long and, for him, very profitable dealings with the local agent of the English East India Company, the easily fooled Richard Cocks. Cocks believed Li was the key to British trade with China and that Captain China's evident excellent contacts among officialdom could get all the necessary permissions and treaties. Li did everything to encourage Cock's self-delusion, including such ingratiating ploys as having the Englishman act as godfather to Li's daughter Ignacia. Cocks was entirely taken in by Li and it paid off handsomely for the Chinese merchant pirate. Over several years

Cocks handed over a fortune in silver bars, which Li said regretfully were necessary to grease the right palms in China. And the more Li lamented that the permissions had not come through, the more silver Cocks shoveled at him. Eventually the directors of the East India Company in London saw all too clearly what Cocks could not see or would not admit to himself: that Captain China was taking them for a very profitable ride without any intention of helping the company get into the China market. Cocks died at sea on the way home after being recalled to London in disgrace for his lavish and fruitless importuning of Li. The Englishman is the archetype of all those western businessmen who have followed since in greed and certainty that they knew how to hustle the East. He is also, perhaps, the first of those rogue traders who gambled outrageously with his company's money, lost beyond redemption, and found himself in such a deep hole he saw no option but to keep digging.

The stern directors of the English East India Company demanded, in 1622, that Cocks retrieve from Li all the silver bullion the swindler had received. But it was much too late. By the time Cocks received the message, Li Tan had moved his center of operations and departed for Taiwan, where he saw the prospect of new and even greater opportunities. While Li had maintained one persona in Hirado as the diligent agent for the English and Dutch, he played a different role at the major port city of Nagasaki. Here he kept his own trading factories and ships with which he did business with Taiwan, southern China, and Southeast Asia. Those ships were well armed and there is good reason to think that with the protection, no doubt for a fee, of the local lord, the daimyo Matsuura, Li's merchant captains were equally active as pirates. Li hoped to make Taiwan a pirate kingdom under his own control, and for the two or three remaining years of his life he was remarkably successful. His Chinese heritage and extensive Japanese experience, plus the compelling salesman's patter that had so effectively duped Cocks, allowed him to bring the Japanese pirates of northern Taiwan and the Chinese of the west and south under one flag. The meeting of the pirate chiefs to create their confederacy was held in a small cove south of Anping. The outlaw chieftains were seduced by Li's vision and swore to accept his leadership of what was not only the first Asian multinational trade conglomerate but also the first semblance of an island government for Taiwan. Author W. G. Goddard, writing in 1966, said:

> The whole situation was nothing short of fantastic, and the closer our investigation of it, the more incredible it appears. From Japan to Java and beyond, the orders of Li carried more weight than the injunctions of Governments.

> His ships, flying [his] tortoise-shell flag, were masters of the seas and the dread of all merchants engaged in legitimate trade. His connections reached from Hirado and Nagasaki in Japan, down the China coast, where members of his family in Fujian were co-partners in the gigantic scheme, right down to Batavia. For a brief period Formosa was the most important spot in the Far East. For twelve months in 1624–5, Li Tan—Captain China—was the uncrowned king of the western Pacific, ruling his maritime kingdom from the island of Formosa.[6]

The same political and commercial phenomenon was described in 1903 by James W. Davidson in slightly less breathless tones:

> The Chinese pirates who resorted to the island as a safe retreat, were as a rule divided into bands, and, according to the scanty historical material which we have at hand, established a rough form of government over their settlements. So admirable was the organization that the different bands lived together without discord and chose their leaders by vote, while a supreme chief was appointed to look after the interests of the combined bands whenever anything arose of common concern. The strongest of them was a powerful band under the leadership of one Gan Shi-sai [Li Tan]. Their exploits brought large returns, and by combining legitimate trade with piratical raids they eventually attained a position so formidable that smaller bands combined with them for their own protection, and thus nearly the whole of the China and Formosa trade was brought under their control.[7]

It speaks volumes for Li's subtlety of intellect and confidence in his own purpose that he created this empire right under the noses of the Dutch without them fully comprehending what was going on around them. More than that, it was Li who encouraged and orchestrated the Dutch move from the Penghu Islands to the harbor at Tayoun, which eventually gave the entire island of Taiwan its abiding name. The Dutch knew about Andreas Dittis, as they sometimes called him, as they began their mission to find a bridgehead into China. They doubtless heard about him from So Bing Kong, the head of the Chinese community in Batavia, the Dutch East India Company's headquarters on Java. The Dutch may not have known that So was the southern manager of Li's pirate empire. They had suspicions, however, and never entirely trusted Li, though they engaged him as their agent to help facilitate their China venture. A note in the East India Company records of 1624 from the commander of the Dutch expedition, Martinus Sonck, then still on the Penghu Islands, to his directors at Batavia said, "Had we been able to use anybody else, we would not have trusted Captain China as much as we are now forced to do for lack of an alternative."[8]

It was Li who suggested a compromise between the Dutch and the Chinese authorities in Fujian, who were violently opposed to the interlopers remaining on the Penghu Islands, which were regarded as sovereign Chinese territory. Li's suggestion was that the Dutch decamp to Taiwan, still a distant, barbarian place in Chinese eyes, in return for an agreement to trade. This became the basis for the East India Company's nearly 40-year presence on Taiwan. Why Li encouraged the Dutch to establish themselves in what was his own kingdom can only be speculated upon now. The Dutch were the naval superpower of the age and Li may well have judged that they would make better allies than enemies, especially if he were confident he could dupe them about the true nature and extent of his own operations. Subsequent events give support to that view. Li's empire not only continued to blossom but did so under the protection of Dutch guns.

In 1625 Li disappeared from the historical record. In Hirado there was a brief report that he had died in Japan, though it is more likely he died on Taiwan. Part of the confusion is because Li had yet another name, Yen Ssu-chi. This was sometimes Romanized as Gan Shi-sai, the name used by Davidson for Taiwan's pirate chief. Davidson was not alone among historians in failing to make the direct connection between Yen and Li Tan. Chinese often adopt altruistic and poetic names, frequently applied to them by others, conveying their aspirations. Li may well have liked the name Yen Ssu-chi, which implied that his visage conveyed the demeanor of one thoughtfully intent on building an empire.

Before he died Li tried to ensure that his empire would be passed into capable hands. The inheritor of the pirate conglomerate was a young man, then about 21 years old, named Cheng Chih-lung. Li's choice was entirely logical. The two men were cut from the same cloth. Cheng nursed his inheritance well. He oversaw the substantial growth of Li's pirate fleet, which achieved such mastery of the southern China seas that the Ming dynasty felt compelled to adopt it as their navy with Cheng as admiral. Then he achieved the ultimate respectability of being appointed a royal prince. His son, Cheng Cheng-kung, better known in the West as Koxinga, took Li's inheritance to its apex of power when in 1661 he drove the Dutch out of Taiwan and established the island as an independent principality.

Cheng Chih-lung's early life was remarkably like that of his mentor, Li Tan, which was doubtless what attracted Captain China to the young man in the first place. There is some suggestion in Dutch records of the East India

Company from the time that their relationship was a close one from the start. The Dutch speculated, based on Li addressing Cheng as "son" and "son-in-law" in messages, that Cheng was at least betrothed as a child and perhaps married to a daughter of Li by his senior Chinese wife. At any rate, Cheng was born about 1603, the eldest son of a minor official in the village of Shih-tsing near Anhai in Fujian province, close to Li Tan's own birthplace. The region was poverty stricken at the time, and as a teenager Cheng, like Li a tailor by trade, left to seek his fortune in the Portuguese enclave of Macau, where an uncle lived. Cheng appears to have worked for Portuguese employers because he learned the language and also converted to Christianity. His baptismal name was Nicholas, but he also somehow acquired the name Jasper, which is "Icoan" in Portuguese. From this combination he became known to most westerners he encountered as Nicholas Iquan and it is under this identity that he appears in the records of the Dutch East India Company. The matter is not necessarily that straightforward because *i-quan* or *yeh-kuan* can also mean eldest son in Chinese.

While still a teenager Cheng abandoned tailoring in favor of petty trade and apparently spent some time in Manila, for he acquired some Spanish as well as Portuguese. Around 1623, when Cheng was about 20 years old, he moved to Hirado in Japan. The exact circumstance of how Cheng came to Li Tan's notice is unclear, but it is obvious that Captain China quickly saw the potential of this talented and ambitious young man. Within a remarkably short time—it can only have been a matter of months—Cheng was acting as Li's righthand man and frequently as his representative on voyages to far corners of the pirate empire. This speedy rise makes most sense if Cheng was a close and trusted relative of Li's.

During Cheng's relatively brief stay in Japan, he married a local woman of the Tagawa clan, who in 1624, just as the Dutch were establishing themselves on Taiwan, gave birth to a son, Cheng Cheng-kung, Koxinga. It was a signal moment in the history of Taiwan that resonates today. Koxinga's life was extraordinary in itself and various interpretations of his heritage and exploits remain potent political symbols for the Taiwanese, the mainland Chinese, and even the Japanese. Koxinga's younger brother remained in Nagasaki all his life, acting as a Chinese translator and, when Davidson wrote in 1903, the family was still there, a source of great pride to local Japanese. If Koxinga's bequests to earthly history were not enough, he is for many Taiwanese adored as a god and there are 63 temples on the island dedicated to his worship.

When Li moved his operation to Taiwan in 1623 Cheng Chih-lung went with him. Cheng played a key role in negotiations between the Dutch and the

Chinese authorities in Fujian in 1624, acting as interpreter using Portuguese as an intermediate language. In this role Cheng was very much in the forefront of Li's policy of trying to persuade the Dutch to move their trading base to Taiwan. But after Li's death in 1625 Cheng broke off his connections with the Dutch, who were as skeptical about his trustworthiness as they had been of Captain China's. Cheng moved his entire fleet from Taiwan to Xiamen in Fujian, which fell to his pirate army after an eight-day siege and from where he launched a reign of piratical terror on shipping in the Taiwan Strait and neighboring seas. A little more than a year after he took over Li's empire Cheng had about one thousand junks in his fleet and was doing a mighty trade selling goods pillaged from hapless merchantmen in the Chinese and Japanese markets. A message in 1627 from the Dutch on Taiwan to the company directors in Batavia notes that a year before a man who had worked as an interpreter for the company, who they called Iquan, had left his job without notice and become chief of a pirate band. The message says he had put together a large fleet, was terrorizing the whole China coast, and made navigation in the region impracticable.

In the spring of 1628 the Dutch decided to rid themselves of the troublesome Cheng, whose fleet now allowed him to attack and capture Dutch, Portuguese, Spanish, and English vessels just as readily as local junks. The Dutch dispatched eight warships "armed with the bravest men" and led by Commander de With to attack Cheng's fleet at Xiamen.[9] It was a disaster for the Dutch. A message of June 16, 1628, from the Dutch Fort Zeelandia on Taiwan to the company officials in Batavia says, "The said commander, on arriving there [Xiamen], was so overwhelmingly attacked by the Pirate's fire-ships that he had to make his escape to Java with the *Vrede* and *Erasmus* without firing a shot, having previously instructed the remaining yachts and junks to return hither [to Taiwan]. But, as we have said, not one of them has appeared yet."[10]

To say that Cheng was infuriated by the Dutch attempt at a sneaky, preemptive attack is to put it mildly. Over the next few weeks Cheng loosed his fleet to take any Dutch ship it could find. A bleakly worded and desperate message from Fort Zeelandia catalogues six Dutch ships captured by Cheng's forces as the pirate chief spent his fury. Several Dutchmen were killed in these encounters and at least 85 captured. Most of these captured Dutch, with their superior weapons technology, the matchlock musket, were persuaded to enter Cheng's service as his personal bodyguard. "Such then is the fruit of this imprudent undertaking," comments the writer in Fort Zeelandia, making it clear that the attack on Cheng's fleet was not universally approved by the Dutch on Taiwan. "No vessel can show itself on the coast of China, or Iquan has it in his power."[11]

Chapter Five

THE HOUSE OF CHENG

It was not only the Dutch who were watching with concern Cheng Chih-lung's burgeoning power and overt control of the south China coast. In Beijing the Ming court was confronting a double threat. In the north Manchu warriors were on the move and demanding the full attention of imperial forces. At the same time the court believed there would be continual pressure from the Europeans, especially at that time the Dutch, to establish colonial trading outposts in the south. The court decided it needed Cheng Chih-lung and his outlaw fleet to contain the Europeans so imperial forces could concentrate undistracted on the Manchu. The man chosen to try to bring Cheng into the imperial tent was Tsai Shan-chi, who had been prefect of Cheng's home district of Chuan Chow. Tsai had known Cheng as a boy and commented publicly and favorably on the youth's evident qualities. The prefect had even tried to encourage Cheng to enter government service and had himself given the boy some instruction in preparation for the preliminary exams. Tsai was disappointed when Cheng decided instead to go to Macao to seek his fortune. But the relationship between student and teacher in China then was a lifelong one, and often still is. The Ming court had reason to be confident that Cheng, even as an adult pirate warlord, would show respect and listen attentively to what his old teacher had to propose.

The seduction of Cheng into the imperial fold did not proceed in quite as straightforward a manner as the court in Beijing hoped. Cheng did indeed agree to meet his old master, Tsai, and did listen with evident enthusiasm to the proposal. Tsai set out the court's basic strategy that it would handle the Manchu if Cheng would deal with the Dutch, but the envoy added that Beijing was considering bringing Taiwan into the empire and would be happy if Cheng expelled the Dutch altogether. This appealed strongly to Cheng, who had never accepted the policy of subtle coexistence with the Dutch promoted by his mentor, the pirate Li Tan. But before making a decision Cheng discussed the imperial proposal with his brother, Cheng Chih-hu, who was a good deal more skeptical of imperial intentions. Cheng should delay a decision, his brother argued, until the court gave firm commitments about the future security and status of the Cheng family. Cheng Chih-lung accepted this position and it was then that another intervention by the Dutch decided the matter.

The East India Company's governor on Taiwan, Pieter Nuyts, got word of the Tsai-Cheng negotiations and decided Dutch interests should be considered. Nuyts requested an invitation to Xiamen and Cheng agreed. After all, while he was considering Beijing's importuning he might as well see if the Dutch were offering anything better. Nuyts duly sailed in a Dutch warship to Xiamen, where he was well received and feasted. To repay the hospitality, ostensibly, Nuyts invited Cheng to visit the Dutch warship. When Cheng and his party boarded, far from receiving Dutch hospitality, they were seized. Nuyts then dictated a treaty he required Cheng to sign in return for his freedom. The treaty was to force Cheng to support Dutch freedom of trade in all the south China ports. Cheng signed, but without any intention of complying. Because of Nuyts's actions, Cheng decided to accept the imperial offer if Beijing would agree to some guarantees.

As soon as Cheng was released from the Dutch warship he contacted Tsai, who set off for the capital immediately with the warlord's terms. The Ming court, increasingly unsuccessful in its efforts to contain the Manchu, agreed. Cheng was appointed commodore of the imperial fleet, essentially his own pirate band then numbering about three thousand ships. In a classic example of poacher-turned-gamekeeper, Cheng was now responsible for the suppression of piracy on the south China coast. He took his responsibilities seriously. When a group of freelance pirates led by Li Kuai-chi and based on the Penghu Islands attacked Kinmen, near Xiamen, in the summer of 1629, Cheng's response was quick and devastating. Li's band was totally destroyed. This and other diligent work to fulfill his imperial mandate earned Cheng much prestige at court, and in 1630 he was promoted admiral.

It is a measure of how secure and confident Cheng felt in his future that in the same year, 1630, he sent for his eldest son, Cheng-kung, Koxinga, still living in Japan, to join him at the grand mansion he had built at Anhui. Cheng's Japanese wife was either not sent for or could not get the necessary official approvals to allow her to leave Japan. She did not leave Japan for another 14 years and never saw her husband again. In Anhui Koxinga lived the life of a princeling, with all the advantages and duties that entailed, and acquired a thorough education in the Chinese classics.

The concept of leadership in China is very different from that in the west. In China, even now, military power, political authority, or the muscle to suppress the people is not enough. The concept of leadership involving the "mandate of Heaven" is no less true for having become a cliché. This notion of the semidivine responsibility to care for the wellbeing of ordinary Chinese is part of the burden of power, and lies as heavy on today's Communist leaders in Beijing as it did on the emperors and their officials in the past. In Chinese accounts of the career of Cheng Chih-lung, therefore, there has been a conscious effort to establish that when he donned the mantle of an imperial official, he also willingly accepted the responsibilities of the mandate of Heaven. This view asserts that a major reason why Cheng accepted imperial overlordship was so he could be in a better position to help the land-starved and famine-stricken people of Fujian province. To this end, Cheng suggested to the governor of Fujian, Hsiung Wen-tsan, that he, Cheng, be commissioned to assemble "several tens of thousands of starving people" and ship them to Taiwan, where the Dutch were beginning to establish agriculture and needed indentured labor with better skills than the aborigines.[1] Because of this initiative, Cheng is frequently held up by Chinese writers as the father of the Chinese colonization of Taiwan. That basic view cannot be contradicted. Yet it is also true that Cheng added handsomely to his already massive fortune with the fees for transporting the laborers. In addition all kinds of other taxes and pay-offs came his way from what was in essence officially approved human trafficking.

On Taiwan, meanwhile, Pieter Nuyts had been succeeded as governor by Hans Putmans, an even more aggressive and trigger-happy officer of the company. Although the Dutch and Cheng had reestablished a low-level working relationship, such as over the supply of agricultural labor, Putmans was outraged that Cheng had torn up the agreement to open up the China coast to Dutch trade. Putmans decided therefore on yet another now-familiar display of Dutch force. In July 1633, Putmans launched a surprise attack on the most powerful portion of Cheng's fleet, then anchored in Quanzhou Bay. The initial attack was dramatically successful and Cheng lost a large portion of his fleet. Confident of his victory, Putmans blocked the harbor of Cheng's capital, Xiamen, and demanded the Dutch be allowed to establish a trading enclave on the mainland as well as freedom of trade with the south China ports. In return the Dutch, according to their Taiwan colony records, were prepared to offer Cheng and the Ming "cannon, gunners and soldiers to fight the Manchu invaders."[2] With yet another example of Dutch duplicity to add to his already well-stocked store of contempt, Cheng dismissed the terms and set about planning a counterattack. There was a standoff for over two months, during which Cheng managed to put together another fleet of war junks. Then, in October and under cover of night, Cheng's fleet attacked the Dutch flotilla blockading Xiamen harbor, setting several of the ships ablaze. Putmans and the remaining ships fled back to Taiwan in disarray. In the sober light of dawn Putmans sifted through the ashes of his adventure to see what could be retrieved. He sent a letter to Cheng saying that if he found the Dutch offer unacceptable—a mild description of Cheng's response if ever there were one—perhaps the admiral could suggest some alternative.

Cheng was happy to oblige. He wrote back saying he would allow the establishment of a Dutch trading post on the mainland at Fuzhou so long as all the goods traveling between Taiwan and south China were transported in Chinese ships. For Putmans this looked like the best he could retrieve from a bleak situation. He would get his trade and his enclave, even though he would not control the shipping. For Cheng the agreement had the advantage of restricting Dutch shipping in the Taiwan Strait as well as keeping the admiral intimately informed with gossip from his ships' captains of what was going on in Taiwan, where the population of Chinese laborers was growing substantially.

In northern China the defensive war against the Manchu was not going well. The resulting famine and displacement of people carried down into the south, providing human fodder for Cheng's business of transporting laborers to Taiwan. As well as sending men into indentured service with the Dutch, Cheng was also transporting independent migrants into growing communities of Chinese in northwestern Taiwan outside the areas then controlled by the Europeans. The Dutch were generally happy with the influx, which allowed the rapid development of the highly profitable sugar cane industry on the island. But now and then notes of anxiety and caution are evident in the Dutch record. A Dutchmen reflecting a little later in the East India Company records on his nation's Taiwan colonial experience, wrote:

> A considerable number of junks kept arriving in Taiwan [from China]. As for those Chinese, they had been driven from China on account of the war, and had been increasingly in Tayoun and Formosa from time to time; until now, they form a colony of some twenty-five thousand fighting men, besides

> women and children. They occupied themselves in trade and agriculture, by which later means much rice and sugar was produced here, so that whole shiploads were annually sent to other places, from which the [Dutch East India] Company derived much profit from customs duty.[3]

The reference to a significant number of Chinese "fighting men" being among the immigrants has led to the thought among some analysts that even in the mid-1630s Cheng foresaw the defeat of the Ming by the Manchu. He was, this view holds, consciously preparing Taiwan as a final sanctuary for the Ming loyalists from which a counterattack on the mainland could be made.

Cheng was certainly a passionate Ming patriot at this time, and an increasingly important one as the dynasty's empire shrank before the Manchu onslaught and the southern navy became the Ming's only significant fighting force. On June 3, 1644, the Manchu captured Beijing and the Ming court removed to Nanjing, which fell on June 8 the following year. The emperor committed suicide and Cheng found himself the last authority of the Ming dynasty. Cheng proclaimed the prince of Tang, Chu Yu-chien, the new Ming emperor and established him on the throne at Fuzhou on the Fujian coast. Soon after the enthronement, in 1646, Cheng presented his son Cheng-kung to the emperor he had created. There is something a little tragi-comic about what followed. The emperor—in reality Cheng's puppet—was pleased with the young man's appearance and bestowed on the 22-year-old the great honor of the right to use the imperial surname, Chu. Thus Cheng Cheng-kung became, in the Fujian dialect, Kuo-hsing-yeh, "Lord of the Imperial Surname," which was heard and pronounced by Europeans as "Koxinga."

By this time the Ming empire had shrunk to three southern provinces, Fujian, Guangdong, and Guangxi. As well as receiving a new name, Koxinga was loaded with official appointments, one of which was as an officer in the imperial bodyguard. In this capacity he was dispatched to guard a pass between Fujian and the Manchu-held neighboring province of Zhejiang. But Koxinga's father failed to send supplies to his son's army. In the autumn Koxinga was forced to retreat to Fuzhou and in October the Manchu armies marched through the pass into Fujian. The emperor Chu Yu-chien wanted to attack them with the remnants of his land army while Cheng and his navy sailed up the coast, landed his forces north of Fuzhou, and attacked the Manchu from the rear. Cheng hesitated and the emperor marched off without him. The Ming army was defeated, the Ming emperor was captured and committed suicide, and the Manchu forces took Fuzhou.

It is certain that Cheng's hesitation, and perhaps his failure to send supplies to his son, was because he was already in negotiations to capitulate to the Manchu. The invaders had for some years pursued a practical policy of guaranteeing Ming officials that they could continue in their positions if they swore loyalty to the Manchu. It had been a highly productive policy as the Ming dynasty withered and was obviously in its death throes. As they approached the Ming dynasty's remaining three provinces the Manchu made the same overtures to Cheng, who was tempted and had heated debates with his son about the issue. Cheng eventually decided to throw in his lot with the Manchu. We are told that Cheng, dressed in the robes of a Ming duke and surrounded by troops and his personal bodyguard of two hundred former African slaves, escapees from the Portuguese at Macau (and replacing Cheng's guard of Dutch musketeers, who had been allowed to return to Batavia), marched into Fuzhou. The Manchu appeared at first to keep to their policy of retaining Ming deserters in their former posts and proclaimed Cheng the king of Pingnan, southern China.

There are several versions of what happened next. One account says that during three days of feasting to celebrate Cheng's defection, Cheng did not notice that he was being gradually separated from the main body of his troops. Then Manchu troops fell on Cheng and one hundred of his African bodyguards died trying to protect their master. Cheng was captured and taken in chains to Beijing, where he was held prisoner. Another version is that having made Cheng their local proconsul and loaded him with honors, the Manchu army prepared to return to Beijing. Cheng, as was his duty, set out to escort them part of the way. Once Cheng was separated from his fleet and army the Manchu captured him and carried him off to Beijing in chains. The two versions are not inconsistent and the differences are only in nuance.

Cheng spent the remaining 20 years of his life as a prisoner in Beijing, but under a fairly liberal regime of house arrest. In 1661 he was executed for refusing to persuade his son Koxinga to hand over the southern fleet to the Manchu. It appears that in his final years Cheng returned to the Christian, Catholic faith. Two priests, the Portuguese Gabriel de Magalhaes and the Italian Luis Buglio, who became his friends in his captivity and whose church he visited daily to hear mass, administered the last rites before his execution.

Ming resistance to the Manchu Qing dynasty did not end with the fall of Fuzhou in 1646. Armed remnants of the old regime remained on the loose in the southern provinces, hiding out in the hills and mountains that rise behind the narrow coastal plain. It was into these hills that Koxinga fled with a retinue of only a few friends after his father's desertion. Here, after much contemplation at a Confucian temple, Koxinga burned his scholar's robes in an emotional ceremony. With defiance in his heart he then left the hills to gain control of what was left of his father's army and fleet, and to take up the cause of the Ming. He went first to Xiamen, where he took command of two of his father's ships and then sailed to the island of Kinmen. Here he began reassembling the Cheng army and pirate fleet. Dutch records tell us that he soon gathered an army several thousand strong and a substantial fleet. In 1647 he was strong enough to extend his territory by capturing and moving his base to the island of Ku-lang-yu, off Xiamen, and went on to capture a number of cities along the Fujian coast. When Koxinga heard in 1648 that a Ming emperor, Chu Yu-lang, had been crowned in exile in western China, the young warlord sent a message of congratulation. He was rewarded for his courtesy by being named the marquis of Wei Yuan (Glory Extended) and subsequently given the title duke of Chang Kuo.

The extended Cheng family was split into factions by the importuning of the Manchu, with some, like Koxinga's father, kowtowing to the new Qing empire and others holding out. In 1650 Koxinga captured Xiamen from his Manchu mandarin cousin Cheng Lien and combined the city's troops with his own. It was the beginning of a major insurrection against the Qing, with fortunes swaying this way and that for over a decade. There was a setback for Koxinga early the following year, 1651, when the Ming emperor Chu Yu-lang ordered him to rescue the Ming governor of Guangdong and Guangxi provinces. Koxinga got only as far as Shantou, just over the provincial border from Fujian, when he heard of a dispute among his subordinate relatives back in Xiamen. He decided dealing with the family in-fighting was more important than the Ming emperor's mission, returned to Xiamen, and executed his uncle, Cheng Chih-kuan.

Over the next two years, as Koxinga's armed power grew in the south and the Ming insurrection gained momentum in western China, especially Yunnan, Sichuan, and Shaanxi, both the Ming and Qing emperors courted him with favors and titles. Koxinga steadfastly refused the Manchu Qing blandishments and even declined the Ming offer of the title prince of eternal peace on the grounds that he had done nothing to deserve it. A year later he was persuaded to accept the Ming decoration. He had by this time established an impressive Ming outpost along China's south coast. By mid-1655 he had built a thorough military and civil administration in Fujian with 72 *chen* (military outposts) and 6 civil administration offices. Koxinga's forces at this time were about 50,000 cavalry and 70,000 infantry, which included an elite Praetorian guard of 10,000 heavily armored foot soldiers known as "iron men," with more men arriving to join up every day.

Koxinga's enclave also became a gathering place for scholars and literati disaffected from the Manchu dynasty. Several of these torchbearers of classical Chinese culture moved further, to Taiwan, beginning the island's tradition as a repository of cultural purity. In this heady atmosphere of defiance against the foreign Manchu invaders, Koxinga ordered Xiamen renamed Ssu-ming-chou, meaning "thinking of the Ming."

Koxinga was not as able a general on land as he was an admiral at sea. It was still his fleet, direct descendant of Li Tan's pirates, that was most impressive and threatening. An eyewitness description of the fleet in Xiamen harbor has come down from Vittorio Ricci, an Italian Jesuit who appears on several occasions in the story of Koxinga and Taiwan, playing somewhat murky roles. "Never before nor since was a more powerful and mighty fleet seen in the waters than that of Koxinga, numbering more than 3,000 junks, which had been ordered to rendezvous in the bays and waters around Xiamen. The sight of them inspired one with awe. This squadron did not include the various fleets he had, scattered along neighboring coasts."[4]

The Manchu made an attempt to destroy Koxinga's fleet, sending a scratch armada of some eight hundred war junks against Xiamen. The enterprise was a failure. The Manchu were no match for Koxinga's captains at sea. A contemporary account says that after the battle "for weeks putrid corpses and tangled wreckage strewed the shores of Xiamen and Kinmen."

The Qing armies were more successful on land. In late 1655 they launched a campaign against Koxinga's battalions and forced him out of a significant portion of his western domains on the south coast. At the same time the Manchu moved against the forces of the Ming emperor Chu Yu-lang in western China. The emperor fled first to Yunnan, from where he sent a message to Koxinga urging a counterattack, then on to Burma and finally to Siam (Thailand) where he was captured. Chu Yu-lang was sent back to Yunnan by the Siamese and was strangled by the Manchu. Koxinga in the meantime raised his largest army ever, estimated at about 170,000 men. Some accounts say this force was only the core infantry and that in addition he had 5,000 cavalry, 50,000 marines, and his 10,000 "iron men." He also attempted to play on his Japanese heritage and asked the shogun to send support, but without success.

In 1658 Koxinga was ready for what he believed would be a decisive attack on the Manchu at their capital, Nanjing, on the Chang Jiang (Yangtze) River. He began by launching seaborne attacks at various cities along the coast, but on September 11 his fleet was caught in a typhoon and he was forced to retire and regroup. Contemporary accounts say he lost eight thousand men and one of his sons in this disaster. After this inauspicious beginning he was ready again by the summer of 1659. While the land army headed north toward Nanjing from Fujian, Koxinga's great fleet sailed around China's southern and east coasts and then up the Chang Jiang (Yangtze) River to the outer defenses of Nanjing, where it united with the land army. This vast force besieged Nanjing's outer defenses, which soon fell. It seemed that victory was certain and that after only 15 years the end of the Manchu dynasty was at hand. But, in the words of A. Grove Day in his book about pirates of the Pacific Ocean, Koxinga "behaved more like a prince than a pirate."[5] He decided to celebrate his thirty-fifth birthday and launched a carousing party that within hours had much of his army besotted with drink. In Nanjing the Manchu defenders quickly heard of the disarray among their attackers and launched a counterattack. A sortie in the middle of the night by the Manchu's most effective weapon, their cavalry, routed Koxinga's drunken army while fire ships played havoc with his fleet in the confines of the river.

It was a bedraggled and dispirited force that dragged itself back to Xiamen with only four hundred battle-scarred junks. The Manchu attempted to press home their advantage, well aware that even when severely mauled, Koxinga's forces were dangerous. A fleet of some eight hundred war junks was assembled by the Manchu and set out to attack the remnants of Koxinga's fleet, by this time holed up in the harbors of Kinmen. At this moment Koxinga's pirate instincts came to the fore. He commanded his crippled and outnumbered fleet so ably that toward evening, after a day-long battle, he maneuvered the Manchu fleet under two lines of his guns. The attackers were wiped out and, it is said, not one Manchu survived to take news of the defeat back to Nanjing.

Despite this great victory Koxinga knew that his days were numbered and the Manchu would keep coming by land if not by sea. This they did in June the following year, 1660. That attack was successfully repulsed, but it confirmed in the minds of Koxinga and his generals what they had already been discussing: They could not hold out forever at Kinmen and Xiamen. A new refuge must be found from which they could rebuild their strength for a further attempt to restore the Ming dynasty.

Koxinga had been casting covetous eyes on Taiwan since he had taken control of his father's forces in 1646. The Dutch had certainly heard rumors that he might attack the island in 1652 when a Jesuit, apparently with information from the ever-watchful Vittorio Ricci, told company officials in

Batavia that Koxinga had "an eye on Formosa, with the view of ultimately settling down in that territory."[6] It seems, though, that Koxinga's firm interest in Taiwan was not aroused until 1659, when his agent on the island, Ho Pin, who had been left as the Cheng family surrogate when Cheng Chih-lung left to attack Xiamen in 1626, fled to the mainland.

The Dutch first suspected around 1657 that Ho Pin was Koxinga's agent on the island. In March that year the governor, Frederick Coyett, used him as an envoy to negotiate a resumption of trade between Taiwan and China after the so-called Kuo Huai-yi Incident, when the Chinese settlers rose up against oppressive Dutch taxation. Part of Ho's mandate from Coyett was to directly ask Koxinga if there was any truth to the rumors that he intended to invade Taiwan. Ho returned in August with a calming letter from Koxinga saying he had no ambitions for the island and that the breech in trade was the fault of disobedient subordinates. Trade was immediately restored. The Dutch were mollified for a while. But in 1659 Coyett discovered Ho Pin was not only Koxinga's agent, he was also levying taxes on behalf of his master on all trade between Taiwan and the mainland. A warrant was issued for Ho's arrest, but he slipped the net and escaped to Xiamen. There he urged Koxinga to take the island as soon as possible. Koxinga was at the time fixated on his pending attack on Nanjing, with all the hopes of an overthrow of the Manchu that entailed, and took little notice of Ho's entreaties.

Taiwan looked a much more interesting option later in the year after the defeat at Nanjing. However, one of Koxinga's commanders, Wu Hao, who had visited Taiwan, said the Dutch were well able to defend the island with their two fortresses and one thousand European troops. The matter was shelved temporarily, but Koxinga was approaching the conclusion that Taiwan offered the most secure prospect for a haven from which to relaunch the Ming cause. In February 1661, Koxinga put the case to his generals and at the same time ordered preparations for an invasion of the island. A fierce debate ensued, with most of Koxinga's leading commanders firmly against the idea. Those from Fujian didn't want to leave their native province for a place with a bad reputation for disease and savage headhunters. Others argued that their forces would be outclassed by the Dutch guns and the impregnable fortresses of Zeelandia and Provintia. Some even suspected, perhaps correctly, that Koxinga was abandoning the Ming cause and was intent on establishing his own principality. One commander, Ma Hsin, suggested what seemed like a compromise. He argued that Koxinga should send a division of troops to scout the island, feel out the Dutch defenses, and see if Taiwan could be taken. This was agreed upon and Koxinga had backing for at least an exploratory invasion. But the situation changed almost immediately when it was learned that a major portion of the Dutch fleet at Taiwan had left for Batavia.

Koxinga's invasion plans were put into high gear. A force of 25,000 soldiers on 400 war junks was assembled at Kinmen. The fleet left its home base on April 21, 1661, and arrived at the Penghu Islands early the next day. The weather turned bad and the army was forced to stay on Penghu for eight days. On the evening of April 29, Koxinga decided to continue, despite the still adverse weather conditions. That night, as the fleet set out, the weather improved and on the morning of April 30 the fleet appeared on the northern horizon to a sentry at Fort Zeelandia.

Chapter Six

THE SIEGE OF FORT ZEELANDIA

At dawn on April 30, 1661, sentries at Fort Zeelandia saw what they had anticipated for nearly 10 years. Koxinga's invasion fleet of over four hundred Chinese war junks was approaching the coast a little north of the fort at the inlet of Luerhman. The Dutch, governor Frederick Coyett wrote later to the company directors in Batavia, were unable to resist such a powerful foe. For the ten years in which successive Dutch governors had anticipated an invasion by Koxinga, they had warned the directors of the East India Company in Batavia that it would be impossible to stop a landing with only their regular garrison of about 1,200 men.

In the frantic preparations of the previous months, governor Coyett and his council had tried their best to block off obvious invasion sites. In an attempt to make the narrow Luerhman inlet unusable for an attacking fleet they had sunk rock-laden barges across the mouth. But it was the time of the spring tides, when the sea level was at least two feet higher than normal. Koxinga moved his troops into the boats with the shallowest draft. They rowed with ease over the obstacles placed in the waterway and streamed ashore. His army of 25,000 was given an ecstatic welcome by thousands of the island's Chinese settlers, who rushed down to the beaches with handcarts to aid the landing. For these early Taiwanese islanders the arrival of Koxinga was an intoxicating moment of liberation, and they mobbed the arriving army. The invasion held the prospect of an end to burdensome Dutch rule and the advent of a familiar Chinese administration with all the formulas of Chinese culture but without the regular chaos of life on the mainland.

Koxinga's landing site was well chosen. It was out of range of the Dutch heavy guns, which far outclassed the Chinese artillery. It also put Koxinga's army between the two Dutch strongholds. To the west of Koxinga's force and across the mouth of the harbor was Fort Zeelandia, built at the northern end of Tayouan, a sparsely vegetated island a mile and a half long and half a mile wide. Tayouan tailed away south toward the shore of the main island. A shallow channel, fordable at low tide, separated the two at the southern end. Fort Zeelandia was an imposing, square brick-built castle with bastions for heavy guns at each corner, designed to cover the harbor entrance.

To the southeast of Koxinga's landing place was Fort Provintia on the main island's harbor shore. Fort Provintia had been hastily built nine years before after an uprising of Chinese islanders. With the help of maps provided by Koxinga's secret agent on Taiwan, the Chinese interpreter Ho Pin, called "Pincqua" in Dutch accounts, Koxinga's forces had not only landed unchallenged but also threatened communications between the two Dutch defending forts. The Dutch position looked perilous but not yet hopeless. Governor Coyett had only 1,140 soldiers, of which about 800 were regular troops. The rest were militia. He had four warships, but only two of those, the *Hector* and the *'s Gravelande,* were true fighting vessels. The others, the *Maria* and the *Vink,* were lightly armed auxiliaries designed for local trade in pirate-infested waters.

There was, however, no shortage of cultural and racial certainty among the Dutch, who were the naval superpower of their age. One Dutchman armed with a musket, they believed, was worth a hundred Chinese armed with bows or swords. There was some reason for this bravado. Dutch matchlock muskets were the first practical portable firearms, but they were crude affairs more like small canons than modern rifles. Pulling the trigger sprung a smoldering length of gunpowder-impregnated thin rope against a primed touchhole, setting off the main charge in the barrel and firing a large lead ball. Matchlocks were slow to load, it was near impossible to keep the match alight in the rain, and they were often as dangerous to the musketeer as to the target. But the Dutch had mastered the infantry discipline necessary to make them effective. Dutch musketeers were as good as any in Europe. In southern Africa and Asia, the unwavering lines of their soldiers and the fearsome noise and clouds of smoke from their guns terrified the local peoples.

It was this certainty of the superiority of their forces that had in part led Coyett's masters, the governors of the Dutch East India Company at Batavia, to disregard the warnings from Taiwan of an imminent attack by Koxinga and the appeals for reinforcements. Coyett did have, though, a large store of ammunition and food supplies for at least six months. Most important, the Dutch had the indomitable spirit of Coyett himself. He held his small and constantly dwindling force together for ten months through an ever-tightening siege made worse by the island's endemic malaria and typhoid.

What Dutch bravado ignored, however, was that Koxinga's army was not the rag-tag collection of farmers and peasants whom they usually faced. It was a well-trained and highly disciplined force of veterans of years of war against the Manchu. It is true that most of the soldiers were armed only with crossbows, swords, and Chinese pikes—only Koxinga's personal bodyguard of two hundred Africans had muskets—and the Chinese cannons were inferior to those of the Dutch. But what the Chinese lacked in armaments they made up for in numbers and experience. A Dutch account of the siege published 15 years after the battle says: "The archers formed Koxinga's best troops, and much depended on them, for even at a distance they contrived to handle their weapons with so great skill, that they very nearly eclipsed the [Dutch] riflemen."[1]

From the early hours after Koxinga's landing the fighting did not go well for the Dutch. On May 1, the day after the invasion, Coyett tried to stop the rest of the Chinese army from landing. The four Dutch warships sailed up the coast with the most powerful, the *Hector,* in the lead to engage the Chinese junks off Luerhman. Koxinga's admirals, Ch'en Tse and Ch'en Kuang, sent out 60 of the largest junks, each armed with two cannons, to engage the Dutch. It seemed at first an unequal fight. The heavy guns of the *Hector* sank eight of the junks and the remaining Chinese vessels scattered to keep out of range of the Dutch man-of-war.

Then the tide of battle turned dramatically. The *Hector* blew up and sank. According to Dutch accounts it was an accidental explosion in the gunpowder magazine, not Chinese action, that destroyed the ship. Some Chinese accounts give greater credit to the attackers. They say the *Hector* was beset by junks that closed in below the Dutch ship's guns. In this version it was the Chinese attack that caused the *Hector* to explode, but the Dutch ship took several of the junks with it.

The sinking of the most formidable of the Dutch warships gave a huge boost to the morale of the Chinese. The Chinese boats swarmed toward the three remaining Dutch ships, which started to head out to the open sea, where they would have the advantage over the junks. But before the Dutch were able to regain the initiative, four junks approached the *'s Gravelande* and the *Vink* from their most vulnerable quarter, the stern, and threw grapple hooks and lines aboard. Chinese fighters scrambled up the ropes, but the Dutch seamen and marines were able to clear the decks and free their ships. The *Maria,* meanwhile, too small and ill-equipped for the battle, headed far out to sea and kept going to Batavia, where it brought news to the Dutch East India Company governors of the attack on Taiwan. The Chinese made one more attempt to destroy the two remaining Dutch warships. They brought out fire ships and managed to attach one to the bowsprit of the *'s Gravelande* with an iron chain. The Dutch ship caught fire, but the crew was able to extinguish the flames. And there the sea battle ended with both sides claiming victory. The Dutch believed they killed at least one thousand Chinese marines. No reliable estimate of the Dutch losses has survived, but the explosion in the *Hector* alone must have killed scores if not hundreds. On balance the Chinese claim to victory is more convincing. The Dutch failed to seriously damage Koxinga's fleet. At the same time, the Dutch lost their most powerful ship and the *'s Gravelande* was seriously damaged. Neither of Coyett's remaining ships took any further part in the war.

On May 1 the land battle went no better for the Dutch. Koxinga began moving about four thousand of his troops toward Fort Zeelandia on Tayouan Island. They marched around Fort Provintia and south, fording the water to the island at low tide. With the approach of the Chinese the townspeople around Zeelandia fled in panic to the fort, which was soon crammed with about three thousand people. Coyett's deputy, and one of those who had loudly proclaimed that one Dutchman was worth a hundred Chinese, the hotheaded Captain Thomas Pedel, demanded to be allowed to lead a sortie against the attackers. It is unclear from contemporary records whether he got Coyett's permission or not. Some accounts insist he took it on himself to reconnoiter and attempt to clear the Chinese from the Zeelandia island. At any rate he took 240 of the most professional soldiers in the fort and set off down Tayouan Island toward the oncoming Chinese. At the same time another officer, Aeldorp, a militia captain whose real job was as a baker's assistant, was ordered to cross the bay to Fort Provintia with two hundred men to reestablish contact with the other bastion and keep communications open.

Captain Pedel's contempt for the fighting ability of the Chinese got the better of him. He divided his small band into two companies, apparently believing his 240 men could catch the 4,000 Chinese in a pincer movement.

Koxinga's troops saw an opportunity and took it. About eight hundred of the Chinese circled behind the Dutch under cover of a hill. When the Dutch opened fire with their matchlock muskets on the main body of Chinese troops, a rain of arrows hit them in front and behind. Many Dutch died in the first few minutes of the engagement. Others threw down their cumbersome muskets and fled back to Fort Zeelandia or ran into the sea. Pedel tried to organize an orderly retreat, but he had lost control of his men, all of whom now dropped their guns and fled. With the Chinese swiftly encircling them, the only escape was to wade out to a Dutch pilot boat, which took them back to Fort Zeelandia. In the rout 118 of the 240 Dutchmen were killed, including Pedel. Most of their muskets were captured by the Chinese and used later against the Dutch.

Captain Aeldorp, ordered to reach Fort Provintia, was no more successful, except he did not suffer the losses of Pedel. Aeldorp's first attempt to reach Fort Provintia met with stiff resistance from the Chinese at Sakkam village. He gave up and returned to Fort Zeelandia. At the same time deputy governor Jacobus Valentyn, in command at Fort Provintia, managed to get a message through to Coyett begging for four hundred troops to reinforce his garrison.

Even though Coyett was governor of Taiwan he did not have an entirely free hand. He was obliged to call a meeting of the 28-man "Council of Formosa" to discuss the request. The council decided they could not send the four hundred men Valentyn wanted, partly because the only safe approach to Fort Provintia was across the bay, and they did not have enough shallow draft boats to carry that many men. Secondly, sending four hundred troops would have left only five hundred in Fort Zeelandia, not enough to repel a determined attack by the Chinese. The compromise was to order Aeldorp to try again to reach Fort Provintia with his two hundred men. There were only two boats available that might make the passage in shallow water, a Chinese boat, which could carry only 60 of the soldiers, and a Dutch pilot boat, which took the rest. Ultimately, only the Chinese boat was able to get to shore and bolster the Fort Provintia garrison. Aeldorp and the remaining 140 soldiers returned to Fort Zeelandia.

While the council had been discussing Valentyn's plea for reinforcements on the afternoon of May 1, it also took stock of the general situation of the Dutch in the face of Koxinga's invasion. Their assessment was gloomy. Fort Provintia, they felt, was likely to be overrun by the Chinese very soon because of its small garrison and the inferior quality and design of its defenses. Fort Zeelandia, they judged, was not in the same immediate danger from the Chinese, but it could not survive a long siege, not least because it had no fresh water beyond what could be brought in across the harbor or by sea. They believed, however, that Koxinga was buyable. They saw him only as a jumped-up pirate. They conceded Koxinga's military successes had made him a significant regional warlord. But in the view of the Dutch he was no more than that. They considered, too, intelligence reports from the roving Spanish Jesuit missionary Vittorio Ricci that Koxinga's main ambition was to establish himself on the Philippine island of Luzon and that he had come to Taiwan only to resupply his army. The councilors were therefore convinced that Koxinga could be bought off and that he would see it was in his long-term financial interests to keep on friendly terms with the Dutch East India Company. The council decided to offer Koxinga an "indemnity"—essentially protection money—to leave Taiwan alone, abandon his invasion, and to go back to the old trading partnership with the Dutch that had pertained before April 30. If Koxinga would not accept this offer the councilors agreed on a second proposal. They would tell Koxinga they were willing to abandon the island so long as all the Dutch people scattered around Taiwan were permitted to come to forts Zeelandia and Provintia and leave the island safely. If neither of these alternatives appealed to Koxinga the council decided the Dutch should defend their forts to the last man and woman.

The council sent a message to Koxinga that evening, May 1, asking for his reasons for attacking the Dutch, with whom he had previously had a sometimes difficult but usually functional relationship. The council suggested negotiations. In the middle of the night of May 1, Koxinga sent a reply to the council's message. He demanded the complete surrender of the Dutch. They would, however, be allowed to leave for Batavia in their own ships with all their possessions, including the fort's cannon, so long as they also demolished the two forts. If they did not agree or tried to hold out against him, Koxinga's army would storm both forts. The council met on the morning of May 2 to consider Koxinga's message. In the meantime they had received dispiriting news from Fort Provintia. Dutch refugees from other parts of Formosa had flooded into the fort, far more accessible than Zeelandia on Tayouan Island. The council was told ammunition at Provintia was running low. The quartermaster, it appeared, had a profitable sideline selling the fort's stock of gunpowder to local hunters. The single well had almost run dry because of the influx of people, and the small garrison was close to collapse through sheer fatigue. The message said Fort Provintia and its people could not stand more than one attack by the Chinese.

Two council members, Thomas van Yperen and Leo de Leonardus, were sent to Koxinga's camp under a flag of truce the following day, May 3. They were instructed to try to gauge Koxinga's intentions and, if convinced he intended to storm Fort Provintia, to surrender it under the best terms possible.

The envoys began by saying to Koxinga that he had always shown a friendly attitude toward the East India Company and asked why he was showing such hostility toward the Dutch now. According to the account of the meeting the two Dutchmen gave to their countrymen later, the Chinese leader replied haughtily that he was under no obligation to explain his actions to them. He added that the company extended friendship toward him only so long as it suited their purpose. There were no genuine bonds of brotherhood or loyalty in his view. Taiwan, he added, was part of China, of which he had been made a prince and administrator of the entire southern coastal region by the Ming emperor. He was free to take back what belonged to him, he told them. To prove he was not intent on enriching himself from the company's assets, he would allow them to leave immediately with their goods, cannon, and people.

"You Hollanders are conceited and senseless people. You will make yourselves unworthy of the mercy which I now offer you. You will subject yourselves to the highest punishment by proudly opposing the great force I have brought with the merest handful of men which I am told you have in your castle," Koxinga prophesied according to the report the two ambassadors made later to the council at Fort Zeelandia.[2]

He then referred to the Dutch setbacks on land and sea after the invasion. "Are these not sufficient proofs of your incompetency and inability to resist my forces? I will give you more and stronger ones. But if you still persist in refusing to listen to reason and decline to do my bidding, and if you wish deliberately to rush to your ruin, then I will shortly, in your presence, order your castle [Fort Provintia] to be stormed. If I wish to set my forces to work, then I am able to move Heaven and Earth. Wherever I go I am destined to win. Therefore take warning, and think the matter over."[3]

De Leonardus and van Yperen replied with arguments that echo to this day. Taiwan, they said, belonged to the Dutch East India Company. That ownership, they pointed out, was enshrined in a 1624 treaty between the company and the Ming empire made when the Dutch agreed to leave the Penghu Islands in the Taiwan Strait. Koxinga refused to listen to this argument about ownership. He dismissed the two envoys with the warning that if they did not agree to his terms by eight o'clock the following morning, May 4, the war would continue. If they agreed to surrender they should fly his flag from the walls of Fort Zeelandia, he told them. If they were intent on war they should fly a red flag.

After their discouraging audience with Koxinga the emissaries van Yperen and de Leonardus were allowed to visit Fort Provintia on their way back to Zeelandia. They found the situation as bad as Valentyn's message had indicated. The two councilors told the deputy governor he was free to negotiate his own surrender with Koxinga if it were in the best interests of the garrison and Dutch refugees. Thus Valentyn surrendered the following day, May 4, on the understanding that he and his people would be treated as prisoners of war. That is not what happened. Koxinga wanted to frighten the Zeelandia defenders into an abject surrender. He therefore ordered the killing of many of the male prisoners while the women were given to favored officers to be concubines.

De Leonardus and van Yperen gave an account of their meeting with Koxinga to the Zeelandia council later on May 3. These were not timid men and even though they realized their position was perilous, the councilors felt there were good reasons to defy Koxinga's ultimatum. The immediate position of the Dutch might look dangerous, but reinforcements could arrive from Batavia at any time, and they maintained a firm belief in their military, cultural, and spiritual superiority, despite the reverses of the first hours of fighting with Koxinga's forces. They were convinced that Koxinga would not have the stomach for a long siege. He was, after all, a rebel on the run from the Manchu on the mainland. He had come to Taiwan because he had been chased out of his last refuge in Fujian province. They still believed their intelligence reports that Koxinga's main aim, after resupplying his army on Taiwan, was to go on to the north Philippine island of Luzon to establish a Ming Chinese principality in exile well away from the Manchu armies. Koxinga, they knew, could be a formidable foe, but his military record was mixed and on that night before Nanjing he had shown a gross error of judgment by getting his army drunk. Something similar might happen. Coyett and his council felt the response they must give to Koxinga's ultimatum was obvious. On the morning of May 4, 1661, a red flag flew over Fort Zeelandia.

On May 5, Koxinga's army began swarming up the island of Tayouan toward the town and Fort Zeelandia while scores of junks patrolled the sea and harbor just out of range of the Dutch cannon. About four thousand of Koxinga's troops moved into the abandoned town below the fort and set up defensive lines. Nothing happened for the next three weeks except for a few minor skirmishes. Then the Chinese moved up 28 guns, which they stupidly sited on the open plain before the fort without any barricades or protection. The Dutch fired at them through the night of May 25, but because of the darkness and the smoke they aimed wide and did little damage. The Chinese launched a barrage of fire at the fort the following morning. Coyett ordered all guns possible to be brought to bear on the exposed Chinese. The powerful Dutch guns had a devastating effect and about one thousand of the attackers were slaughtered and the plain strewn with dead and wounded. Seeing the Chinese had abandoned their cannon, Coyett decided to send out a small group of sailors and musketeers to disable any that were undamaged. There was a simple way to do this in the age when cannons were fired by lighting gunpowder in a small touch hole, which then set off the main charge in the breech. The gun could be made useless by driving an iron spike into the touch hole. The spiking party rushed out and succeeded in disabling the surviving Chinese guns as well as capturing 32 of the invaders' battle banners before coming under fire from archers hidden in the town. Three of the party were killed and a few wounded by arrows as they ran back to the fort.

After experiencing the superiority of the Dutch guns, Koxinga's men decided to blockade Fort Zeelandia and wait the garrison out. "The enemy was in no hurry, seeing that those inside [the fort] were closely surrounded, so helpless that they could scarcely have broken a straw; whereas the enemy possessed beautiful and fertile grounds, in which the soldiers, who had roamed the seas for so long, might now rest in a leisurely manner; and, as a matter of fact, they took their full swing of comfort," says a contemporary Dutch account.[4]

The siege continued throughout June, the monotony broken only by the occasional arrival of letters from Koxinga calling on the defenders to surrender. He pointed out that even if Batavia sent them two thousand men, the most the company could dispatch in the ships available, it would not be enough to defeat the Chinese, who were prepared to keep the siege going for ten years if need be.

Meanwhile the little sloop *Maria,* which had broken off from the sea battle on May 1 and put out to sea, reached Batavia. The voyage took 50 days because the adverse monsoon winds forced the captain to take a long detour around the Philippine islands instead of sailing the direct route through the South China Sea. The news that Koxinga had indeed attacked Taiwan caused a commotion among the directors in Batavia, who had just dispatched Hermanus Clenk to take over as governor of Taiwan. Clenk carried with him a letter from the directors in which they set out all Coyett's sins based on the reports of the previous governor that Koxinga was no threat. So when the *Maria* arrived with news that Coyett had been right all along the directors rushed to cover their embarrassment and retrieve the situation. A relief fleet was hastily put together with the hope of overtaking Clenk and getting back the letter before it was delivered. But, we are told, the directors had a hard time finding anyone to command the reinforcements. While everyone wanted to be governor of Taiwan when it was a peaceful and productive place, no one was eager to rush to Fort Zeelandia under siege. The man picked by default to lead the relief fleet was Jacob Caeuw, "a person so defective in the power of speech, that one almost required an interpreter to understand his words."[5] That was how he was described a few years later by a supporter of governor Coyett. Caeuw not only lacked the communication skills of a natural commander, but he was not a soldier. He was a lawyer. His entire martial experience, according to the Coyett loyalist, was as a student at the Academy at Leyden in Holland, when he would run his sword "through the windows of decent people's houses."[6] Doubtless these escapades involved drinking beer with fellow students. So, under the command of an incomprehensible amateur soldier the so-called Succor Fleet set off on July 5, 1661.

Caeuw's ships never did catch up Clenk and the now evidently libelous letter of indictment of Coyett and other Taiwan councilors. Clenk arrived at Fort Zeelandia on July 30 and, instead of the quiet and peaceful country he expected to find, saw the castle flying the blood red war flag and the Chinese army circled around. He decided not to go ashore but anchored well away from the hostilities. A wiser man might have seen that under the circumstances he should keep the letter from the Batavia directors to himself for the moment. But Clenk was not a wise man and even though he had no intention of involving himself in the siege, he managed to get the indictment sent ashore to Coyett and the Fort Zeelandia councilors. The scathing opinion of their masters in Batavia was not, to say the least, a great boost to morale in the fortress, where after nearly three months of the siege, disease and bad well water were beginning to take a fearful toll on the defenders.

The Zeelandia garrison had lost its best troops and its only professional officer on May 1 when Captain Pedel was ambushed and he and most of his 240 soldiers were killed. The manpower of the forts had been further depleted on the same day when Aeldorp managed to land 60 men at Fort Provintia, leading only to their early capture and the execution of many. By the end of July Aeldorp, the baker's assistant, was the only officer left in Zeelandia. There had been others like Aeldorp, who were officers in name. Most, however, were ordinary soldiers who had been given officers' titles in the months before Koxinga's arrival as a sop to persuade them to stay on Taiwan when their tours of duty were over. Disease and fatigue had cut through these untrained officers, the remainder of the troops, the merchants, wives, children, and loyal Chinese in the castle. Only four hundred able-bodied men remained to mount the defense. In this atmosphere the letter brought by Clenk weighed heavily on everyone. It meant there was little hope of support from Batavia. The seasonal winds were now blowing from the south, which meant it would be perhaps two months before those besieged in Fort Zeelandia could send a message back to company headquarters. Then the winds would change and, even if they managed to get Batavia to change its attitude, it would likely be close to a year before relief could arrive.

Clenk was still refusing to come ashore, his enthusiasm for taking up the post of governor now completely vanished. His opportunity for a pretext to leave came a few days after his arrival when a storm blew up and he insisted his ship would be safer in the open sea than at anchorage. Once clear of Taiwan he decided he needed water and rice, so he headed for Japan. He stopped en route at Keelung and managed to do yet another disservice to Coyett and the defenders at Fort Zeelandia by taking on board the 170 Dutch troops there. Both Dutch forts at Keelung and Tamsui were thus abandoned, which Coyett didn't discover until he managed to send a ship to the north to try to collect the outlying garrisons for the defense of Fort Zeelandia.

On the way to Japan Clenk encountered a Chinese junk loaded with cargo from Batavia. It seemed to Clenk like a good moment to turn pirate, so he seized the junk and divided the cargo among the officers, only to discover to his horror the captain of the junk had a free pass from the Dutch East India Company. Clenk's powers of decision failed him yet again. He thought of going to Japan and selling the cargo there. But the existence of the pass was bound to become known, with unpleasant results. Clenk therefore decided to try to cover up his crime. The pass was torn up, the junk was sunk, and the crew was abandoned on a desert island without water or food. Clenk sailed off confident that he had destroyed the evidence. However, the junk crew was picked up by a passing fishing boat that took the sailors to Batavia, where they told their story to the company directors. Clenk may have been a rotten leader, but he was an expert sycophant. His friends rallied around and he was sent home to Holland without a stain on his record.

On August 12, almost as soon as Clenk left Taiwan, the relief fleet of ten ships commanded by Caeuw arrived and the mood of the garrison lightened immediately. "The sick lying in their cribs, the men from behind the walls, and everyone else, looked upon it as succor from heaven, far in excess of their expectations," says the council's daily journal.[7] The weather was still bad, but the next day the garrison and ships' crews managed to unload over two thousand pounds of gunpowder, other essential provisions, and many of the soldiers. The storm worsened and Caeuw's fleet was forced to put out to sea to weather it. The fleet tried again to unload on August 16, but without success. It put to sea again and was away 28 days. Meanwhile Coyett and his council learned from those who had landed that the fleet was bringing only seven hundred men. This would only bring their strength back up to what it had been at the start of the siege and offered no hope that they could break out and take the battle to Koxinga.

The swift arrival of the relief fleet startled Koxinga. He had been confident in his information that Batavia would not lend serious support to the besieged fort and, not knowing of the epic voyage of the *Maria,* did not believe any help could arrive so soon. But any anxiety Koxinga felt was soon dispelled. A small ship of the relief fleet, the *Urk,* was wrecked on the coast of Taiwan by the storm. Its crew was captured and tortured before being killed. From them Koxinga learned there were only seven hundred soldiers on the ships. Koxinga decided the Dutch in Batavia were either short on resources or didn't care about Taiwan. He was now confident Fort Zeelandia could not expect further relief before the end of 1661 and he was sure the Dutch garrison would capitulate before help arrived.

There were about six hundred Dutch settlers, clergymen, and teachers living in the island's hinterland, mostly in native villages scattered around western Taiwan, at the time of Koxinga's invasion. About one hundred living in northern Taiwan managed to escape to Japan, and some gathered at Fort Zeelandia and at Provintia for safety as the expectations of invasion rose. But several hundred were still in the countryside when Provintia was surrendered and Zeelandia besieged. With the Dutch soldiers bottled up in Fort Zeelandia, the greatest threat to Koxinga's troops as they fanned out over the island was the indigenous warriors. Koxinga took this threat seriously, especially from among the natives who had become Christians and might therefore be expected to maintain some loyalty to the Dutch. His policy was as harsh as it was effective. He reasoned that the most direct way to break the bonds between the natives and the Dutch was to kill the Dutch in as humiliating a way as possible while at the same time lavishing gifts upon the aborigines. The campaign to hunt down the Dutch in the hinterland went on for months. Those who managed to get messages to Fort Zeelandia, whose stories were recorded in the day book, spoke of even Christian villages slowly turning against the Dutch and warriors sometimes killing and beheading their pastor or schoolmaster. If caught by the Chinese, the Dutch were usually crucified as an object lesson to the native villagers. One particularly poignant account is the story of one of the missionaries, Anthonius Hambroek, who with his wife and children was captured by Koxinga's men. On May 25, 1661, Koxinga sent Hambroek to Fort Zeelandia with one of the Chinese leader's letters demanding surrender. Hambroek had to leave his wife and children behind as hostages to assure his return. When Coyett refused to surrender, Hambroek was urged to stay at the fort as he and his family were bound to be killed because of the failure of his mission. The emotional pull to remain was intensified by the discovery that two of his daughters from whom the family had been separated during the chaos of the invasion were among the refugees in the fort. But Hambroek decided his duty was with his wife and other children. The two daughters, says the fort daybook, "hung about his neck, overwhelmed with grief and tears to see their father ready to go where he knew he must be sacrificed by the merciless enemy."[8] The fate of Hambroek is recorded by Caeuw, the commander of the relief fleet. Two native boys got into the fort in October and said they had seen Koxinga fly into a rage the previous month and order the decapitation of all the Dutch male prisoners, Hambroek among them. The wives were given to Koxinga's captains as concubines and the small children were sent to China. Koxinga himself took one of Hambroek's teenage daughters—"a very sweet and pleasing maiden" according to Caeuw—as one of his concubines.[9] In August there was also a killing of captive Dutch from the hinterland and Fort Provintia; Koxinga believed they had been inciting the aborigines against the Chinese. The Dutch reports say five hundred men were either beheaded or "killed in a more barbarous manner."[10] Many women and children were killed too, but others were "preserved for the use of the commanders, and then sold to the common soldiers. Happy was she that fell to the lot of an unmarried man, being thereby freed from vexations by the Chinese women, who are very jealous of their husbands,"[11] says the fort's daily journal.

The results of these incidents are still evident in some parts of southern Taiwan. There are areas where the people have decidedly European features and even occasionally the red or auburn hair common among seventeenth century Dutch.

Coyett and his council were disappointed by the small number of soldiers Caeuw had brought them. But the reinforcements were welcome nonetheless, and Caeuw's ships, of which five remained at Fort Zeelandia, added considerably to the defenders' firepower and maneuverability. The new arrivals were keen for a fight and the council decided to try to clear Koxinga's troops from the town below Zeelandia and thus ease the pressure on the fort. The ships would first try to destroy Koxinga's junks tied up near Fort Provintia and then get behind Zeelandia town, where they could bring their guns to bear on the

Chinese lines. At the same time four hundred men from the fort would sally out and attack the Chinese from the front. The attack was launched on September 16, but the weather foiled the scheme. The ships were first becalmed and then caught by an adverse wind that made it impossible for them to reach their appointed attack points. Part of the attack plan was that soldiers in rowing boats would make for the beaches behind the town under cover of the ships' guns. The rowing boats foolishly pressed ahead without the protection of the becalmed big ships. They were routed and the warships didn't do any better. Two were stranded on the mud by the retreating tide, one was blown to bits by the Chinese guns, and a fourth was set on fire by a Chinese fireboat. The Dutch losses, along with many wounded, were one skipper, one lieutenant, one color-sergeant, and 128 men. The Chinese lost about 150 men. After this failure and with even the new arrivals now succumbing to disease and bad water, several other plans were hatched, but most of October passed with only skirmishes between the two sides.

On November 6 the prospect of relief arrived from an unexpected quarter. A letter arrived from the Manchu governor of Fujian province. The governor said he had heard of Koxinga's invasion and "he therefore offered what assistance he could command to destroy this pirate once and for all with their combined forces," say the fort's records.[12] The council debated the offer for nearly three weeks and on November 26 decided to send three of their most powerful warships plus two supply ships to help the Manchu try to take Koxinga's remaining island outposts on the China coast. Caeuw eagerly offered to command the expedition. It seems to have slipped everyone's memory that only a month before Caeuw had been saying he felt it was time for him to return to Batavia and argue the case with the directors for more support for Fort Zeelandia.

Caeuw should have sailed straight to the China coast and coordinated an attack with the Manchu forces. Instead he sailed directly to the Penghu Islands, where he anchored until strong winds caused three of his five ships to lose their anchors and drove them back to Fort Zeelandia. They were quickly repaired and sent back to Caeuw at Penghu. While the three ships were away Caeuw decided he had had enough of warfare, which was a good deal less fun than breaking windows with his sword. He ordered his captains to sail for Batavia, much to the disgust and anger of his officers and crew, who felt they were abandoning their comrades. The ships stopped at Thailand, then called Siam, on the way to Java. Caeuw went everywhere with a personal bodyguard of six soldiers, apparently for protection against his own men rather than the Thais. The kingdom had a rule that foreigners were allowed only a small number of lightly armed attendants. Caeuw and his bodyguard, all wearing full armor according to the records, were so upsetting to the Thais that they nearly disrupted the entire trading relationship with the East India Company. When Caeuw finally did make it back to Batavia he gave a fanciful account of conditions at Fort Zeelandia and why he was not still there supporting the besieged Dutch. He was charged with neglect of duty but got off with a small fine and suspension from duty for six months, after which he was reinstated and promoted.

When the three repaired ships got back to Penghu and found Caeuw gone, they returned to Fort Zeelandia. The news of Caeuw's desertion caused great dismay, not only for the loss of the troops and supplies on his two ships but because it destroyed any hope of an alliance with the Manchu. The garrison and refugees in the fort felt totally betrayed and abandoned. But there was worse to come as the siege entered its final weeks.

Hans Jurgen Radis had arrived at Taiwan with Caeuw's relief ships and was one of the few experienced and professional soldiers at Fort Zeelandia. He had fought in several European wars, but he was one of those crafty individuals who are found in every army and whose only loyalty is to personal survival. With Caeuw's desertion removing the last hopes of victory or relief from Batavia, Radis thought self-preservation was his first duty. He decided to abandon his comrades and sell information to the Chinese about the sorry state of affairs in Fort Zeelandia in return for his own life. He did more than that. Radis also told Koxinga how he could capture Fort Zeelandia or at the very least make continued resistance by the garrison untenable. Radis slipped out of Fort Zeelandia one night, crossed the lines, and demanded to be taken to see Koxinga. There he described to the Ming prince how, if the Chinese could capture one of the fort's outposts, known as the Utrecht gun redoubt, which they ought to be able to do with few men and at little cost, their guns could dominate the fort. Koxinga saw the logic of the plan, gathered together all his forces on the island, and marshaled them on the plain of Tayouan away from the fort during January 1662. The Chinese prepared the assault on Utrecht by digging trenches and throwing up sand barricades to protect their guns. The assault on Utrecht began on January 25, and, despite a brave defense by the Dutch, the redoubt was in total ruin the following morning. The Dutch gunners retreated to Fort Zeelandia, but before going left a bomb of four barrels of gunpowder on a long fuse in the underground magazine of Utrecht. Many Chinese soldiers who had scrambled into the abandoned redoubt died when the barrels exploded. Koxinga himself was almost killed in the explosion. He had wanted to be among the first at the captured redoubt but was warned against it by Radis, who told him it was common among Europeans for troops abandoning an emplacement to leave a bomb behind.

With the capture of Utrecht the Chinese expected to have Fort Zeelandia at their mercy, but Coyett remained defiant. He listed for the council reasons why they should be resolute, but the loss of Utrecht had been the last straw for most of the defenders. Coyett's list of reasons to be hopeful was, admittedly, fanciful—one argument was the likelihood that Koxinga was running short of gunpowder after the more than 2,500 rounds fired at Utrecht—and the councilors replied with a list of their own.

The councilors said the Dutch soldiers were demoralized and their provisions, though plentiful, were damaged and inedible. Koxinga now controlled the high ground and Fort Zeelandia could expect no meaningful help from Batavia. They might be able to fend off one or two full attacks on the fort, but the losses would be great and they would eventually be overcome. To save lives in a lost cause, the councilors urged Coyett to surrender. Coyett agreed with the majority decision, a message was sent to Koxinga, and after six days of negotiations a treaty was signed on February 1, 1662.

The 18-point treaty was more generous than the Dutch had reason to expect. They had to abandon the fort with its artillery, money, and trade goods but were allowed to take enough stores and ammunition to get them safely to Batavia. The Dutch were allowed to take their private possessions with them as well as some money. All prisoners held by the Chinese were to be freed, including those held in China, and any Dutch who had avoided capture were to be given free passes to leave. Koxinga agreed to provide more ships for the voyage to Batavia if the company's vessels could not hold enough people. Until the Dutch left, the Chinese would be responsible for providing food for them. And when they left the Dutch soldiers would march out of Fort Zeelandia with drums beating, their banners flying, their guns loaded, and the fuses lit. And that is the way it happened on February 12, 1662.

The end of the siege was not the end of the torment for Coyett. Someone had to pay for the company's loss of its most consistently profitable colony, and no one in Batavia was about to accept any blame. All the mistaken, malicious, and ill-informed criticisms of Coyett were revived, and he was charged with a host of offenses. A court in Batavia, unsurprisingly, found him guilty, took all his possessions, and sentenced him to two years in prison. On his release he was banished for life to the northern Indonesian region of Banda. There he languished for ten years until 1674, when a campaign by his family and friends in Holland bore fruit. They persuaded several members of the government and the Prince of Orange to write to the Dutch East India Company demanding Coyett's release. Under such pressure the company had no option but to accept. But they insisted Coyett go straight to Holland and stay there. They did not want such an able and experienced man working for anyone else in Asia.

Chapter Seven

THE PRINCE WHO BECAME A GOD

In the nearly four hundred years since Koxinga's expulsion of the Dutch from Taiwan and his death only a year later, he has been deified as an example of the ideal Chinese prince. He epitomizes the system of meritocracy that has been at the heart of Chinese government and administration for several millennia. Koxinga was a warrior but also a classical scholar, poet, and musician whose learning and skills capitalized on the hard and grubby work of his pirate father to better the Cheng family. Koxinga even became an adopted royal prince.

Once he had captured Taiwan, Koxinga proved himself an able and far-sighted administrator who mapped the course of the island's development reaching right into the second half of the twentieth century. As a dispenser of justice he was brutally stern, following a Chinese tradition that still survives under the Communist Party in mainland China and that is the constant target of human rights complaints in a more liberal age. Above all Koxinga demonstrated that essential element of a Chinese leader whether he be prince or Communist Party secretary-general: a clear and diligent concern for the welfare of the Chinese people. It is this quality more than any other that gives a Chinese leader legitimacy in power.

Koxinga's legend has benefited from his early death at age 39. He was called to sit in Paradise beside the departed Ming emperors, to whom his loyalty never wavered, before the inevitable corruption of absolute power could soil his record. He thus retains the luster of those who die young and at the height of their powers. The nature of Koxinga's legends and the significance of his victory over the Dutch, however, vary depending on from which side of the Taiwan Strait they are viewed. To the Communist government on the mainland, Koxinga, or Zheng Chenggong, as he is known there, was a nationalist military hero who first demonstrated to the Chinese they could overcome European colonial instincts and superior technology. By this view Koxinga lit the beacon that guided future generations to expel foreigners from occupation of Chinese soil and unite the Motherland. There was the defeat and removal of the Japanese from their colonial conquests of much of China at the end of the Second World War. There was the expulsion of Europeans and Americans from the largely self-governing enclaves in Shanghai, other spots on the coast, and inland river ports with the Communist Revolution in the late 1940s. And there was the voluntary return of Hong Kong by the British in 1997 and of Macau by the Portuguese in 2000.

In Beijing's eyes Koxinga was also the man who firmly and irrefutably made the island of Taiwan an inalienable part of China. Before Koxinga, the mainland made no claim to own Taiwan. After Koxinga there can be no doubt, in Beijing's view, that the island and its people belong to the mainland. Koxinga, then, can also be said to represent the Beijing government's drive for Greater China: the determination of the current generation of Chinese leaders to establish the country's contemporary boundaries at the furthest markers of the old imperial empire. Those include Tibet and the largely Turkic Muslim northwestern province of Xinjiang as well as the high reaches of the Himalayas, where Chinese and Indian troops remain in confrontation over disputed territory. Modern leaders in the ten countries of Southeast Asia wonder, aloud sometimes, whether the Chinese vision includes their subjugation to the old role of vassal states paying tribute to the imperial court in Beijing. In Hanoi, Phnom Penh, Bangkok, and Kuala Lumpur, the wonder of China's extraordinary economic and military growth in the closing decades of the twentieth century is mixed with questions about its implications for their own sovereignty.

Mainland leaders at the beginning of the twenty-first century have tried to enlist Koxinga's name in the campaign of threats and inducements aimed at pressing Taiwan's 23 million people to capitulate to Beijing's rule and sovereignty. On one of the islands off Xiamen there is a 16-meter-high statue of the warrior pointing a threatening finger out across the Taiwan Strait. Whether he is pointing at the ghosts of the Dutch or at modern-day Taiwanese who resist the embrace of the People's Republic of China is left to the viewer's imagination. Beijing portrays Koxinga as the essential Chinese cultural nationalist "fighting to retake Taiwan from the foreign colonizers," to quote the official mainland handbook available at the statue for visitors.[1] He was "the great nationalist who recovered Taiwan from Dutch imperialists, restoring it to its proper place in Chinese territorial domain."[2] In 2002, to mark the three hundred and seventy-eighth anniversary of Koxinga's birth, the mainland lavished an extraordinary amount of attention on him. There was a full-length feature film, two television miniseries, a competition for playwrights, many conferences, three first-class postage stamps, and four souvenir phone cards. Tour groups were led around his grave and the Zheng Chenggong Memorial Museum. When Nan'an, Koxinga's mainland hometown, close to the port city of Xiamen, held a ceremony in February 2002 to mark the three hundred and fortieth anniversary of the victory over the Dutch on Taiwan, the mayor, Chen Chenggong, invoked the hero's name as a bond across the Taiwan Strait. "Nan'an is willing to make the Zheng Chenggong culture a bridge to strengthen exchanges and co-operation with Taiwan, so as to be the pioneer region of economic and cultural exchanges towards Taiwan," mayor Chen said in a speech quoted by local newspapers.[3]

In the eyes of many Taiwanese, such blandishments cannot obscure the five hundred or so missiles aimed at Taiwan from the coast of Fujian province. Nor can they camouflage the clear indications, set out in detail in Pentagon intelligence assessments, that the prime aim of China's military reform and modernization is to be able to carry out its perennial threat to invade the island. And in a reaffirmation of Taiwan's regional geopolitical and economic significance, first spotted by the pirate Li Tan and exploited by the Dutch, Chinese military strategy for capturing the island is predicated on being able to defeat or neutralize American forces in the Pacific.

Mayor Chen's invocation of Koxinga as a symbol of brotherhood across the Taiwan Strait drew little echo on the island for deep historic and cultural reasons too. All the Koxinga activity on the mainland was largely in response to an awakening interest in him on Taiwan. The island started producing documentaries, biographies, and revised school and college textbooks about Koxinga as the transition to democracy progressed and the sense of a Taiwanese identity bubbled to the surface. On the island Koxinga is seen as the original ancestor, the man who created the free nation-state of Taiwan. In the context of contemporary politics he is the symbol of the beginning of "Taiwan consciousness," of the evolution of a separate national entity. As the guide at the Koxinga memorial hall at Tainan, once Koxinga's capital, puts it: "Before Zheng Chenggong there were no Chinese on Taiwan. He brought all the people over and made this a safe place for them."[4] That is not true, but raising a ghost for modern propaganda wars inevitably involves distortion.

The position Koxinga occupies in Taiwanese awareness goes well beyond his political stature as the father of the nation. Koxinga is as much a spiritual being as a political one. He is the patron saint of the island's liberty and is recognized as a god. Around the island there are over 60 temples dedicated to the worship of the man generally known on the island as Kaishan Shengwang, "the Sage King who Opened up Taiwan." In the view of many islanders, Koxinga did not restore China's rule, but heroically led persecuted, fearful, and dissident Chinese to a new land of hope and promise away from the chaos of the mainland.

When talking about Koxinga today, many Taiwanese mention early in the conversation that he was half Japanese. Mainlanders seldom if ever refer to Koxinga's Japanese mother. She was the daughter of a poor samurai and Koxinga's father, the pirate, merchant, and latterly Ming dynasty admiral Cheng Chih-lung, married her while he controlled Sino-Japanese trade. No one knows her name for sure, but sometimes she is called Tamura Matsu. Tamura was her family name and Matsu may be a fanciful addition because it is the name of the queen of Heaven and goddess of the sea, the patron goddess of seafarers, usually written in English as "Mazu." Mazu is thus one of the most important gods on Taiwan, and there is a legend on the island that she was Koxinga's mother. The legend is very similar to the Greek myth of the hero Aeneas, son of King Priam and the goddess Aphrodite.

Cheng Chih-lung, Iquan, was an absentee father. Koxinga was born on August 28, 1624, and brought up by his mother at Hirado until he was six years old. The core of his personality was thus formed in and by Japan, and in the milieu of a Japanese aristocratic family at that. This has resonance today with the elder generation of Taiwanese who grew up under the period of Japanese colonial rule of the island, from 1895 until 1945, and who often attended Japanese schools, colleges, and universities. Men like Lee Teng-hui, who was Taiwan's first freely elected president in 1996 and in semi-retirement is one of the island's most outspoken advocates of internationally recognized independence, often speak and read Japanese better than they do Mandarin Chinese. One of Lee's speechwriters once told this writer that the former president has difficulty reading many Chinese characters. If when writing a speech for him, they came to a character with which they knew he would have difficulty, they would substitute a Japanese version.

The Japanese have often been as avid as mainland Chinese and Taiwanese to claim Koxinga for their own when the occasion suited. The first play about the prince, *Kokusen a Kassen,* "The Battles of Koxinga," was written in the eighteenth century by Chikamatsu Monzaemon and first performed in the old Japanese imperial capital of Kyoto. Koxinga's elevation to god status on Taiwan also has distinct Japanese Shinto connotations. After the Japanese annexed Taiwan as a colony in 1895 they attempted to establish kinship with the island's people by dedicating Koxinga's temple in his old capital, now called Tainan, as a Shinto shrine. Similarly, the Japanese historian Yosaburo Takekoshi, writing in 1905 in the early years of Tokyo's possession of Taiwan, made this assessment of Koxinga:

> Inheriting tact and talent from his father and a sound judgement and daring from his mother, he was full of great ambition roused by the tendencies of the age, and proved himself to be a hero, gifted with great governing and organizing powers. His deeds in Formosa proved him a statesman of no ordinary mould. He was the leading spirit of the government and he alone gave life and vigor to the whole institution.[5]

So Yosaburo attributed Koxinga's masculine qualities of martial heroism and administrative ability and sagacity to his Japanese blood and cultural heritage. This fitted nicely with Japanese assertiveness of the time, its industrial revolution and determination to catch up with the American and European nations as a military and colonial power.

Ancestor worship is a form of early religious development common to many cultures. In China it blended with Taoism and Confucianism, but in Japan it reaches its zenith in Shintoism and the belief that the emperor is a direct descendant of the god who created the Japanese. In Shintoism all dead ancestors become gods. Koxinga on Taiwan assumes a role similar to that of the emperor in Japan: he becomes the spiritual and political father of his people. But on the island Koxinga's transformation from pioneer creator of the nation to communal god precedes the period of Japanese colonial rule. The deified paternity of Koxinga was an abiding force on the island, especially during the two hundred years leading up to 1895, when the mainland Manchu Qing dynasty had control over the western third of Taiwan. There were scores of uprisings against Qing overlordship, very many of them in the name of Koxinga and his loyalty to the deposed Ming dynasty. These uprisings continued into the early years of Japanese rule, though by this time the insurgents abandoned the demand for the return of the Ming and aimed at the establishment of a Taiwanese republic.

The very different views of Koxinga on the mainland and Taiwan are nicely encapsulated in the accounts of that moment when his army crossed the sandbar into the Luerhman inlet on April 30, 1621. Myths that even the forces of nature obeyed Koxinga, swelling the waters so his fleet could land quickly, grew and have survived on the island. In this vision there is more than a touch of Moses parting the Red Sea to lead the Jews out of Egypt. For very many Taiwanese the myth has much the same function as it does in Jewish history. Koxinga is their liberator and patron saint, leading his people to the Promised Land. President Chen Shui-bian's vice president, Annette Lu, once made this exact comparison in a speech, saying Koxinga was like Moses who "led his people to the land of milk and honey."[6] It is significant that his temple images usually portray him not as a warrior but as an imperial sage. For Taiwanese, though, the spiritual reference is to Mazu, the queen of Heaven and patron saint of seafarers whose protection was essential to all islanders be they fishermen, pirates, traders, or simple migrants crossing the treacherous waters of the Taiwan Strait. Koxinga's navigation of the perils of Luerhman inlet showed divine intervention by Mazu and was yet another indication that he possessed the mandate of Heaven.

In contrast, on the mainland the story of Koxinga's landing is used only as a demonstration of his military expertise. The story of the invasion is regularly recounted as a morale booster in the training of People's Liberation Army marines. It is drummed into them as a model to follow one day if ordered to invade the island. Koxinga's example tells the marines that superior tactics can overcome a better-equipped enemy. They are extolled to adopt the "Koxinga spirit."[7]

Koxinga began asserting his rule over Taiwan in mid-May 1661 soon after Fort Provintia had surrendered and the main Dutch force was bottled up in Fort Zeelandia. At Peikang, the main Chinese coastal village north of Tayouan, which is now well inland through silting, he held an audience with the leaders of the Chinese community, many of whom were guardians of the Cheng family interests, appointed by Koxinga's father. He was congratulated on the recovery of Taiwan from the Dutch, though victory was still ten months away, and given gifts. As the siege wore on Koxinga kept only the minimum number of troops necessary to enforce the blockade under the command of his most able lieutenant, Ma Hsin, at Tayouan. The rest of his forces were dispersed around Taiwan, cajoling the indigenous tribes into submission where possible and pacifying them by force when necessary. Thus when the Dutch left with all the pomp, ceremony, and pride they could muster on February 12, 1662, Koxinga already had a good idea of the extent and possibilities of his new domain.

His first move was to erase all vestiges of Dutch rule and to build in their place all the institutions of a classic Chinese, Ming administration. One of the first acts of liberators in all ages has often been to rename the places they have conquered. It is a sound psychological move, drawing a line under the vanquished regime and emphasizing the dawn of a new age. Sakkam was given the cumbersome name of Tung-tu Ming-ching, usually abbreviated to the more handy Tung-tu. The southern part of Taiwan was designated a prefecture and divided into two districts. Fort Zeelandia was demolished and a new, Chinese castle built that, as An-ping-Chin (City of Peace), became Koxinga's official residence. The city that has grown up on the site is now called Anping, and restored remnants of Koxinga's castle are still there. On the mainland Koxinga's son, Cheng Ching, was put in command of Xiamen and the family's remaining possessions around the city. Trustworthy officers were assigned to the Penghu Islands.

With the basic structure of his administration in place, Koxinga set off to tour Taiwan accompanied by a bodyguard of about one thousand heavy infantry, archers, and artillerymen. Koxinga's progression northward was a charm offensive. At every village and settlement he held court, listened to local gripes, and distributed gifts of clothing and tobacco. Word spread ahead of the entourage of the goodness of the new prince, and, Chinese records say, at every stop people clamored to see Koxinga.[8] He traveled as far as Tamsui and the island's northern ports, noting all the way the fertility of the soil and casting especially appreciative eyes over the plains land still held by the aborigines.

Koxinga returned to Anping with an agricultural development plan. At the castle, military and civil officers were assembled to hear what was a broad policy statement, an enunciation of principle that would be studied, mulled over, and fleshed out over the coming months and years.

"In order to establish our rule over this island we must have food for our subjects," Koxinga said. "With insufficient food in a house even a family, in spite of the ties which bind them together, finds it difficult to live happily. So in this island, notwithstanding the patriotic spirit of our subjects we cannot hope for tranquillity unless we can provide them with the necessities of life. Again with few of our subjects engaged in agriculture we are not provided with the necessary of all munitions of war—abundant food to support us while fighting the enemy. Hence our soldiers, whose occupation is to guard us against our foes, should prepare for battle by engaging during times of peace in agriculture."[9]

The style and content of Koxinga's speech could have been delivered by any Chinese leader before and since. It is the perennial concern in governing China that there are too many people and, despite the country's size, not enough arable land to provide for them with any confidence of long-term security.

Koxinga was in the happier situation of having plenty of land available for the population under his control. The task he set his officials was to bring forward policies that would encourage the development of the surplus of good land on Taiwan. A four-tiered plan was developed. Officials and Koxinga's family and clansmen were given large grants of land, which they owned and worked with hired labor. This had the effect of creating a significant gentry class of major landowners who lived off the rents of their tenants. This class became the political establishment of Taiwan and in later years easily shifted its allegiance from the Cheng family to the Qing dynasty, then to the Japanese, and finally to Kuomintang. It was not until a major land reform program began in the 1950s that the control over land by the gentry was broken, and by that time many of the major landowners had diversified their investments and become captains of industry.

In order to encourage agricultural development, Koxinga offered free grants of undeveloped land to Chinese who had already been on Taiwan before his army arrived and to new emigrants from the mainland. Pioneer farmers were exempt from land tax during the three years it took to clear their plots and bring them into production. If they managed to bring the land into profitable production earlier and started paying land tax, their subsequent assessment was reduced. Greater concessions were given to groups of people who formed themselves into rural villages, usually a clan or extended family. The caveat to being granted free land was that all able-bodied men had to undergo a period of military training so they could be called up to militia defense forces should the island be attacked.

The last element in the land development plan was Koxinga's professional soldiers. He had 72 garrisons, known as *chen,* around the island, each with one thousand troops. In addition his navy is said in contemporary records to have been made up of 20 *chen.* How many men and ships that describes is unclear. At any rate, soldiers and sailors were required to produce food when not engaged in military duties. Land was provided around garrisons and barracks for this purpose. As well as making the troops nearly self-sufficient in food, this policy had the added benefit, contemporary records say, of giving the soldiers no idle moment to create trouble.

On the mainland the Manchu Qing dynasty inadvertently gave a huge boost to Koxinga's call for pioneers when in 1662 it ordered the evacuation of all villages and towns on the South China coast and the depopulation of a swath of land 15 miles (24 kilometers) inland. The regulation was an attempt to stop an invasion of the mainland by Koxinga and deprive him of the support of local people. It was ruthlessly applied and the south coast was turned into a scene of death, desolation, and famine. Tens of thousands of people managed to slip across the Taiwan Strait and chose the option of free land on the island, despite its evil reputation for disease and fierce aborigines, rather than being made penniless beggars on the mainland.

The Manchu were just as suspicious of scholars, writers, and poets as they were of the Fujian and Guangdong peasantry. They saw scholarship and writing as subversive occupations. When raids began on the homes of men with libraries, about a thousand of the so-called literati from the Ming tradition fled to Taiwan. They were welcomed with open arms and reinforced the notion that the island was a sanctuary where Ming culture could gather its strength for a victorious return to China. But these writers and philosophers also formed the nucleus of a particular scholastic and artistic tradition on Taiwan. The original literati and their descendants came to play a significant role at several points in the island's story. They were central to the ill-fated founding of the Taiwan Republic in 1895, to resistance to Japanese occupation in the first half of the twentieth century, and to Taiwanese opposition to the Kuomintang in the second half of the century.

Koxinga's policy of giving land to small farmers preceded by three hundred years the "land to the tiller" policy of Sun Yat-sen, which was one of the three pillars of the republican revolution in China in 1911. Koxinga's son Cheng Ching continued the agricultural development policy with even greater success, making Taiwan one of the major food-exporting nations in Asia.

Having set the island on a course toward self-sufficiency and military security, Koxinga turned his mind to his passion: the defeat of the Manchu dynasty and the restoration of the Ming. Koxinga thought that if he could weld Taiwan to the Chinese diaspora in Southeast Asia he could form an alliance strong enough to defeat the Qing regime in Nanjing. The first target for inclusion in Koxinga's empire of exiles was the Philippines, where some 13,000 Chinese lived around the Spanish colonial outpost of Manila. On April 24, 1662, Koxinga sent his friend, the Dominican friar Vittorio Ricci, to Manila with an abrupt letter demanding that the Spanish pay him annual tribute. He threatened to deal with them as he had done the Dutch only two months before if they did not comply. Ricci was received by the Spanish governor, Don Sabiniano Maurrique, but it is unclear whether Koxinga's letter was delivered or its contents spelled out. The Spanish were on edge after the ouster of the Dutch from Taiwan and highly suspicious of Ricci and the local Chinese, known as Sangleys. Maurrique and his troops moved to preempt any uprising. They seized two Chinese trading junks and ordered the local Chinese to remain in their ghetto, called Parian. Somehow, and it is now unknown whether it was purposeful or accidental, a Spanish officer was killed in the marketplace. The governor was delighted. He had been purposefully heavy-handed with the junk captains and the Chinese ghetto in the hopes of stirring up outrage that would justify retaliation. Maurrique was ready with eight thousand infantry, one hundred cavalry, and well-placed artillery. The death of the officer was the pretext the governor needed to attack. How many of the 13,000 Chinese population around Manila were killed in the ensuing slaughter is not known. According to a Spanish historian of the time, Juan de la Concepcion, the original intention of the governor was to kill all the Chinese in Manila.[10] He only ordered a halt to the killing when it was pointed out to him that the colony needed Chinese merchants and tradesmen in order to survive. "Therefore they made a virtue of necessity and graciously pardoned in the name of His Catholic Majesty all who laid down their arms."[11]

Many of the Manila Chinese managed to escape and get to Taiwan, where they told their story. Koxinga got a firsthand account, too, from Ricci when he returned. Koxinga was furious and ordered the preparation of a fleet and army to attack the Spanish at Manila. It never sailed. Koxinga fell ill at the beginning of May 1662 and died some time in June, aged 39. There have been numerous causes cited for his death. A bad cold that turned to bronchitis, tuberculosis, and malaria are just some of them. But drama must attend the deaths of great men. Chinese accounts say Koxinga changed into ceremonial robes, bowed to the sacred testament of the first Ming emperor and then, with the precious document in his hands, turned to his courtiers and said, "How can I meet my Emperor in Heaven with my mission unfulfilled?"[12]

Then he leaned forward with his face in his hands and died.

Some records say that after Koxinga's death his councilors met under a plum tree by the Confucian temple that the prince had built and where he used to sit and contemplate the future of Taiwan. The councilors swore a blood oath to continue Koxinga's aim of driving out the Manchu Qing dynasty and restoring the Ming empire. To that end they formed the San Ho Hui secret society, also known as the Tien Ti Hin, the Heaven and Earth Society, and the Hung Society. It was one of the first of the Chinese triads. For most of their centuries of existence the triads have been seen primarily as Chinese nationalist organizations, usually dedicated to restoration of the Ming dynasty. Their criminal activities have often had a Robin Hood revolutionary flare. It is only in the last century that triads have become exclusively criminal gangs. Both Sun Yat-sen and Chiang Kai-shek were triad members. Chiang, indeed, started his career as a hit man for the Green Gang, which controlled drug trafficking in Shanghai in the 1920s and 30s. At various times in the last 50 years questions have been raised about the influence of the Green Gang within the Kuomintang government in Taiwan, especially among the military that came to the island with Chiang in 1949.

Even in orderly families the succession and inheritance can be a problem on the death of the patriarch. It is likely to be much more so, irrespective of the cultural context, when there is a wealthy and promising little principality at stake. The permutations become even more complex when polygamy is practiced, even when, as in Chinese culture, there is a strict hierarchy among wives and concubines. Cheng Ching was Koxinga's eldest son by his first wife and thus the obvious choice for the succession. The problem was that Koxinga had been outraged by his son's outlandish and disrespectful behavior, and ordered him executed. Cheng Ching was a wild and dissolute youth who had affairs with many women after his wife failed to have children. One of the women was a former wet nurse to Cheng Ching's younger brother, and she gave birth to a son. Under Chinese ritual custom this affair was considered incest and Koxinga was apoplectic with rage when he heard about it. At the time, Cheng Ching was Koxinga's viceroy in Xiamen, governing the Cheng family's mainland holdings. A messenger was sent to the military commander at Xiamen with orders to kill Cheng Ching, the baby, the mistress, and Cheng Ching's mother, one of Koxinga's wives, for failing to exercise better control over the family. The order to kill Koxinga's heir presented the senior officers with a serious problem. They decided the order was unreasonable. They killed only the mistress and her son and sent the heads to Taiwan with a petition asking that the lives of Cheng Ching and his mother be spared. Koxinga was determined and sent back fresh orders for the execution to be carried out.

What could have turned into an open conflict between father and son was avoided by Koxinga's death. The seeds of internal conflict had been sprouting for some time. Many of the senior officers at Xiamen and on islands under Cheng control were unhappy with Koxinga's instructions to abandon the mainland and move to Taiwan along with their families. There were plans for an open revolt against Koxinga and the establishment of a separate pro-Ming enclave on the mainland under Cheng Ching's rule. Koxinga's death forestalled the mutiny.

The news of the second refusal to obey his order to execute Cheng Ching reached Koxinga around the same time he heard about the massacre of the Chinese in Manila. Some historians contend these two emotional upheavals caused his death. Others go so far as to say Koxinga committed suicide in his anguish.

Cheng Ching declared himself his father's successor on June 30, 1662, in Xiamen. He was already aware he was going to have to struggle to win his inheritance. Koxinga's anger with his son was so evident that the Cheng family members and officials on Taiwan decided he couldn't possibly have intended Cheng Ching to take over the principality. There was even talk of a will disinheriting Cheng Ching. The officials and military commanders on Taiwan chose Cheng Ching's uncle and Koxinga's brother, Cheng Shih-hsi, to succeed Koxinga.

Meanwhile, on the mainland, the Manchu learned of the death of Koxinga with relief and delight. They knew of Cheng Ching's wayward youth and thought he might be easily coerced into accepting Manchu sovereignty. The governor of the Manchu-controlled areas of Fujian province, Li Shuai-tai, was summoned to the capital for a conference. It was decided that if Cheng Ching would agree to demonstrate his submission to Beijing by handing over all the official seals and edicts of the Ming dynasty as well as shaving his head and growing a pigtail, he would be given a high position and wealth. His past sins would be forgotten. Just in case this was not inducement enough, the Manchu also mobilized a considerable army.

Governor Li met Cheng Ching in Xiamen. During the interview the young leader showed diplomatic skills that had not been apparent before. He successfully played for time without arousing Li's suspicions. Cheng Ching told the governor that he was willing in theory to submit to the Qing dynasty. Some accounts say he begged for some time to consider the details of the proposition and to persuade his officers and officials to follow his lead. Others say he asked that Taiwan and the Xiamen enclave be associated with China only as a tributary state, like Korea, and not as an administrative part of the nation. Hand-in-hand with this suggestion went the request that he be exempt from shaving his head and growing a pigtail queue. Cheng and his advisers made these suggestions knowing full well Beijing would not allow him to avoid this humiliating demonstration of submission. The requirement that all Chinese shave the front of their heads and grow a long queue at the back in the Manchu manner was a powerful everyday symbol of the Qing empire's authority. It was a precondition of being accepted into the empire. As such it is very similar to the demands by the Beijing government today that Taiwan acknowledge the "one China principle" before there can be any discussions about future constitutional relations between the two states.

Governor Li set off happily for the capital, carrying Cheng Ching's conditions and feeling he had accomplished his mission. The menacing Manchu troops were withdrawn. This gave Cheng Ching time to attend to his main purpose, which was to gather his fleet and an army in order to invade Taiwan and remove his uncle. As this was a family affair Cheng Ching observed the courtesy of sending a messenger ahead announcing he was coming to take over governance of the island. Cheng Ching also hoped some of the commanders on Taiwan would be induced to defect, knowing that Koxinga's son was about to invade.

It didn't work. When Cheng Ching's fleet arrived at Taiwan his army's landing was strongly opposed and there was a fierce battle. Cheng's soldiers did, though, manage to kill the commander of the defending forces. During a lull in the battle one of Cheng's commanders called out: "Here is Cheng Ching. The commander of your forces is dead. Let us all join the standard of the true son of our late beloved King!"[13] The passion of this appeal loses something in translation, but it did persuade many of the defending officers to lead their soldiers over to Cheng Ching's side. He welcomed them warmly. Cheng Shih-hsi was then invited to meet his nephew. Cheng Shih-hsi, seeing that many of his soldiers had already switched sides, readily relinquished leadership to Cheng Ching. Both men blamed their conflict on devilment by ambitious officers and underlings, a useful fiction frequently used in Chinese diplomacy. A few officers were executed to give veracity to the story, and Cheng Ching was declared the rightful heir to Koxinga. He established his court in his father's castle at Anping.

This victory and Cheng Ching's assumption of his father's position did not make him secure in power. His grip on Xiamen was tenuous. Through the summer and autumn of 1662 the Manchu kept up diplomatic pressure on the Ming loyalists. Many of Cheng Ching's senior officials were tempted with blandishments and secretly negotiated with the Manchu for pardons and positions in the Qing dynasty administration. Among them was Cheng Tai, a cousin of Koxinga and the family member with direct control over the Chengs' fleet and trade interests and therefore a power in his own right. Cheng Tai, as part of the negotiating process with the Manchu, sent to the capital in October 1662 six official Ming seals and three imperial edicts. He also sent an accounting of the Cheng family domain. This listed 2,156 officers, an army of 412,500 men, 5,000 war junks, and a population of three million people.

A showdown between Cheng Ching and Cheng Tai was inevitable. It came quickly, early in 1663. When Cheng Ching invaded Taiwan in November 1662 and his forces killed the defending commander, Huang Chao, a search was made of Huang's camp. Letters were found from Cheng Tai urging Huang to support the leadership of Cheng Shih-hsi, Koxinga's brother. Cheng Ching did not act immediately after learning that his cousin was an enemy. He bided his time. Over the winter of 1662 relations between the two men deteriorated. Early in 1663 Cheng Tai got his fleet ready for instant flight, loaded his hoard of silver bars, and even had his family living on board. In the mean time he was carrying on half-hearted negotiations with the Manchu. But he didn't trust them and feared that if he submitted he would meet the same fate as Iquan, Cheng Chih-lung: imprisonment in Beijing and finally execution. Attempting to play both sides and believing that Cheng Ching was in Taiwan, Cheng Tai went to Xiamen in July 1663, taking with him a gift of 100,000 ounces of silver for the military campaign against the Manchu. It turned out that Cheng Ching was in Xiamen and a banquet was organized to mark Cheng Tai's generous donation. In the middle of the meal Cheng Ching excused himself to go and change his clothes—perhaps he purposefully spilled food on himself. While he was away two of his officers produced the letters found in Huang's camp. Cheng Tai was arrested almost before he realized he was in a trap. Even as this drama was playing out soldiers were sent to take over Cheng Tai's fleet. One commander with 180 ships and over 7,000 men escaped the net and defected to the Manchu. The rest were put under commanders loyal to Cheng Ching. Cheng Tai committed suicide while imprisoned at Xiamen.

The Dutch, meanwhile, were sniffing around to see if they could regain a foothold on Taiwan. A fleet of 12 ships under the command of Admiral Balthasar Bort was sent in June 1662 by the company directors in Batavia with this purpose. The fleet anchored first on the mainland, where there were negotiations with the Manchu governor of Fujian, Li Shuai-tai, over a joint attack on Taiwan. These talks came to nothing and Bort contented himself with piratical raids on the Taiwan coast. The Batavia directors sent a more powerful fleet of 16 ships, 1,386 sailors, and 1,234 soldiers in July the following year, 1663. Two weeks later another 17 ships were sent, the combined fleet being the most powerful the Dutch had ever deployed off the southern China coast. This fleet did work in coordination with Manchu forces against Xiamen, where Cheng Ching had taken personal command. The Ming forces were defeated in several hotly fought skirmishes, but Cheng Ching despaired of being able to hold on to Xiamen. In April 1664 he abandoned the city and its surrounding area, but kept control of Kinmen and some smaller offshore islands, and took his family to Taiwan.

Cheng Ching saw that the Dutch might be a continuing problem. He sent a message to the fleet pointing out that there were still about one hundred Dutch men and women on Taiwan who had been kept as hostages as part of the agreement between his father and Frederick Coyett. They should have been released many months before, and Cheng offered to release them now as part of a trade agreement with the Dutch. He offered to let the Dutch set up a trading establishment either at Tamsui or Keelung if they would abandon their links to the Manchu. The Dutch decided their best long-term interests lay with the Qing dynasty on the mainland. The fleet did, however, storm and capture Keelung, which the Dutch held for five years, but it was never a profitable trading post and they eventually abandoned it. Instead of seeking a trading arrangement with Cheng Ching on Taiwan, the Dutch in 1665 sent an embassy to Beijing. The envoys were treated to all the attention, feasting, and presents that are still showered on high-ranking visitors to the Chinese capital. As they left, the Dutch were given a sealed envelope that they believed contained a treaty allowing them trade access to the mainland. When they finally opened the letter and had the contents translated they discovered the Qing dynasty had graciously decided to enroll Holland as one of the nations privileged to be a tributary state of the Chinese empire. This allowed Holland to bring gifts to the emperor in Beijing and receive presents in return, in Manchu eyes a far more gracious, honorable, and civilized exchange than the grubby business of trade. It is unlikely the Dutch ever fully appreciated the honor bestowed upon them.

Chapter Eight

DELIVERANCE AND DEFEAT

Cheng Ching's seventeen-year reign was Taiwan's first Golden Age. He proved a worthy guardian of his father's dream for the island and kept the family pledge to attempt to restore the Ming dynasty. But he never gave up his taste for debauchery, which shortened his life. When Cheng Ching died on March 17, 1681, at age 39 like his father, he had overseen a great burst of agricultural, industrial, commercial, and administrative development on the island. Yet this was also the beginning of the end of the Cheng dynasty on Taiwan. Cheng's designation of Cheng Ko-tsang, a son by a concubine, as his successor set off a family feud that ended with submission to the Qing dynasty in Beijing. Taiwan became for two hundred years an ignored and ill-used outer island of the Qing empire until its colonial occupation by Japan in 1895.

An essential quality of leadership is the capacity to pick and delegate authority to able lieutenants. In his desire to turn Taiwan into a model outpost of the Ming imperial system, Cheng Ching was fortunate to have available the outstanding scion of a family of administrator-scholars, Chen Yung-hua. Chen was drafted into the Cheng family administration at Xiamen by Koxinga in 1650 and later made Cheng Ching's tutor, the beginning of a lifelong relationship, as is still common among Chinese teachers and their students. As a leading advisor at Xiamen, Chen planned the campaign by Cheng Ching after his father's death to overthrow Cheng Shih-hsi's usurpation on Taiwan. When Cheng Ching established himself on the island, Chen was made the chief planner and day-to-day administrator of the government. Chen was also given military responsibilities as commander of the elite *Yung-wei* brigade. In the 1670s, when Cheng Ching was away for several years fighting in the Ming cause on the mainland, Chen was the de facto ruler of Taiwan.

With Taiwan's population burgeoning because of the Manchu scorched earth policy in the mainland coastal regions, Chen's first task was to divide the Chinese areas of the island into controllable administrative sections. The existing prefectures established under Koxinga were divided into wards under chiefs responsible for civil administration. Areas where Chinese lived outside the prefectures and that were not yet developed enough for that status were divided into 32 *li* under the control of superintendents. Within each *li* were villages headed by chiefs, and each village was divided into ten sections or *chia.* The *chia* were divided in turn into groups, called *pai,* of ten households. An elder headed each *pai* with the responsibility of gathering and reporting information on such things as births, deaths, and marriages, and also maintained collective responsibility for order among the ten households. The heads of *chia* carried the powerful incentives of reward or punishment for the activities of households under their watch.

The so-called *pao-chia* system for maintaining social order has a long history in China, right up to recent years in Communist China. It is an important element of Chinese social culture for foreigners to understand because it is one of the clearest expressions of the difference between a society based on the rights of the individual and one organized on the concept of group responsibility to which the individual must always submit. Outsiders coming from the western tradition often see the *pao-chia* system as a malignant form of authoritarian control under which every act by the individual is watched and noted by neighborhood spies. The system has indeed been used for that purpose on many occasions. The Japanese used *pao-chia* not only on Taiwan but on the mainland in Manchuria in the 1930s and 1940s. Chiang Kai-shek and the Kuomintang retained the system on Taiwan during the period of martial law from the 1940s until 1987. In Communist China the system began to break down only with the launch of economic reform in the late 1970s. The end of the centrally planned, collectivized economy put tens of millions of people out of work and sent many of them tramping around the country in search of jobs. The *pao-chia* system only works among a sedentary population. It cannot function when many millions of people are itinerant. But even though *pao-chia* is largely a thing of the past, the social and cultural concepts on which it is based are still very much alive. It is in part why Chinese communities even in the overseas diaspora tend to be more cohesive than counterparts from other cultures, why consensus decision making remains pervasive, why the common good is always an overriding factor, and why *guangxi*—a network of contacts—is often effective.

When Cheng Ching took control of Taiwan, the most pressing need was agricultural development, which Cheng addressed by bringing virgin land under cultivation. Surviving records have been analyzed in several different ways by historians, who have come up with diverse estimates of the island's population at this time. A reasonable estimate, though, is that the ethnic Chinese population was about 100,000, equal to that of the indigenous peoples, at the time of Koxinga's death in 1662. When Cheng Ching died in 1681 the Chinese population was probably about 400,000. Chief minister Chen Yung-hua decided that the quickest way to boost food production for the ever-increasing population was to expand the military farm system started by Koxinga. Even then it took three years for positive results, and it was not until 1665 that a significant increase in food production was evident. In all, about 40 military farms were established on the plains of western Taiwan during Cheng Ching's reign.

The pioneer work done by the military to clear land and bring it into production trespassed on the hunting grounds of Taiwan's indigenous peoples. The pushing forward of the boundaries of Chinese occupation created a great deal of resentment among aborigines and led to several serious uprisings. To try to ease the tension the Cheng administration eventually separated the settlers and aborigines with a boundary line running roughly down the western side of Taiwan's central mountains. This division, called the "red line" for the color of the markers, kept aboriginal eastern Taiwan outside any effective government administration until after the arrival of the Japanese in 1895. Until 1887, when Taiwan was designated as a province of China, officials disavowed any responsibility for or control of what happened east of the red line. Even today there are regulations on what mountain land may be used for and who may own it, with aborigines given preference.

Administrator Chen and the natural inclinations of the Chinese settlers emphasized the production of the staple food, rice. More than 15 major irrigation schemes were constructed to store water from uneven annual rainfalls and regulate its flow to rice paddies. These schemes involved large ponds for water storage and networks of ditches to transport the water to paddy fields during the dry season. With this system Taiwanese farmers were able to get two or three crops a year, and the island became a significant rice exporter to other parts of Asia.

Chen was less successful in encouraging the production of cash crops, such as sugarcane and tea, for export. Despite the construction of a basic refinery for producing marketable sugar, production was only about two-thirds of what it had been during the Dutch colonial period. Tea production, another crop pioneered on the island by the Dutch, was even less popular among farmers. The planting of tea bushes requires significant capital investment and a consistent market to make it profitable. There was no dependable market at the time. The harvesting of camphor wood and the distilling of camphor oil for export to Japan did become a significant cash industry. But the harvesting method then employed required felling the trees, which were mostly in aboriginal areas, and this thus led to tensions and skirmishes—usually headhunting expeditions on the part of the native Taiwanese—that continued right into the period of Japanese occupation.

The Chinese settlers had rebelled against the tax regime under the Dutch, but the burden under the Cheng was at least as heavy. Koxinga continued almost all the Dutch taxes, and Cheng Ching added new ones as the military and administrative costs of government increased. The Dutch land taxes were almost unaltered. In 1683, when the island submitted to the Manchu Qing dynasty and an accounting was made, land tax receipts were the equivalent of nearly 13,000 metric tons of rice. Revenues from a host of other taxes ranging from fishnets to oxen and salt exports to licensing monks brought in 76,469.69 *taels* of silver, equivalent to 2,168 metric tons of the precious metal.

As well as leading to a population explosion on Taiwan, the closure of the coastal region on the mainland had two significant economic effects on the island, one positive, one negative. During the Dutch period fishing was a major industry around the island, with several hundred fishing boats harvesting large catches of primarily gray mullet and shrimp each year. (Grey mullet, by the way, is still known on Taiwan as "harder," its Dutch name.) With the closure of mainland coastal villages this industry dropped off to almost nothing. A few Taiwanese fishing boats worked the island's coast, but they in no way filled the breach left by the absent mainlanders. A positive result of the closure of the mainland ports was that Taiwan had to develop a ship building industry both to sustain its lifeblood commercial industry and to maintain its navy. This grew into a substantial enterprise and hundreds of vessels were built on Taiwan during the two decades of Cheng rule. The ships were of two main types: war junks known as *fu-chuan* and trading ships called *yang-chuan.* Some of the merchantmen built on the island were large vessels by the standards of the period. The records of one *yang-chuan* built in the island's shipyards in 1682 indicate it was 77 feet (23.47 meters) long and had a beam of 24 feet (7.32 meters). The ship had 25 compartmentalized holds and could carry about 132 tons. It was designed for a crew of 83 men.

Once the island had become self-sufficient in food and was producing a surplus, trade was essential to provide the wealth for further development and to maintain the large military force necessary to deter Qing encroachments. Over three hundred years later that equation has not changed. Modern Taiwan keeps a large military force with sophisticated and expensive weaponry to deter invasion by mainland China.

The Manchu ban on contact between the mainland and Taiwan was only partially successful. There was a considerable nighttime smuggling trade between Xiamen and the island. There appear to have been two main commodities. One was mainland silk, which the Taiwanese sold to Japan, the island's largest trading partner at the time. Another commodity was young women, kidnapped on the mainland to become wives for Taiwan's pioneer farmers. Young Chinese women are still induced to come to the island in significant numbers. Mostly they come as wives of Taiwanese businessmen who have companies in China and who spend much of their time on the mainland managing their factories. There is a darker trade, however. Many young Chinese women are lured to Taiwan with offers of lucrative jobs in "public relations" or the "entertainment industry." This modern traffic is more overtly prostitution than it was in the Cheng era. Taiwan is one of the hubs in an Asian network of women trafficking that is far more profitable than the drug trade, of which Taiwan was and is a regional hub.

As well as silk, Cheng Taiwan sent locally produced sugar and deerskins to Japan, as the Dutch had done. Taiwanese merchants bought Japanese swords and armor but also wracked up considerable surpluses in silver and gold. There was also substantial trade with the Philippines and Southeast Asia, though not, of course, with the Dutch at Batavia. The British made some overtures to establish a trading house on Taiwan in the 1670s. The Cheng administration was encouraging at first, believing that the British would help them recover the business of exporting sugar to Persia developed under the Dutch, and which had been an important money-maker. The Cheng were also keen to get British arms, ammunition, and experts to train Taiwanese in the manufacture and use of modern guns. On several occasions the British East India Company did provide guns, gunpowder, gunsmiths, and gunners as an inducement to a trade agreement. But when Cheng Ching and his ministers found the British were primarily interested in getting a corner of the trade between Taiwan and Japan in both local and trans-shipped Chinese goods, negotiations went cold.

It was not only pioneer farmers who found Taiwan to be a land of opportunity and a sanctuary from the mayhem of the mainland. The Cheng dynasty attracted many hundreds of scholars and writers who either wished to escape political repression under the Manchu or wanted to live and work in the cultural atmosphere of a classical Ming administration. Chen Yung-hua saw the encouragement of arts, letters, and spiritual life as an essential adjunct to economic wellbeing if Taiwan was to be a true expression of Ming China in exile. In 1665 Chen urged Cheng Ching to agree to the construction of a Confucian temple, a building usually representing the heart and soul of Chinese communities. The temple in Cheng-tien prefecture was completed and dedicated in February 1666, with Cheng Ching playing the lead role in the ceremonies.

Parallel with the opening of the temple, Chen recommended the establishment of an education system offering the classic Confucian curriculum. This was the first educational opportunity for Chinese on the island as the Dutch had only been interested in schools for the indigenous Taiwanese. Primary schools were built in every village and a high school in Cheng-tien prefecture. Later, a college, the Institute of Highest Learning, was established as students graduated through the school system. Once qualified students became available, around 1670, the daunting but essential element in Chinese meritocracy was offered: examinations to qualify for civil service posts.

The construction of an education system was made possible by the influx of scholars and writers from the mainland. The most eminent of these lived by writing and philosophizing, but many worked as teachers. One of the so-called literati, Shen Kuang-wen, came to Taiwan while it was still a Dutch possession and served as a policy adviser to both Koxinga and Cheng Ching. In the early 1680s he started a *Chu Yuan Shih-she,* a poetry club dedicated to the memory of China's first great poet, Chu Yuan, who lived in the third century B.C. Chu drowned himself after writing a passionate poem about the evils of his times. The Dragon Boat Festival, a feature of the year in most communities of the Chinese diaspora, is a symbolic hunt by Chinese poets, writers, and thinkers for the body of the man who inspired them. Very many towns in China had such poetry clubs as cultural centers, but the founding of a shih-she in Taiwan had far-reaching effects. The work and discussions of the literati inevitably strayed into politics—one reason why the Manchu campaigned against the literati in China—and the clubs became centers of resistance to Qing rule, and later to the Japanese. This heritage also produced the dissident Taiwanese who campaigned against the military dictatorship of Chiang Kai-shek, and it remains an important strand in what is now known as the development of "Taiwanese consciousness."

By the early 1670s Cheng Ching had kept faith with his father, Koxinga, by making Taiwan a vibrant repository of the Ming culture in exile. There remained another overriding duty Cheng Ching was bound to perform for his father. That was to attempt to defeat the Qing dynasty in China and restore the Ming. Cheng's opportunity to undertake this crusade came in December 1673 with the outbreak of the Rebellion of the Three Feudatories.

The Manchu had conquered China with the help of many Ming dynasty mandarins and military leaders who had been seduced into switching loyalties. Among these were three Ming generals who, as rewards for their help, were made princes and given large feudal land holdings, feudatories. Prince Shang K'o-hsi was made a prince of Guangdong province, Prince Keng Chi-mao was given feudal rights in Fujian, and Wu San-kuei was set up in vice-regal splendor in Yunnan province in the far southwest. These men became powerful regional warlords with their own armies, and they were increasingly independent of rule from Beijing. The Qing emperor Kang-hsi believed they had become too powerful and decided to do away with their principalities. By a happy chance for the emperor, Prince Shang in Guangdong was having trouble with his ambitious son, Chih-hsin, who had decided that it was time for his father to retire and for power to pass to him. Shang Chih-hsin forced his father to send a message to Beijing asking that he be allowed to retire and go to his home province, Liaoning. The Kang-hsi emperor couldn't believe his luck. The elder Shang's wish was granted, but instead of Shang Chih-hsin coming into his princely inheritance, the feudatory was abolished. It must have been a bad day in the Shang household when that message arrived.

The abolition of the Guangdong feudatory created high anxiety in Yunnan and Fujian. Wu, the prince of Yunnan, sent messengers to Keng Ching-chung, who had inherited the Fujian feudatory from his father, with an audacious suggestion. In what may seem in hindsight to have not been a very clever move, Wu and Keng decided to test the mood in the court at Beijing by offering their own resignations. They may have hoped the emperor's response would be a reaffirmation of their princely holdings. Or they may have just been trying to convince the emperor of their loyalty. Wu and Keng had for some time been plotting a rebellion and feared the emperor might have learned of their plans.

Their fears were confirmed. The emperor accepted the princelings' offer to retire and dispatched imperial officials to take over the administration of the feudatories. As their bluff had been called, Wu and Keng had no options but to submit or to fight. They chose to fight. Wu launched his rebellion in Yunnan and the west in December 1673 and Keng in Fujian joined the uprising in March 1674. Shang Chih-hsin, the third feudatory, came into the war on the side of the Qing emperor, apparently thinking this would be the best way to get his principality back. But many of the leading characters switched sides and allegiances several times before the war was over.

Cheng Ching was enticed into the war early with promises of territory in the border region between Fujian and Guangdong provinces. The rebels, however, fought each other as much as they did the Manchu, who took advantage of the squabbling to slowly tighten the net around the southern provinces. Early in 1680 the Qing dynasty sent an armada down to Xiamen to attack Cheng Ching's fleet. The fleets met in battle on March 21. The result was indecisive, but many Cheng commanders believed their fleet had been destroyed. The flood of defections to the Manchu became a torrent. Within a few days Cheng Ching concluded he could no longer hold his remaining mainland possessions. On March 28 he ordered the abandonment of Xiamen and Kinmen. His remaining forces were ordered to retreat to Taiwan.

The last year of Cheng Ching's life was devoted to self-indulgence, debauchery, and sensual pleasure in his numerous palaces and pavilions. Unhappiness with the Cheng dynasty began to be evident on Taiwan for the first time. The conscription into the army of one out of ten able-bodied men was highly unpopular, and there was little love for Cheng's chosen successor, Cheng K'o-tsang, his son by a concubine. Cheng K'o-tsang had been designated the head of state while his father was away fighting on the mainland. Chen Ching died of dissipation on March 17, 1681.

The disquiet about Cheng K'o-tsang was most intense within the faction-riven Cheng family court. Misgivings about Cheng Ko-tsang's suitability to assume the family mantle of power were fed by Feng Hsi-fan. Feng was the father-in-law of Cheng K'o-shuang, a boy of only 11 and Cheng Ching's eldest son by his wife. Cheng K'o-shuang was thus the legitimate heir. Feng first marshaled the support of Cheng Ching's younger brothers and then went to see Koxinga's widow, the Lady Tung. Lady Tung never liked the concubine who was Cheng Ko-tsang's mother and was easily persuaded to set aside her son's orders for the succession. On March 19, 1681, two days after his father's death, Cheng K'o-tsang was invited to his grandmother's palace, where he was seized by his uncles in the garden and strangled. The boy Cheng K'o-shuang was proclaimed Cheng Ching's successor, and his uncle Cheng Tsung was named regent. But the real power was in the hands of the corrupt and devious Feng Hsi-fan.

The two years after the death of Cheng Ching, until Taiwan submitted to the Qing emperor, was a period of chaotic palace intrigue and civil unrest. The resources of the island were depleted after six years of war. Most of the brightest and best among the younger Taiwanese leaders had either been killed in the war against the Manchu or had surrendered to the Qing emperor. The older leaders were dying off, too, among them Chen Yung-hua, the master craftsman of Taiwan's development. Late in 1682 there was a serious uprising of indigenous Taiwanese. Aborigines in the north rebelled against forced labor laws imposed on them by the commander at Keelung, Ho Yu. The revolt spread to the south but died out after forced labor was ended. The island was in such disarray that there was famine early in 1683.

Within the ruling family there was constant squabbling for power among the brothers of Cheng Ching. But the main trial of strength was between Feng Hsi-fan, the power behind Cheng K'o-shuan's throne, and the commander of the navy, Liu Kuo-hsuan. In December 1682 it was discovered that three senior officials were in contact with Qing officials on the mainland and were plotting the capitulation of the island. Among the information they had supplied to the Qing commander, Shih Lang, was that the Penghu Islands, the traditional stepping stone to conquest of Taiwan, were weakly defended. Feng used this incident to get his opponent, Liu, out of the way. Liu was sent to reinforce the defense of Penghu.

It was too late. Shih Lang had been preparing to capture Taiwan since 1668. Shih was motivated by revenge. He had been a senior naval commander in the Cheng fleet, but, like so many others, had switched allegiance to the Manchu. As a result, most of his close relatives had been killed by the Cheng family. He was at first unable to arouse in Beijing any interest in capturing Taiwan, but that changed with the death of Cheng Ching. The Qing emperor instructed Shih in 1681 to work with Fujian officials and to invade Taiwan as quickly as possible. Shih refused to share control of the operation, and his stature with the young Manchu emperor Kang Hsi was such that his request was granted. Shih also refused to be rushed into invading Taiwan before he was ready. He was well aware of the internal discord among the island's rulers and knew that time was on his side. He assembled a relatively small but highly trained force of about 20,000 soldiers and 300 war junks. Shih dispatched his fleet to Penghu on June 29, 1683, but victory was far from certain despite the careful preparations. Liu Kuo-hsuan had substantially boosted the defenses of the outer islands with a garrison of 20,000 troops, 80 warships, and scores of smaller craft. Although Liu's fleet of war junks was outnumbered, it fought well when the naval battle started on July 1. Shih's fleet was forced to retreat with heavy losses. The timely arrival of two hundred more war junks to reinforce Shih's force changed the equation and he attacked again on July 7. This was the last action by the navy that had been born nearly one hundred years before in Li Tan's pirate conglomerate. But its skill and esprit could not overcome the weight of numbers against it. Losses on both sides were great, but it was a victory for Shih and the Qing. The estimates are that Liu lost 12,000 of his 20,000 soldiers and 134 ships. In addition 165 officers and nearly 5,000 men surrendered and changed sides in the course of the battle.

News of the defeat shattered what little common purpose there was left on Taiwan. The Keelung commander, Ho Yu, immediately sent a message to Shih Lang on Penghu offering to submit to the Qing. Liu, who managed to escape the defeat of his forces at Penghu and return to Taiwan, urged Feng Hsi-fan to surrender. Feng agreed and a letter offering capitulation was sent to Shih on July 22 in the name of Cheng K'o-shuan. Yet even as defeat loomed Feng tried to negotiate for concessions. He sought autonomy for Taiwan and wanted to avoid demonstrating ultimate submission to the Manchu by wearing the queue. This may have been the first proposal for the concept of "one country, two systems," enunciated by paramount leader Deng Xiaoping in the 1980s, that remains the mainland's plan for a peaceful unification of the island with China.

In 1683 Shih Lang certainly did not think "one country, two systems" was an acceptable idea. He refused to send Cheng K'o-shuan's letter on to Beijing. On August 22 another letter arrived at Penghu also in Cheng K'o-shuan's name, this one offering unconditional surrender. Shih's first act was to send officials to Taiwan to oversee the shaving of heads and wearing of the queue pigtail, which demonstrates the power of this symbolic act of humiliation and submission. Shih went to Taiwan on September 23 and five days later accepted the formal surrender of Cheng K'o-shuan.

"When kneeling at the feet of Your Majesty, I look upon China's greatness which has existed in unbroken brilliancy for ages, I cannot do otherwise than acknowledge that it is the will of Heaven which has vested you with the supreme power to govern the nine countries [of China],"[1] said Cheng's letter to the emperor. It was a clear confession that the Cheng family and the Ming had lost the mandate of Heaven.

Beijing was magnanimous in victory. The 17 Ming princes found living on Taiwan, among them the acknowledged heir to the previous dynasty's imperial throne, were allowed to live out their days in China. Cheng K'o-shuan was ordered to go to Beijing, which he resisted for a while, fearing the fate of his great-grandfather Cheng Chih-lung, Iquan. But he had to obey and was treated kindly in the capital. He was even given the hereditary title of Hai-chung Kung, the "Sea-quelling Duke."[2] Writing at the end of the nineteenth century, the historian James W. Davidson reported that descendants of Koxinga still carried the title.

There is a temptation to see a parallel between the era of the Cheng dynasty and modern Taiwan. Chiang Kai-shek can be seen as the counterpart to Koxinga, the father of the nation. Chiang Ching-kuo, the generalissimo's son, fostered the island's development as Cheng Ching did. The strength-sapping palace intrigues of the 1680s have some of the characteristics of Taiwan's furious political infighting under Lee Teng-hui and Chen Shui-bian. The comparison is sharpened because of the large number of Taiwanese businessmen who have, with their investments on the mainland, switched allegiance from Taipei to Beijing. The difference now is that Taiwan has powerful allies in the United States and Japan, and the advent of democracy on the island means that there can be no political accommodation can be made with Beijing without the consent of the Taiwanese.

Chapter Nine

A STATE OF CONSTANT REBELLION

When news of Shih Lang's victory in Taiwan reached Beijing, courtiers suggested to Emperor Kang-hsi that he incorporate a reference to the conquest of the island among his many titles. The emperor dismissed the idea. "Taiwan is outside the empire and of no great consequence," he replied.[1] That was the prevalent view of the island in Beijing at the time. China was seen as a complete nation and empire in itself. If other states and territories were wise enough to emulate Chinese culture and social order, well and good. But conquest and empire building in the European style were not the Chinese way. There were even tentative overtures made to the Dutch to see if they were interested in buying Taiwan back. They were not. The emperor asked for opinions from his advisers about what to do with the island and the dominant view was to abandon the place.

"Taiwan is nothing but an isolated island on the sea far away from China, it has long since been a hideout of pirates, escaped convicts, deserters and ruffians, therefore, there is nothing to gain from retaining it," said one report to the emperor. "On the other hand, the Penghu islands, being an important military strongpoint, need to be retained and used as a front base in the eastern China Sea. As for the Han immigrants currently living on Taiwan, they should all be shipped back to their homes in China."[2]

Shih Lang fought a lone battle arguing for incorporation of the island into the empire. "Taiwan is a natural shield for the four south-eastern provinces of China, namely Guangxi, Zhejiang, Fujian and Guangdong," he wrote. "It is not only abundant in fertile soil, but also in farm products and natural resources. Even if Taiwan is to be abandoned, the policy of shipping immigrants back home is impracticable, for immigrants would flee to the mountains [of Taiwan] grouping with aborigines and escaped convicts from the Mainland, and attack the coastal regions of China. This will cause trouble in the future. Furthermore, the Dutch may try to occupy Taiwan again and the safety of Penghu Islands will be jeopardized." Shih put extra emphasis on the threat from the Dutch and their "unrivalled" and "exquisitely built" ships. "If this rich island fell into their hands, so that their ships and men had a base of operations, they would be in a position to rally allies and supporters from all sides, in order to peep at our shores from the advantageous position of a nearby base. It would then be sowing the seeds of trouble and our coastal provinces would have no moment of peace in future."[3] This argument got the emperor's support and a decree was issued on May 27, 1684, that Taiwan be annexed as part of Fujian province and a garrison established of 10,000 soldiers. But Shih didn't entirely win the day. The policy toward Taiwan dictated by the emperor was a compromise between the two arguments presented to him. In essence it agreed to take the island into the empire, but in such a way so as to emphasize that Taiwan was "of no consequence."

Some responsibility for setting the grudging tone by which China governed Taiwan for the next two hundred years belongs to Shih. To persuade the court he couched his case for taking possession of the island in defensive terms and only as a measure for maintaining China's own security. Only in passing did he exhibit enthusiasm for the possibilities presented by developing Taiwan. The island would be administered by the empire only to prevent it from becoming a pirate base, a nest of conspirators against the dynasty, or a strategic threat to the coastal provinces. That attitude, with its strong tones of a reluctant colonial administration, permeated the official view of Taiwan until the 1880s. It was the place to send low-paid, demoted, or third-rate officials who, predictably, practiced the art of institutionalized graft far more avidly than even their colleagues on the mainland. The level of corruption was made worse by an edict saying that soldiers and officials could only be posted to Taiwan for a maximum of three years and no Taiwanese could be recruited into the administration. Those assigned to the island were also forbidden to take their families with them. The intention of this order was to prevent officials and soldiers from identifying with the islanders and perhaps making Taiwan a bastion of revolt against the empire. It had the opposite effect, because those sent to the island, the dross of the empire anyway, felt driven to squeeze as much under-the-counter income out of Taiwan as they could during their brief stay. The result was that for two hundred years the island was in an almost constant state of civil unrest. Taiwan became renowned in folklore for seeing "one major rebellion every five years and one minor rebellion every three years."[4]

An early attempt was made by the Qing dynasty to remove "bad elements" from Taiwan. Soon after the submission of the Cheng family, more than 100,000 of the Chinese on Taiwan—probably about a quarter of the settler population—were rounded up and shipped back to their hometowns and villages on the mainland. Historical records differ on how these people were selected. Some say they were all the officials and soldiers of the Cheng dynasty. Others say it was people with criminal records. As both categories of people amounted to the same thing in the eyes of the court in Beijing, the nuance is probably immaterial. Those permitted to remain on Taiwan were men with wives and children or people who owned a business or property. Even these men had to apply to the Taiwan-Xiamen Military Command Branch Office for permission to stay, a costly procedure requiring much palm greasing. At the same time, what was intended to be a strict immigration policy limiting who could go to the island was proclaimed. This was never enforced consistently, and when the policy was followed stringently, it only meant that would-be pioneers on Taiwan had to pay larger bribes to officials. The policy had three essential elements. Those wanting to move to Taiwan had to get written approval and a passport from the authorities in their hometowns as well as from the Taiwan military command and the coast guard. Stowaways and smugglers would be subject to severe punishments, in theory. The families of pioneer immigrants would have to stay at home as hostages, guaranteeing the good behavior of their menfolk. Men on Taiwan would, eventually, be able to send for their families, thus affording another opportunity for bribes. Banned from going to Taiwan under any circumstances were people from eastern Guangdong province because it was a "well-known pirate den and the residents of this region are customarily thieves."[5] Eastern Guangdong was actually an area populated mostly by Hakka. This element in the policy is evidently the result of Shih Lang's known prejudice against the Hakka.

The immigration policy did little to prevent or regulate the flow of people wanting to move to Taiwan and farm its fertile and abundant land. The Chinese population in 1683, when the Qing dynasty took control, can be estimated at about 400,000, going by the poll tax on adult males for that year. In 1811, when a census was taken, there were just over two million Chinese in a quarter of a million households. Seven years later another census found the population had increased by 545,000. This is far more people than can reasonably be accounted for by the natural increase of population. Further evidence of constant illegal immigration is the regularity with which the authorities had to add new administrative districts or subdivide existing ones.

Failed official attempts to manage population growth and development on Taiwan were not limited to restrictive immigration policies. One regulation prohibited the private importation of iron and iron products to Taiwan. Only government agencies were allowed to bring in iron and there were only 27 licensed blacksmiths on the island. The aim of this rule was to limit the availability of farm implements and thus deter development. The regulation was also an attempt to keep weapons out of the hands of the island's temperamentally rebellious people. An additional attempt to stop Taiwanese from arming themselves was a prohibition on the transportation of bamboo, which could be used for making spears. Both regulations were utter failures. The restriction on iron importation simply created a ready market for smuggling from the mainland, an inherited skill among Taiwanese and their Fujianese cousins anyway. And attempting to restrict the possession of bamboo on subtropical Taiwan, where the plant grows in wild abundance, was futile to the point of silliness.

The determination and hard work of the Chinese pioneers defeated every effort, legal and corrupt, by the officials to curtail development of Taiwan. When the Qing took over, Taiwan rice production was confined to the south of the island. Within 20 years, however, irrigation schemes and the opening up of land for agriculture in the north and east of the island had added 68,800 hectares for rice production. Most of these paddies could produce two crops a year, and Taiwan became the grain basket of southern China. An issue of the newspaper *Guangzhou Register* in 1833 noted that three hundred Taiwanese junks had transported rice to Fujian that year while others carried sugar and camphor to Guangzhou. A contemporary historian commenting on Fujian said, "if violent storms prevent the shipment of rice [from Taiwan] a scarcity immediately ensued and great distress was felt."[6] Modern historian Hung Chien-chao says that by 1890 there were 450,000 hectares of land on Taiwan dedicated to rice production, which averaged 150,000 metric tons a year.

Sugar production started by the Dutch and enhanced by the building of refineries under the Cheng continued under the Qing. Until the European powers forced China to open itself to foreign trade in the mid-nineteenth century, all Taiwan's exports, including sugar, were meant to go to the mainland. There was smuggling of Taiwanese products to other destinations, of course.

But the sugar industry developed rapidly with freer trade. In the late nineteenth century Taiwanese sugar was sold to the Philippines and Australia, but Japan was by far the largest market.

The Qing administration of Taiwan is often described as "colonial," and there are strong arguments to back that view. The island was governed exclusively by officials from an alien elite. Attempts were made to keep civil order using only a garrison from the mainland. The garrison was bolstered only occasionally by local militias, which were usually recruited from among the aboriginal tribes. This approach suggests the Qing authorities did not trust or respect the Taiwanese. The restrictions on immigration and land development also have echoes of a colonial enterprise. Tax harvesting by the administration is a common feature of colonies. Until the final years of the Qing era there was little in the way of government-inspired infrastructure development. The people of Taiwan were treated very much as an underclass. There was no encouragement, for example, for Taiwanese to enter the mainstream of the Chinese civil service, even though tuition was made available in 1686. The lowest-level examinations were first held in 1695, and some of those who passed went on the following year to take tests to become second-degree holders. But because Taiwan was only a district of Fujian province these examinations had to be held in the provincial capital Fuzhou, not on the island. For an islander to even gain passage to Fuzhou was clearly a significant barrier to Taiwanese becoming part of the Chinese mainstream. There is no record of an islander passing the second-degree examinations until 1729. In the entire two hundred years of Qing rule Taiwan produced only 251 second-degree holders. The third and highest-level civil service examinations were always held in the Chinese capital, Beijing, and there is no record of Taiwanese taking part until 1822, when eleven men from the island sat for the tests; only one qualified to become a government official. As far as can be determined, no Taiwanese civil servant ever worked on the island during the Qing tenure.

An early, positive action by the Qing officials was to try to assemble a full picture of Taiwan and its peoples. In 1714 three Jesuits, Fathers De Mailla, Regis, and Hinderer, were commissioned to make a complete survey. The three priests traveled throughout the island, in the forested mountains of the aboriginal tribes as well as the western plains, and compiled the first detailed descriptions and maps of Taiwan. The maps, prepared mostly by Regis, and the descriptions of the mountain tribes, written by De Mailla, had profound effects on Taiwan. They revealed that there was a good deal of fertile land on the island's northeast and eastern coasts. And in the northeast there was coal, gold, and hot sulfur springs, providing one of the three ingredients for gunpowder.

Over the following decades, settlers from China began moving into these new areas. That brought them into competition and conflict with the indigenous peoples of the mountains.

Like the Dutch before them, the three priests nursed strong European cultural prejudices. They saw the native Taiwanese as noble and innocent savages, friendly and trusting. De Mailla brushed off headhunting as almost a childish idiosyncrasy. The Chinese, on the other hand, were portrayed as greedy, devious, and cruel. De Mailla told with relish the following story: A band of Chinese gold prospectors visited a native village and saw some nuggets, on which the villagers put no value, displayed in one of the huts. The Chinese were welcomed by the villagers, and before leaving the Chinese staged a feast as an apparent act of thanks for the hospitality. But when they had got the villagers drunk they killed all of them, burned their huts, and made off with the gold. Such stories of the Chinese dealings with the tribes are plentiful, but the relationship was not entirely one of exploitation. To a significant degree the assimilation of the tribes on the island's western plains, for example, was achieved by marriage. There was a saying at the time that all Taiwanese grandfathers came from China and all grandmothers were already on the island. This was a predictable result of first the Dutch and then the Qing attempts to restrict immigration to Chinese males. The children of these unions were considered Han Chinese. Some communities of natives on the plains did survive independently, but they were slowly assimilated, especially after the Qing authorities started providing schools in their villages early in the eighteenth century. Eventually over two hundred schools were opened for both assimilated and mountain aborigines. It was not until the late nineteenth century, shortly before the island was ceded to Japan, that a secondary school was opened for indigenous Taiwanese. The assimilated indigenous Taiwanese were known as "cooked savages," while the tribes in the mountains were known as "raw savages."

In 1729 the Qing administrators proclaimed the "Mountain Sealing Order," which prohibited Chinese settlers from venturing into or cultivating land in the hill country of the aborigines. This order has often been given the overly generous interpretation of an attempt by the authorities to protect the mountain tribes from the depredations of the Chinese pioneers. Even if that were the case, it tends to underline the colonial and constantly tense relationship between the Qing administrators and the Chinese settlers on Taiwan. There were, for example, similarly angry relationships between British settlers in Kenya and Rhodesia in east and southern Africa and the government's colonial office in London. The British government wanted to protect some of the rights and the land of the indigenous peoples against the expansionist drive of the colonists. In the cases of both Rhodesia and Kenya this conflict between London and its expatriate settlers led ultimately to brutal wars of "liberation" by the indigenous peoples. A more realistic view of the Mountain Sealing Order is that the Qing government wanted to prevent rebel settlers from escaping into the mountains and perhaps forming a common cause with the tribal warriors against the authorities. A line separating the plains from the mountains was established and marked with regular military outposts, but the segregation policy was ultimately no more successful than limiting immigration from the mainland. Some Chinese merchants were licensed to trade with the aborigines, and their cheating and exploitation of the aborigines more than made up for whatever protection the segregation policy offered. The merchants were hated by the tribal villagers and were the cause of the 12 serious uprisings by aborigines during the two centuries of Qing rule.

On the Chinese side of the mountain boundary, animosity between the rulers and the ruled was much worse than in the mountain villages of the aborigines. In the 212 years of Qing rule there were at least one hundred major and minor uprisings or incidents of mob violence. Many of the minor riots were between factions of the settlers themselves. De Mailla wrote:

"Though they are industrious, yet the emigrants have deservedly a reputation for insubordination and lawlessness. They associate much in clans and clannish attachments and feuds are cherished among them."[7]

Among those clannish attachments was the San Ho Hui, the triad secret society formed with a "blood oath" by Koxinga's councilors after their leader's death in 1662. The triad became powerful on the island and attracted many members, especially among the young, single male pioneers, for whom it was a substitute for the security of a family. Most of the 15 major uprisings against the Qing were under the banner of the San Ho Hui or its offshoots, such as the Small Sword Society and the Hung Society. Even when contemporary records don't mention a specific triad involvement in an uprising, in almost all cases they speak of the conspirators swearing oaths or ceremonially drinking blood before taking up arms. These are usual triad rites.

There is good reason to think that triads in their early form, as patriotic Ming partisan groups, were first established on Taiwan during Koxinga's lifetime before the San Ho Hui was created. The secret societies on Taiwan had their birth on the mainland in the declining years of the Ming dynasty among a group of eight honest officials who were outraged at the decadence and corruption they saw around them. They formed a secret society with the aim of promoting reform at court. But they were too late to prevent the overthrow of the Ming by the Manchu and instead launched a revolt in China against the new dynasty. The rebellion was defeated and one of the eight leaders, Wong Shuen Shan, fled to Taiwan. There he wrote a book, called the *Kam Toi Precious Records* for the name of a mountain on the island, setting out a plan of action to defeat the Qing dynasty. The book was given to Koxinga, who, by one account, used it as a blueprint for his unsuccessful attack on the Manchu at Nanjing. On his deathbed Koxinga is said to have given the book to one of his grandsons, who, when the Qing took Taiwan in 1683, threw the book into the sea and committed suicide. A nephew of Koxinga, Cheng Kuan Tat, was among the group of Ming loyalists who took refuge with the famous Fighting Monks of Shaolin Monastery in Fujian province, where the first real triad, the Heaven and Earth Society, was born.

It is important to understand the historical role of the secret societies that have become known as triads and are now seen merely as criminal gangs. They have been key to revolution in China. Sun Yat-sen, the founder of the Chinese republic in 1911, was a triad member from an early age, as was Chiang Kai-shek, leader of the Kuomintang and military dictator on Taiwan from 1949 until his death in 1976. Even China's Communist Party shows strong historic and cultural influences from the triads. In the mid-1990s China's chief economics minister Zhu Rongji, later the prime minister, referred to the triads in a public comment as "patriotic organizations." Indeed, the Beijing Communists in 2004 used triads in Hong Kong to threaten and intimidate two popular radio hosts and some political activists who were seen as stirring up public sentiment in favor of political reform in the territory.

The triads' evolution stems directly from the Confucian concept of the emperor—or Communist Party general-secretary—ruling by the mandate of Heaven. Confucius dictated that the ruler must govern with benevolence, probity, righteousness, and mercy. If the ruler failed to keep that pact with his subjects, they had not only the right but also the duty to rise up and depose him. Justified rebellion against the unjust or undeserving ruler is thus deeply embedded in Chinese culture.

The first mention in Chinese records of a secret society of rebels comes in the story of the overthrow in 25 A.D. of the usurper Wang Mang. A society called the "Red Eyebrows" was instrumental in the ouster of Wang and the restoration of the Han dynasty. In a portent of things to come, the Red Eyebrows continued to exist after their patriotic duty was done, but they survived only as outlaws and bandits. And in yet another foreshadowing, the Han dynasty turned on its mentors and massacred them.

The Chinese genius for administration contributed to the propensity for rebellion. The carefully structured system of officials and ministries evolved in

China as an effective way of managing such a large and populous country. But it was impossible for the imperial court to keep watch on what was happening in the provinces, where the local administrators usually operated as unaccountable petty princes and inevitably became corrupted by unbridled arbitrary power. This made jobs in the civil service highly attractive and lucrative. Entry into the civil service was based on merit and only accomplished by passing a series of formidable examinations in the Chinese classics. Available civil service positions each year were limited; thus each round of examinations produced many thousands of educated young men, frustrated by failure to pass the exams and beholden to their families who had invested in their tutoring. This great lake of unemployed men furnished the class of often seminomadic scholars, writers, and artists—the literati—who have always provided the philosophical underpinning of Chinese revolt. A modern manifestation of the literati is the Chinese dissidents who influenced the student demonstrations at Tiananmen Square in 1989 and, more recently, the subversive Internet discussion groups that so worry the Communist authorities.

In a society where authority seldom lived up to the idealistic concepts of Confucius, ordinary people had to protect themselves. This was achieved both by the emphasis on family loyalty and by the setting up of trade and craft guilds, as happened in Europe, too, before the ascendancy of the rule of law made such mutual protection organizations less necessary. Several guilds and merchant associations were formed on Taiwan during the rule of Cheng Ching, and several had their roots in the pirate confederacy of Li Tan. The usefulness of the guilds depended on trust among the brotherhood. Trust was secured by the swearing of oaths and mystical initiation ceremonies that often included the drinking of animal blood. It is only a short leap from a secret society established for trade purposes to one with political objectives. Trade associations were therefore natural partners and sources of membership for triads. Contemporary records of the many uprisings on Taiwan during the Qing dynasty concentrate on the "ruffians" and "unsavory characters" who led the fighting. But several accounts also mention links to local business interests.

The origins of the Ming loyalist triads go back to the invasion and conquest of China by Chinggis Khan and his son Kublai Khan in the thirteenth century. The hub of resistance to the Mongols was a secret Buddhist organization, the White Lotus Society, one of whose adherents was the monk Chu Yuan-chang. The White Lotus Society changed its name several times to avoid detection, the Incense Smelling Society being the most disarming name it assumed. When the society's members rose in open rebellion against the Mongols in the 1340s, however, they adopted the no-nonsense name of the Red

Turban Rebels. In 1368 the Mongols were driven out of China, and the monk Chu Yuan-chang became the first emperor of the Ming dynasty. The White Lotus Society remained largely invisible through the three centuries of Ming rule. The arrival of the Manchu and their conquest of China in the mid-seventeenth century also brought persecution of secret societies. The White Lotus Society changed its name to the Hung Society and then to the Heaven and Earth Society. It retained a strong religious identity from its Buddhist past but became more and more political in purpose as the Manchu advanced south.

The center of Heaven and Earth Society membership was in Fujian and Guangdong provinces, which were also the core of Ming loyalty and the source of immigrants to Taiwan. The unstable frontier communities on Taiwan, with their large populations of single young men and exiled literati, were a natural breeding ground for triad societies. Taiwan also provided the other necessary ingredients for triad growth and activity. It represented the last bastion of Ming loyalty and resistance to the Qing. And the island was cursed with an officialdom that had clearly lost the mandate of Heaven, if it ever possessed it. Rebellion was a sacred duty.

In theory Taiwan was under the jurisdiction of the governor of Fujian province. He should have visited the island once a year to ensure it was being run according to imperial edicts. In reality the governors seldom risked the stormy passage across the Taiwan Strait, with its notorious Black Current. Subordinate mandarins and magistrates on Taiwan were left to their own devices, which involved arbitrary measures and extortion well beyond the institutionalized corruption on the mainland. A finely crafted system of bribery and fraud quickly became established after the Qing acquired the island. Each position in the administration came to have attached to it a segment of the economy from which the official would extract bribes for licenses or divert taxes in order to pad a meager salary. The following list of officials and their exclusive spheres of graft was compiled by Robert Swinhoe, a British diplomat in Xiamen who was sent to Taiwan as vice-consul in 1861.[8] It thus represents a picture quite late in the Qing era, but the system was well-established by Swinhoe's day and is probably representative of the Manchu colonial period. Chief magistrates took a rake-off from the taxes levied on harvesting camphor trees. Prefects took court fees and pocketed a percentage of the salt tax, which they were in the doubly fortunate position of assessing themselves. District magistrates took all court fees in lesser cases. Port controllers had the power to commandeer any boat required for transporting rice to China. Whether a junk was seized or not was entirely at the whim of the controller and decided by how much the owner was prepared to pay to be left alone.

The first major rebellion came after local officials declared a government monopoly on the camphor industry and in 1720 had over two hundred people decapitated for illegal harvesting. The insurrection was raised by Chu Yit-gui, described in contemporary accounts as a duck herder and "worthless character." But Chu had the royal surname of the Ming dynasty, and in the temper of the times that was a beacon for discontented Taiwanese. The rebellion spread throughout the island within a week under the banner of "Destroy the Qing, Restore the Ming." The garrison troops scored victory after victory in their brushes with the rebels. These setbacks only increased popular discontent and support for the insurgents, whose strength grew with every defeat. Fresh troops were sent from the mainland, but the rebels were able to occupy the island's capital, Taiwanfu, now Tainan. Chu Yit-gui was crowned emperor and the era of the Qing dynasty on Taiwan declared over. Most of the Qing officials fled the island for Fujian. Chu's empire lasted less than a year, however. An army of about 22,000 men was collected at Xiamen for the invasion of Taiwan. As this imperial force was only half the size of the rebel militias, free pardons were offered to any insurgent who surrendered. Only the leaders would be executed. This new army landed at Tamsui and quickly demoralized the rebels with a series of military victories. The emperor in Beijing had, meanwhile, received accurate reports on the reasons for the rebellion and he saw there was justification for the uprising. He sent a decree to the troops saying there were to be no massacres of the rebels as it was clearly disloyal and corrupt local officials who were at fault. New civilian administrators were dispatched to try to win over the Taiwanese. This tactic was successful. Most of the insurgents surrendered quickly, some of the leaders among them. Chu Yit-gui fled into the mountains, where a village headman betrayed him to the imperial forces. Chu was taken to Beijing and crucified.

To try to ensure corruption among officials didn't become a problem again, a censor was assigned to Taiwan with responsibility for maintaining the honesty of the administration. This reform was not effective for long. Within a decade corruption was as bad as ever, and discontent among the Taiwanese was again rife.

In 1731 a "freebooter" called Wu Fu-sheng, together with a gang of about 30 followers, took advantage of an imperial garrison campaign against aborigines to attack and capture a thinly guarded armory at Kang-shan. Wu used pro-Ming, anti-Qing slogans as a rallying cry, and his force quickly swelled to over 300. Over the following days Wu attacked official buildings in several nearby towns before government troops arrived and he was defeated in an eight-hour battle. There was a remarkably similar uprising, also triad inspired, in the same area of Taiwan in 1768, that took the island garrison a month to put down.

A much more serious uprising flared up in 1786, after the secret societies had divided Taiwan into northern and southern spheres of influence. A violent quarrel arose among two factions of the northern triad. Government forces intervened. They arrested some gang members and confiscated property that seemed to be at the heart of the feud. This did not calm matters. Then a more senior officer decided the triads had been dealt with too leniently. He ordered the arrest and execution of several dozen triad leaders and the burning of their villages. The leader of the northern Heaven and Earth triad, Lin Shoan-wen, raised the Ming loyalist banner, marched on Changhua, and captured it. Lin's army then captured a nearby government camp and killed over two thousand men, women, and children in the attacks. With Changhua and much surrounding territory in their hands, the rebels set up an administration with Lin as ruler. Rebel forces fanned out across the island with little opposition from the government troops. By the time word of the rebellion got to the mainland, only Taiwanfu and Tamsui were not in rebel hands. Early in 1787 soldiers were sent from China, but it took nine months of hard fighting before Lin's army was defeated and all the captured towns repossessed. Well over 50,000 troops had to be sent from the mainland to put down the insurrection. Lin himself fled first into the lands of the mountain aborigines and then to his home region in the north. Repression and reprisals by the imperial forces, however, persuaded Lin's triad brothers to consider the common good over the safety of an individual member. He was handed over to the authorities, who sentenced Lin to the death of a thousand cuts. This was the punishment for rebels until 1905. It involved the slicing of small pieces of skin and flesh from the condemned man's body over many days until he finally died.

There was another triad uprising in 1795, when the rebels managed to capture Lugan and Changhua before they were defeated by government troops. In 1800 an offshoot triad, the Small Sword Society, captured Chiayi before their uprising was put down two weeks later. The San Ho Hui triad led an 1833 uprising that captured Taiwanfu and in which 2,000 imperial troops were reported killed, though that is probably an exaggeration. The last major insurrection against the Qing on Taiwan coincided with the Taiping Rebellion on the mainland started in 1850 by Hung Hsiu-chuan, who claimed to be a younger brother of Jesus Christ. The Taiping revolt did not spread to Taiwan, but it led to a great deal of insecurity on the island because government troops had to be diverted to China. In response, some of the triads set up district vigilante groups to maintain order after their own fashion. One such group in and around Changhua was led by Tai Chao-chun, who had established his own triad faction, the Eight-Trigram Society. In 1861 a local mandarin lost patience with the overzealous violence of the triad vigilantes, ordered them off the streets, and had one leader arrested and executed. The mandarin then ordered the subprefect in Tamsui, Chiu Yueh-chin, to disband the vigilantes there. A perhaps overly colorful account of this incident recorded by the British diplomat Swinhoe says that Chiu went out into the city with a detachment of soldiers but was quickly surrounded by an infuriated mob.[9] Chiu found progress impossible in his sedan chair. (European chroniclers, by the way, always found it amusing that Chinese commanders went into battle in sedan chairs. The Europeans did not seem to feel this struck the right tone of martial leadership.) Chiu then "got out and commenced to run from the scene, but seeing that his corpulency would not admit of much more than a waddle, he consented to the suggestion of his chief attendant, and mounted his back. This servant, like the majority of [Chiu's] followers, sympathized with the rebels, besides having private grudges against his superior, so after having carried his master a short distance, he permitted one of the [vigilante] braves to thrust a spear in [Chiu's] back, and, as he fell crying for help, the chief attendant settled up old accounts by deliberately carving off the unfortunate officer's head."[10] The triad soldiers then marched on Changhua, which fell on March 19. Chiu's head was displayed on the city gates.

The uprising now turned into a pro-Ming, anti-Qing rebellion. After triad leader Tai Chao-chun took control of Changhua he declared himself grand marshal and ordered his followers to cut off their queue pigtails, the symbol of subservience to the Qing. Tai then adopted some of the forms used by the Taiping leader Hung, though this is the only connection between the two rebellions. Tai had himself made the eastern prince of his rebel government while three of his generals were designated princes for the north, south, and west. The triad army besieged several cities on Taiwan's west coast but was unable to capture them. Troops were sent from the mainland, and local landowners raised a militia. They managed to contain Tai's forces, but the rebellion dragged on for two years. It eventually collapsed because of internal dissent and rivalries among the rebels. Tai surrendered and was executed in January 1864. Tai's rebellion was the last uprising with a strong pro-Ming element. It was, however, far from being the final uprising or the end of triad involvement in Taiwan life.

Even as Tai's rebels were rampaging through western Taiwan, the center of gravity in China had shifted forever. China's defeat by Britain in the two Opium Wars of 1841 and 1856 forced Beijing to allow the country to open up to foreign trade and the establishment of semi-autonomous colonial enclaves. From the signing of the Treaty of Tientsin in 1858, the main threats to Taiwan were not internal. They came from western nations and Japan, which saw the island's geopolitical and commercial importance and were casting covetous eyes in its direction.

Chapter Ten

THE WOLVES CIRCLE

Taiwan's disappearance into the cold embrace of the isolationist Chinese empire in the late seventeenth century did not erase the island from the memory of outsiders. Interest in Taiwan as a potential hub for regional trade and power remained strong. One reason for the persistent interest in Taiwan, at least in England and France, was the most extraordinary piece of fraud by a man who went by the name of George Psalmanazar. Who this man really was remains a mystery. He was probably born in southern France around 1680 and seems to have decided on a life of confidence trickery at an early age. He adapted his alias from the name of an ancient king of Assyria, Shalmaneser, and first appears pretending to be a mendicant Irish Catholic on a pilgrimage to Rome. To give some verisimilitude to this story he stole a pilgrim's cloak from a church. However, as he was frequently in the company of other pilgrims, among them real Irish ones, he soon had to abandon this identity. Too many people quickly discovered he knew nothing about Ireland. He went to London in 1703 and made the sensible decision to adopt a new nationality and persona that was unlikely to be challenged by anyone possessing superior or real knowledge. Psalmanazar decided to become a Formosan on the basis that there were unlikely to be many if any Taiwanese in London who could expose his fraud. The arrival of this exotic gentleman from an unknown island at the other end of the Earth soon became the talk of London, and he was feted by high society. Psalmanazar created an entirely fictitious life, including a diet made up exclusively of heavily spiced raw meat "because that is the way food is prepared on Formosa." Such was his glamour and reputation that in 1704 he published a book entitled *An Historical and Geographical Description of Formosa, an Island Subject to the Emperor of Japan, Giving an Account of the Religion, Customs, Manners, etc. of the Inhabitants, Together with a Relation of What Happened to the Author in His Travels.* The book was a best-seller and went into an expanded second edition that was also translated in French. To cap it all Psalmanazar was invited to teach the Formosan language, a gibberish tongue he made up as he went along, at Oxford University. Some people began to nurse doubts about him when his gibberish translations of the same English passage differed from one occasion to another. But he was a charming charlatan and many were willing to overlook the evidence of his roguery. Among his closest and most loyal friends was Samuel Johnson, author of the first English dictionary, whose diaries suggest he saw through Psalmanazar's act but didn't care.

Psalmanazar was able to keep the fiction going for so long partly because this was a new age of philosophy in Europe. John Locke had just published a series of essays on the human condition, including one called *Identity and Diversity.* Psalmanazar's account of the lives of the people of Formosa appealed to an audience entranced by the complexities and influences of culture on nationhood. Although he worked on the principle that whenever any of his outrageous descriptions of Formosa were challenged, he would counter it with something even more mind-boggling, Psalmanazar was eventually discredited. Even that he turned to good account and wrote a book, another best-seller, confessing his duplicity. But with Psalmanazar's help Taiwan remained an island of public interest, even though it may have been for entirely fraudulent reasons.

There is some speculation, probably wrong, that another extraordinary character who next kept Taiwan in the public eye was inspired by Psalmanazar. Count Maurice August de Benyowsky was born in Hungary, served for several years in the army of the Austro-Hungarian Empire, went to Britain and Holland to learn navigation, and then fought the Russians as a cavalry commander in the armies of the Polish confederacy. He was captured in 1770, then aged 29, and banished to the Kamchatka peninsula in the Russian Pacific. Benyowsky and several other exiles escaped by seizing a ship. The Russian governor's daughter, Aphanasia, who was consumed by a mighty sexual passion for the Hungarian count, went along for the ride, even though she knew he had a wife in Europe awaiting his return. The 94 escapees and their ship first got to Japan, then went on to the Ryukyu Islands, and in August 1771 reached

Taiwan. Benyowsky and his party landed on the island's eastern shore roughly where the Tropic of Cancer bisects Taiwan. This was, of course, the aboriginal region of the island, and the first encounter with the local indigenous tribe was bloody. Two of the count's men were wounded by arrows, and about six of the native Taiwanese were killed when Benyowsky's crew responded with a musket volley. The escapees sailed north up the coast and found a good harbor, which Benyowsky named Port Maurice after himself. Here they had the good fortune to meet a Spaniard, Don Hieronimo Pacheco, living with the local tribe. Pacheco had been the port captain at Manila but had had to flee the Philippines after killing a Dominican monk he discovered in "criminal intercourse" with his wife. Pacheco also killed his wife. He had lived among the tribe for eight years and was able to act as interpreter. For several months Benyowsky and his small army gave decisive help with their cannon and muskets to the local tribe in their wars with their neighbors. As a result Benyowsky concluded a treaty of eternal friendship with the chief before leaving for Macau, where he and his crew caught a French ship for Europe. In France Benyowsky wrote a book about his adventures and advocated the colonization of Taiwan. The French government was taken with the evident buccaneering talents of the count but was not so entranced by Taiwan. He was commissioned instead by the French to found a colony on Madagascar, off the east coast of Africa. He spent three years there but, according to his own account, resigned over serious disagreements with his masters in Paris. France wanted him to claim the island as a French colony and subdue the natives. Benyowsky's preference was to make nation-to-nation treaties of friendship with the local chiefs. Back in Europe in 1783, Benyowsky tried to get the British interested in Taiwan, but without success. He then went on to America, where the government was equally unenthusiastic about Taiwan. In 1784 he left the United States for Madagascar to help the local people fight the French, who were pursuing possession of the island in a manner more to their tastes. Benyowsky was killed in battle against the French in 1786.

After Benyowsky's visit in 1771 there are no records of other foreigners visiting Taiwan by accident or design until 1824, when two British ships attempted to trade with the island. Both called at Taiwanfu, the site of Fort Zeelandia, now called Tainan. But the Dutch harbor was already entirely silted up and the fort rebuilt by Koxinga was well inland. Neither ship could get closer than three miles to the coast. The second of the two ships went on to Keelung, where the captain ordered a survey of the harbor. British ships called again in 1827 and 1832 but with equally little success at finding a practical harbor or local interest in regular trade.

Events in India now set off a ripple effect that eventually washed onto the shores of Taiwan as they had hundreds of years before when land-hungry Austronesian peoples found refuge on the island. By the late eighteenth century Britain was having a hard time raising revenue to pay for the enormous cost of running and developing its Indian empire. At the same time British merchants were being blocked by Beijing from breaking into the China market. They were only allowed to trade at Guangzhou for a few months each year and then required to leave, usually for the Portuguese enclave of Macau. Added to these restrictions was the Chinese preference for using silver as a currency medium. There just was not enough of the precious metal around. The British found the solution to both their problems in the fields of the newly acquired Indian state of Bengal. That commercial salvation was the opium poppy.

Arab traders had introduced opium to Asia in the seventh century A.D., and the Portuguese had taken over the business when they began to dominate the region. The Portuguese also introduced tobacco to China from their Brazilian colony in the 1500s. Smoking tobacco mixed with opium became a fashion in China, and all the European and American traders quickly appreciated that drug trafficking created a self-sustaining market. The British, however, with the greatest imperial demands for trade and the naval power to enforce them, pushed opium trafficking to its limits. A government monopoly was enforced over Bengal poppy growing, and the demand for opium in China grew dramatically as more and more addicts were created. In 1821 the British exported 270 tons of opium to China. By 1838 the trade had reached 2,400 tons.

The Chinese court became alarmed as opium addiction spread through the bureaucracy and army, dulling the efficiency of these state institutions and beginning to undermine the economy. In 1800 the emperor banned the importation of opium. British merchants, backed by the Royal Navy, simply ignored the repeated edicts from Beijing and carried on using the drug as the currency of trade either openly or with the aid of Chinese smugglers. In 1839 Chinese imperial officials in Guangzhou lost patience with the British and had several thousand tons of the Indian opium seized and thrown into the harbor. These were the days before the telegraph, and it took about a year to send a message to London and receive an answer. The task of protecting British interests was left by force of circumstance to the officers and diplomats on the spot. The British Empire was acquired not in "a fit of absence of mind," as historian J. R. Seeley wrote in 1883, but in an absence of communication when freebooter adventurers on the colonial frontiers were beyond the control of policymakers in London. Naval officers of the Asian fleet in cahoots with outraged British merchants fought and won the so-called First Opium War against China before London knew much about it. To give the merchants a secure base for their trading, Britain took as its prize the island of Hong Kong under the August 1842 Treaty of Nanjing, much to the disgust of the British government, which felt it had acquired a "barren rock."

The ease with which a few British warships and their crews overcame imperial Chinese forces and barged their way into China sparked a feeding frenzy in Asia among Europeans and Americans. The door to China had been forced ajar. It was evident another shove would spring it off its hinges. It was just a matter of time, opportunity, and excuse. Every act that could be portrayed as an example of Chinese perfidy was logged and tallied for a day of reckoning that would surely come soon.

Two incidents chalked up against the Chinese happened near the end the First Opium War, and both happened on Taiwan. Late in 1841 the British transport ship *Nerbulla* struck rocks near Keelung. The circumstances sound very like those in the opening chapters of Joseph Conrad's novel *Lord Jim,* for the European officers of the *Nerbulla,* two Filipinos and three Indians, took to the boats and left the bulk of the ship's company, described as "240 British Indian natives," to their fate.[1] The *Nerbulla,* like Lord Jim's *Patna,* did not sink, however. After five days the weather improved and the ship drifted off the rocks and into Keelung Bay. The survivors were all captured by the Chinese and kept in chains for several months. Then, in March 1842, the British brig *Ann* was blown by a storm onto the shore near Tamsui. The 57 people on board, including 14 Europeans and Americans, 5 Chinese, 34 British Indians, and 4 Portuguese and Malays, were captured by Chinese soldiers and imprisoned in chains with the survivors of the *Nerbulla.* On August 13, 1842, all the survivors of the two ships, 197 people at that point because several had died of maltreatment and disease, were taken to a field and decapitated. A Chinese who witnessed the executions said later the islanders paid a bitter price for killing the foreigners because a tremendous storm hit Taiwan, even as the decapitations were in progress, and up to 2,000 islanders died. "That was the judgment of Heaven for beheading the foreigners," the Chinese witness told a British chronicler. "But it was done in revenge for your soldiers taking Amoy [Xiamen]."[2]

Reading just the British accounts leaves the impression that the *Nerbulla* was an innocent transport ship whose passengers were subjected to a foul massacre. The Chinese accounts give a different story, and the truth is probably somewhere in between. The second version is that the *Nerbulla* was an armed troop transport ship and the "British Indians" were Sepoy troops. On September 30,

1841, the *Nerbulla* shelled one of the forts at Keelung. The Chinese batteries replied and damaged the British ship so that it ran aground. About 30 of the crew died as they tried to abandon the ship, and the Chinese took 132 prisoners. In October a British gunboat was sent to Keelung to try to secure the release of the prisoners, by paying ransom if necessary. When it appeared negotiations would be a long and tedious business, the British shelled the Chinese gun emplacements. Some marines landed to try to storm the fort but were beaten back. Early in 1842, after the passengers and crew of the *Ann* were taken prisoner, an order was received from Beijing to execute all prisoners taken in the Opium War. The order was not carried out immediately, however. In the meantime the emperor decided that killing the prisoners would not help the treaty negotiations with the British and issued a counterorder. This arrived at Taiwan too late to stop the executions. The British senior diplomat in the region, Sir Henry Pottinger, made a hotly worded complaint to the governor of Fujian province, and the Chinese military commander in northern Taiwan was punished, but only by being demoted.

The number of European and American merchant ships badgering to get into the China trade by fair means or foul in this period grew dramatically in response to the evident weakness of imperial rule in Beijing. More shipping meant more wrecks, especially during typhoons and on the forbidding east coast of Taiwan, which bordered the sailing lanes to America and Japan. Accounts from the period speak of shipwrecked crews meeting more cruel and brutal fates at the hands of the indigenous tribes or even the Chinese on the island than would have been inflicted on them by the sea. A particular affront to the certainty of European ethnic superiority—which included Americans at the time—were reports of shipwrecked sailors and officers being kept and bought and sold as slaves by both the Chinese and indigenous Taiwanese. The British, Americans, and Prussians—this was before the emergence of the German state—all dispatched naval expeditions to Taiwan in the 1850s to search for their nationals reputedly being held as slaves, but they had no success. There was much public criticism in Europe and America of the leaders of these expeditions for not being diligent or courageous enough in searching for the prisoners. One who came under criticism for his lack of diligence was a certain Captain Abbot of the U.S.S. *Macedonian,* which was detached from the fleet of Commodore Matthew Perry's "Black Ships" then attempting to establish contact with Japan. Abbot was pilloried in the popular press for apparently having relied on fruitless inquiries by his Chinese steward before deciding there were no imprisoned Americans to be found. However, Abbot did manage to make a thorough survey of the coal deposits on Taiwan in the neighborhood of Keelung, where he landed, so the mission was not a total failure. Abbot's report was so favorable that Perry, when he got back to the United States, wrote a recommendation to the secretary of state pointing out that Taiwan was very attractive as a site for an American Far East trading center and advocated occupation of the island. Civil war was looming in America and Washington was in no mood to contemplate foreign adventures. Perry's views did, however, arouse much more interest in Europe and in Japan.

All these incidents and many similar ones on the mainland were added to the catalogue of perceived acts of violence and duplicity by China against foreign traders and missionaries. The lust to finish the work of knocking down China's barriers to the activities of foreigners begun in the First Opium War grew beyond reason. The strength of the passion is obvious in the frailty of the excuse that set off the next war. On October 8, 1856, Chinese officials in Guangzhou boarded a Chinese junk, the *Arrow,* that they believed was smuggling opium. The junk was registered with the British in Hong Kong and flew the Union Jack. In the course of searching the *Arrow* the Chinese officials hauled down the Union Jack. When reports of the incident arrived in Hong Kong, there was consternation among the colony's merchant opium dealers. This, they held, was a gross insult by the Chinese to the British flag and a clear challenge to the protection guaranteed all those who sailed under the Red Ensign. The British were joined by the French, who used the excuse of the murder of one of their missionaries a few months before to become involved. They captured Guangzhou in December 1856. It was another swift victory and display of the weakness of imperial China against the modern armies of Europe. The court in Beijing was presented with the Treaty of Tientsin, which required the opening up of scores of ports to trade, freedom for missionary work, the exclusion of foreigners from Chinese law, and legalized dealing in opium. It was more than the court in Beijing could bear. In 1858 the emperor refused to ratify the treaty. Retribution was as swift as the first invasion and even more devastating. British and French troops marched on and captured Beijing in 1860 and then, in an act of outlandish cultural desecration, looted and burned the Summer Palace. The Treaty of Tientsin was ratified.

Under the terms of the treaty China was required to open four of the ports on Taiwan as well as allow missionaries to propagate Christianity on the island. The port of Tamsui was opened to foreign merchants in 1862, Keelung in 1863, and Anping (now a suburb of Tainan) and Takao (now Kaohsiung) in 1864. It was the British who led the pack of industrialized nations eager to take advantage of the opportunity when the gates of Taiwan were opened to trade. Soon after the ratification of the treaty, Robert Swinhoe, then based in

Xiamen, was posted to the island, where he took up lodgings in Taiwanfu. Illness forced him to leave the island shortly after his arrival in July 1861, but he recovered and returned in December, convinced he should establish the British consulate either in Tamsui in the north or Takao in the south. The silting up of the harbors around Anping and Taiwanfu was killing trade in that part of the island. Swinhoe opted for Tamsui and first camped for a year on a British receiving ship—essentially a floating warehouse considered safer from theft and riot than storage space ashore. He then managed to get permanent occupation of the old Spanish fort Santo Domingo, and this remained the British consulate on Taiwan until 1972. Once in Tamsui Swinhoe quickly realized that a lot of trade deals were done farther up river at Banka, now part of the capital Taipei, and a British subconsulate was opened there in 1862.

Formal arrangements like treaties and consulates very often follow patterns of contact and commerce that are already established. European and American merchants were doing some trade with Taiwan before the Treaty of Tientsin, but not much. Most of the commerce appears to have been in the hands of an American called Mooney who exported camphor, tea, sugar, and rice. But he only imported opium from his receiving ship anchored off Anping. After the treaty and the opening of the four ports Mooney found himself facing a good deal of competition in the drug trade. More and more of Taiwan's products were exported, but there remained only one substantial import: opium. This free-for-all rocked Taiwan's already cantankerous society, and the sense of violation was heightened by the busy work of the Christian missionaries. The Qing authorities had trouble with the British merchants, who scrambled to avoid the rules on dealing in camphor, still a government monopoly. And several missionaries were roughed up by Taiwanese, both aborigines and Chinese, who objected to the persistence of the door-to-door salesmen of Christianity. The emperor's officials on the island had no more power to control and regulate the unruly foreigners than did their counterparts on the mainland. In 1868 the foreign powers forced another treaty on Beijing that included provisions to end the government camphor monopoly, allow foreign merchants to travel freely on Taiwan, and forbid what the document described as "slanderous talk" against Christianity.

The Treaty of Tientsin opened Taiwan not only to merchants and preachers but also to the gunboats of the foreign powers. The gunboats, their armaments, and marines became the court of final appeal for foreign traders and missionaries who got into trouble on Taiwan. In 1868 a British gunboat was dispatched to Tamsui after a patriotic mob had barred two agents of Dodd and Company from taking up residence in a house they had leased in Banka. The local magistrate reluctantly agreed to punish the mob leaders. In the same year two British gunboats shelled Fort Zeelandia, and marines were landed both at Anping and Takao after a number of attacks on missionaries and Christian churches in southern Taiwan. Sometimes, but only very occasionally, the foreign consuls and their gunboats actually backed the Qing authorities against encroachments by their nationals. Supporting the orders of Chinese officials, in 1869 a British gunboat was sent to the eastern coast near Nanao to dismantle a colony established by a German opium merchant and a British camphor trader. The two complied after the show of force.

Among these foreign, armed interventions the so-called *Rover* Incident stands out because it introduced to Taiwan the American consul in Xiamen, General Charles Le-Gendre. He became the architect of Japan's acquisition of Taiwan as a colony in 1895 and was even at one point promised appointment as governor of the island for the Japanese. In March 1867 the American barque *Rover* was driven onto rocks off Hengchun at the southwestern tip of Taiwan. The captain, his wife, and the crew were able to escape the sinking ship in lifeboats, but they landed on Taiwan's southeastern shore in the territory of the Kaolut tribe. The tribal warriors swept out of the forest and killed all the survivors except a Chinese sailor who hid at the first sign of the attack. The sailor managed to get to Takao, where he informed the British vice-consul what had happened. A message was sent to the American senior diplomat in Beijing, who requested that a British gunboat investigate the incident. A gunboat, the *Cormorant,* sailed from Takao to the Kaolut territory and sent out a landing party, which was attacked by warriors. The British seamen were too few to respond effectively. They retreated to their ship and shelled the native village. Le-Gendre in Xiamen and American diplomats in Beijing first pressed the Chinese authorities for urgent action against the Kaolut, because there was still some hope that members of the *Rover*'s crew were alive and being held prisoner. The Chinese said they had no authority over the aboriginal areas of Taiwan and declined to get involved. Washington was equally reluctant to intervene, but finally in June 1867 Le-Gendre was assigned two ships, the *Hartford* and *Wyoming,* together with 181 officers, sailors, and marines. This expedition fared no better than had the British. The Americans found progress through the jungle and mountainous terrain difficult. They were under almost constant sniper fire from concealed native warriors whose weapons, luckily, were more an irritation than a serious threat. Only one officer was killed. But the Americans decided their task was impossible and withdrew.

Le-Gendre, however, was determined to deal with the Kaolut. In September 1867 he badgered the Qing authorities at Taiwanfu into agreeing to send a considerable force of Chinese soldiers to the Kaolut territory. From Le-Gendre's description of what followed it is unlikely the Chinese seriously intended to follow through on their promise. He received lavish greetings and hospitality when he arrived at Taiwanfu and then reviewed the troops who were to be sent on the mission. But when Le-Gendre suggested that, as everything seemed to be ready, the troops should leave right away and that he would accompany them, there was consternation among the Chinese officials. The American general speculated the Chinese plan was to pack him off back to Xiamen, well feasted, and then to send the heads of some aborigines to the provincial governor a while later with the message that retribution had been exacted. Actually going on an expedition into the territory of the Taiwan aborigines was not part of the plan.

Under a torrent of badgering from Le-Gendre the Chinese finally decided they'd better send the expedition into the mountains. But there was no enthusiasm for the venture and Le-Gendre showed little surprise in his subsequent report that the Chinese foray was defeated by the jungle, mountainous terrain, and hidden enemy just as the Americans and British had been. After this failure Le-Gendre tried another tack. He spent time seeking out and cultivating intermediaries so that he was able to arrange a meeting with the chief of the Kaolut, Tooke-tok. The American general and the headhunter chieftain struck up a friendship, and Le-Gendre concluded an agreement that the Kaolut would not only not kill shipwrecked crews in their territory but would care for them and help them to safety. The Kaolut firmly adhered to their side of the bargain.

It was on the basis of this special relationship Le-Gendre developed with the Kaolut that the Japanese hired him when the crew of one of their merchant ships was massacred by another southern Taiwanese tribe, the Botan, in December 1871.

The events that led from the wreck of the Japanese ship, a large fishing and trading vessel, are highly significant in the story of Taiwan in the late nineteenth century and, indeed, into the first half of the twentieth century. This incident led to Chinese tacit admission that Japan had sovereignty over the Ryukyu Islands, which had previously sent tribute to the emperors in both Beijing and Tokyo. Beijing also admitted that its sovereignty over Taiwan extended only to the western, flatlands third of the island. This confession remains one of the arguments put forward today by Taiwanese independentists to counter Communist China's claim to historic ownership of the island. Japan's large military expedition to Taiwan in 1874 was not only its first experiment in acting like a European power after the Meiji Restoration and its accompanying industrial revolution, it was a practice run for its colonial expansion a decade later into China, Korea, and Taiwan itself. The firsthand experience of Japan's new capabilities against the Botan moved factions in Beijing to belatedly attempt their own modernization program. This led to Taiwan being separated administratively from Fujian and being designated a province in its own right. There was also a brief period of modernization on Taiwan, when the island's development far outstripped mainland China. This in turn fostered the first stirrings of the modern awareness of a distinct and separate Taiwanese identity. And that bred the declaration of the Taiwan Republic in 1895, which survived for only a few months before being crushed by the Japanese army.

That is a large blast of history to fill the sails of one Ryukyuan fishing boat, the *Miyako*. The ship had a crew of 69 and it ran aground near Hengchun on the western coast of Taiwan's southern tip on December 18, 1871. Three sailors drowned in the wreck and 66 made it to shore in the territory of the Botan. Of the survivors 54 were killed by Botan warriors and 12 managed to escape to Fangshan, about 20 miles to the north, where they arrived on January 1, 1872. The 12 sailors finally made it home to the Ryukyu Islands in the spring. There they told their story to the local dignitary, the satsuma, and asked for compensation and future protection. The satsuma then made a decision that affected the future course of the Ryukyu Islands' history. He sent the sailors' petition to Tokyo, not to Beijing. The Tokyo government was delighted to receive this indication that the Ryukyus were acknowledging Japanese sovereignty. In October 1872 the islands were incorporated in the Japanese empire as a prefecture.

After the arrival of Commodore Matthew Perry and his fleet in Tokyo Bay in 1854, the Japanese court looked out on the world for the first time in two hundred years and decided it would like to be part of it. But Japan wanted to be part of the world only on its own terms. That, it envisaged, meant accepting the benefits of western industrialization, but not the western cultural influences that, going by their activities in China, the Europeans and Americans insisted were part of the package. Japan launched into its own vision of modern Asian imperialism with the Meiji Restoration in 1868. Gaining territory and resources was part of the imperial Japanese calculation from the start. The envelopment of the Ryukyu Islands not only had merit in itself, but was also a stepping-stone on the way to the greater prize of Taiwan. But Japan was new to the European game of imperial conquest. It was neither sure of the rules nor certain how the other players would react. Tokyo therefore moved cautiously. It first sent its consul at Xiamen, Kabayama

Sukenori, and a student, Mizuno Jyun, to Taiwan as "spies," according to a Japanese account. With them went the now retired American general and consul Charles Le-Gendre to investigate the situation on the island. Le-Gendre was hired on a retainer of 12,000 yen a year because of his experience with the Kaolut tribe, neighbors of the Botan. The Japanese court then took the occasion of the accession of the Kuang-hsu emperor in May 1873 to send an ambassador to Beijing with the aim of testing the Chinese waters regarding Taiwan. With the ambassador, Soejima Taneomi, went Le-Gendre and Yanagihara Sakimitsu, who had experience negotiating with the Chinese. Yanagihara was sent to the Chinese foreign ministry, the Tsungli Yamen, to see how Beijing would react to a Japanese punitive expedition against the Botan. The Japanese emissary was told clearly by the Beijing officials that China regarded the aboriginal territory on Taiwan as outside its jurisdiction. Beijing would take no responsibility for what happened there and would not punish the tribe for past or future offenses.

Tokyo chose to see Beijing's disavowal of responsibility as tacit agreement that Japan could take any action it chose in eastern Taiwan. It also took Beijing's stance to be acknowledgment of Japan's sovereignty over the Ryukyu Islands. With these formalities successfully completed Japan wasted no time in preparing its expedition to Taiwan. The Bureau of Taiwan Barbarian Territory Affairs was set up in some secrecy because Tokyo was still unsure how the European powers would react to what it was about to do. In charge of the bureau and of planning and leading the expedition was an army lieutenant general, Saigo Tsugumichi, with Okuma Shigenobu as his assistant and Le-Gendre in the background as principal adviser. There were other American hired guns too. Lieutenant Commander Douglas Cassel of the United States Navy was taken into the Japanese service with the rank of commodore, and a lieutenant in the United States Army Engineers, James Wasson, was made a colonel in the Japanese army.

Japan's efforts to keep their preparations secret were doomed, especially in the gossipy atmosphere of the port city of Nagasaki, from where the enterprise to Taiwan was to be launched. Not least of the telltale signs that something big was up was that Japan had no transport ships large enough to carry the 3,600 troops of the expeditionary force and their equipment to Taiwan. They needed to charter transport ships, and that inevitably aroused interest and rumors. Saigo and his team arranged to charter the British steamship *Yorkshire* and with the backing of the local American diplomat also booked the Pacific Mail Company ship *New York.* Then, for some reason that has never been explained, the American diplomat, a Mr. Bingham, recanted on previous support for the Japanese enterprise. He objected to Americans taking part in the expedition without the written permission of China and he worked successfully behind the scenes to make sure the *New York* was not available. The loss of the American ship was a blow to Saigo's plans and when the expedition finally left in mid-April 1874, the hastily acquired second ship was too small and crowded. Fortunately for Saigo the weather was calm. The Japanese called first at Xiamen, where they staged a full rehearsal of their planned landing on Taiwan. They landed on May 7 at Hengchun, where they set up their base camp.

The setting up of the headquarters camp immediately revealed some serious weaknesses in Japan's first outing as an imperial military power. Eyewitness accounts by Europeans and Americans say the Japanese had learned contemporary infantry tactics and the use of weapons well enough.[3] They had not paid the same attention to all the organizational matters of transportation, communications, and supply—command and control in modern military jargon—essential to keeping an effective army in the field. Part of the Japanese problem was cultural. Soldiers were traditionally a superior class in Japan, meaning they were above doing menial tasks or manual labor. This meant that on landing they had to recruit from among the local aborigines a labor force about equal in size to the 3,600 men of the expeditionary force. There were days of bargaining with local villagers before a labor force was assembled, but it never worked very effectively and it was two weeks before Saigo was ready to move against the Botan.

There were eighteen tribes in the vicinity of the Japanese landing, of which the Botan were only one, though marginally the largest. In the early days after the Japanese arrival a good deal of information was gathered about these tribes, many of which quickly made peace pacts or succumbed after brief skirmishes. The Japanese soon discovered that the aborigine population of the area was far smaller than anticipated. The Botan and their close allies could muster only four hundred warriors at most. The Japanese came upon the main Botan village on June 22, fought a brisk skirmish with the warriors, and burned the village.

The irony was that on the way to the Botan village the Japanese came across the graves of the *Miyako* crew, whose deaths had justified the invasion. From local people the Japanese learned what had happened. The Botan had captured the crew, and thinking they were Chinese, had taken them to the nearest Chinese-speaking village in the hopes of getting a reward. The Chinese didn't recognize the Ryukyuans and were not inclined to give the $100 the Botan were demanding in ransom. This attitude did not change when the

Botan threatened to kill the Ryukyuans on the spot unless the money was paid. With no money forthcoming the Botan carried out their threat. Indeed, some reports say the Chinese joined in the slaughter.

By the end of June 1874 the purposes of the Japanese expedition had been achieved, but Saigo showed no inclination to take his army home. Chinese officials began to be concerned that Saigo intended to capture the whole of Taiwan. Many diplomatic protests were sent to the Japanese, and the authorities in Fujian dispatched reinforcements of five hundred men and some light artillery to their Taiwan garrison. Patriotic excitement was aroused in both Japan and China. For a while this fervor spawned street demonstrations both in Japan and Xiamen as a general war between the two countries seemed imminent.

Of particular concern to the Chinese was the involvement of the Americans with the Japanese expedition. Charles Le-Gendre had stayed in Nagasaki at the time of the invasion, partly to manage the resupply of Saigo's forces and partly because of Washington's unease about his involvement. But because of Le-Gendre's former official position as Washington's consul, the Chinese found it hard to believe his involvement didn't signify American backing for the Japanese enterprise. To try to calm Chinese fears the American consul in Xiamen went so far as to print and widely distribute a handbill calling on all Americans involved to withdraw from the Japanese armed expedition. There were, of course, only three Americans involved and they took no notice. Washington's sensitivity toward China, or at least that of its diplomats in Fujian, can be seen in what happened to Le-Gendre in July. He was sent to China by the Japanese as part of a diplomatic team dispatched to try to come to some peace settlement with the governor of Fujian. But when he arrived in Xiamen, Le-Gendre was forcibly detained by a marshal attached to the American consulate with the assistance of marines from the U.S.S. *Yantic* and sent under guard to Shanghai. Cooler heads prevailed in Shanghai and he was released. Le-Gendre then joined up with Japanese diplomats heading for Beijing to try to negotiate a settlement. Talks went on for three months and an agreement was finally reached with the Chinese foreign ministry on October 31. China gave in on every point. It acknowledged Japan's right to protect its subjects and to seek redress for those harmed in the aboriginal part of Taiwan outside Chinese control. At the same time China promised in future to exercise control over those eastern areas of the island. China also agreed to pay 500,000 ounces of silver, 100,000 of which was compensation to the families of the Japanese sailors killed by the Botan, and the rest as recompense to Japan for the roads and buildings it had constructed during its Taiwan expedition. General Saigo left

Taiwan with his whole force on December 3, 1874, and ten days later was received in Tokyo "with much honor and distinction."

The results of Japan's Botan expedition and China's acceptance of Tokyo's terms reinforced the weak and feeble image of the Beijing court. The "sick man of Asia" could not fight and would always give in. This perception sometimes led to miscalculations by the foreign powers and the underestimation of efforts that were being made by some Chinese officials to reform and modernize China. The Japanese incursion on Taiwan troubled senior Chinese official Shen Pao-chen, the architect of China's attempts to build a modern navy. When the Sino-Japanese agreement over the Botan Affair was signed in 1874, Shen urged the court to take Taiwan more seriously. He volunteered to make an inspection of the island and to recommend a program for its reform and development. Shen's report was politely received and then shelved. But it did have a profound influence on officials and literati on Taiwan. So when France picked a quarrel with China in 1884 and decided to use Taiwan as a bargaining chip, it found itself dealing with a rather more robust society than the surrender-prone court on the mainland.

James Davidson, writing in 1903 on the basis of eyewitness accounts of the French invasion, said: "The campaign was unique in that foreign forces were not always the victors and that France, one of the greatest military powers in the world, was forced to admit that the actual results of the campaign frequently failed to correspond with the carefully laid plans, that the anticipated victories, in at least two instances, were victories for the Chinese."[4]

The French failures, Davidson continued, were due to "the mistaken judgment of the French authorities, who were so convinced of the feebleness of China as well as so over confident of their own strength that they endeavored to carry on warfare, under the name of reprisals, with a small force and insufficient funds."

The Franco-China war of 1884 grew out of France's efforts to acquire colonies and protectorates in eastern Southeast Asia—Cambodia, Vietnam, and Laos—then called Annam. In the north of this region, called Cochin China, and bordering China's Yunnan province, there were frequent skirmishes between French and Chinese troops. Early in 1884 Paris and Beijing signed an agreement aimed at lessening the tension, but the skirmishes continued. Both sides were to blame. For example in June 1884 the French cruiser *Volta* sailed into Keelung harbor on Taiwan. The captain demanded a supply of coal for his ship's bunkers, and when the local Chinese officials were slow in making the delivery he threatened to open fire on the harbor's forts. On July 12 France sent an ultimatum to Beijing demanding implementation of the agreement as well as a large payment for recent injuries. When no immediate response came from Beijing a squadron of 12 French warships sailed to the Fujian provincial capital Fuzhou and bombarded the city on August 23. China declared war on France.

The war was already well under way on Taiwan. Two small French warships entered Keelung harbor on July 22 and on August 4 were joined by a gunboat and the battleship *La Galissoniere,* under the command of Admiral Sebastian Lespes. The admiral promptly demanded the surrender of the fort commanding the harbor, which was armed with modern German Krupps guns. When the Chinese refused, the French opened fire at a range of about one thousand yards (one kilometer) and demolished it. French marines landed, raised their flag over the ruins of the fort, and occupied parts of Keelung. Chinese reinforcements were rushed from Tamsui and contained the French advance. There was a stalemate for nearly a month with some small engagements, but no decisive battles. Late in September the French senior admiral Amede Courbet arrived at Keelung with 11 warships. He ordered Lespes to attack Tamsui while he attempted to take Keelung. Courbet launched the second assault on Keelung on October 11, but after a ten-hour battle the Chinese managed to hold the French to a draw. Meanwhile Lespes had attacked Tamsui on October 8. The French fared no better there. The defenders held position after a six-hour battle. But in order to meet the threat to Tamsui the Chinese had to divert troops from Keelung. With the defenses there weakened, Courbet was able to take Keelung on November 2. There followed another stalemate while the French enforced a blockade around Taiwan, preventing reinforcements and munitions from reaching the Chinese. On March 3, 1885, French troops from Keelung marched on Taipei, the trading center inland from Tamsui. The French were stopped at the gates of the city and after a two-week siege abandoned the attempt to take Taipei.

The man responsible for mounting the spirited Chinese defense against the French was the governor of Fujian province, Liu Ming-chuan. He personally led his troops in battle and marshaled them with a flexibility and imagination unusual if not unique among Chinese commanders of the time. But Liu was an unusual man who, with the departure of the French, launched Taiwan on a decade of reform and construction that put the island at the forefront of Chinese modernization.

Chapter Eleven

A MODERN PROVINCE

Liu Ming-chuan was undoubtedly clever enough to have taken the classic Chinese scholastic route to advancement, position, and wealth. However, his lowly birth on a small farm in Anhui province and lack of a source of funds from family patronage precluded embarking on the lengthy and expensive progression through the civil service examination process. Anyway, Liu was a young man in a hurry and from the start demonstrated an impatience that was both part of his genius and a political weakness. He chose the other well-worn route to fame and fortune in China: that of the gangster warlord. In his late teens Liu decided the life of a peasant farmer was not for him. He abandoned the family plot of land and set off to seek his fortune in the big city of Luchow, as the Anhui provincial capital was then called. Liu arrived as the provincial governor T'ao Chu was trying to break the power of a small group of merchants who had not only monopolized the salt trade but established hereditary rights over this commerce. T'ao Chu directed that anyone could deal in salt so long as they bought their supplies from the provincial government and paid cash in advance. Liu, then 18 years old, saw an opportunity. He went into business with the help of forged permits allowing the purchase of government salt and the backing of a gang of armed youths he called the Band of Fiery Insurgents, Ming-tzu Chun. Liu's violent retainers dissuaded competition and within a couple of years the young farm boy controlled the entire salt trade of Luchow and the surrounding countryside.

The outbreak of the Taiping rebellion in 1851 gave Liu the chance to make another leap up his chosen path to advancement. He quickly made the transition from local bandit and warlord to respected and loyal royal servant much as Koxinga's father, Iquan, had done three centuries before when he changed titles from pirate chieftain to imperial admiral. When the Taiping rebels advanced on Luchow in 1854, it was clear to everyone that the city's feeble garrison stood little chance of fending off an attack. Liu called on the governor and suggested his Band of Fiery Insurgents be made into a local militia. The governor agreed and over the next seven years, in many campaigns against the rebels, Liu showed himself to be a military leader of great talent. In 1862 Li Hung-chang, who was to become one of the most notable statesmen of the last decades of the Qing empire, was delegated by Beijing to raise an army to drive the remaining Taiping out of Anhui province. Li readily accepted Liu's offer to amalgamate the Fiery Insurgents militia into his army and from then on the farm boy–turned–gangster rose steadily in the official hierarchy. Liu's gift for military command was essential to a string of victories over the rebels. Li Hung-chang was a generous patron and overlord. By the time the Taiping rebels had been defeated, Liu he had acquired a multitude of honors and had been appointed a baron of the first class. He was only 31 years old.

Two portraits of Liu have come down to us. The earlier one shows the buccaneer, the gambler, and the leader of men. There are the piercing, calculating eyes set off by a raffish drooping moustache and a goatee beard. In the later picture the goatee has been shaved off, though the moustache remains. The difference in the impression conveyed is striking. The face in the second portrait is now serene, and one writer has described it as monklike.[1] There is certainly an ethereal, spiritual glow in the eyes not evident in the hard focus of the first picture. Liu has achieved the Chinese ideal of putting far behind him the cruel acts along his road to success and sits contented as an elderly sage secure in the respect he commands.

By the mid-1860s Liu had become a gentleman. He abandoned banditry, built himself a mansion on a country estate in Anhui, and for over ten years led the life of a respected member of the landed gentry. He also set about acquiring the education that had eluded him as a soldier, salt trade racketeer, and farm boy. His home became a gathering place for local gentry and literati to meet and debate the issues of the day.

Liu's passage from bandit to scholar came at a time when China's educated and creative classes were much alarmed at the depredations of the western powers and the affects of these intrusions not only on the country's sovereignty but also on its cultural sanctity. Liu's thinking developed along the lines of the self-strengthening movement, which held that China should reassert itself by adopting the benefits of western industrialization, especially military power, but should hold fast to the Confucian pillars of social values and structure. This movement closely followed the Meiji Reformation in Japan, where western-style industrialization was being pursued without any ground being given on the country's cultural individuality or political sovereignty. Liu's chance to apply his new thinking came in 1880 when his old mentor, Li Hung-chang, summoned him to Beijing. China had signed a treaty with Russia by which Moscow returned the far northwestern Xinjiang province, which the Russians had occupied in 1871. The problem was Russia had refused to give up the mountain passes leading to neighboring Russian-controlled Turkestan. Control of the passes gave Russia effective continuing military dominance over Xinjiang and the ability to sweep into China any time it chose. Li thought Liu was the man to address the problem. Liu contemplated the situation and decided that as there was no hope of dislodging the Russians from the mountain passes by diplomacy, the answer was to deter Moscow by ensuring China could speedily move large numbers of troops to the region if need be. He advocated building railways from Beijing to the north and northwest. The concept of locomotive transportation as a boon to trade—itself still a despised activity—and the defense of the empire had not yet penetrated the closed and intrigue-ridden world of the court behind the high walls of the Forbidden City. Such assaults on the harmony of China's mother earth, disturbing the *feng shui* by the laying of steel track, cutting through her hills, and tunneling through the mountain homes of sacred dragons, seemed more outlandish and outrageous the deeper the message traveled into the mazelike multitude of palace courtyards. By the time Liu's recommendation reached the heart of decision-making power it was beyond comprehension or contemplation. A few courtiers who had traveled to Europe or North America spoke up for Liu's plan, but the tide of isolated conservatism was against him.

Disappointed and disgusted at the rejection, and with all it implied about the chances of the court accepting notions of self-strengthening, Liu returned to his country estate. However, rejection by the palace only increased Liu's resolve to explore the concepts of modernization within a Confucian society. For the next three years his country home became again a hotbed of debate on ways and means to revive China. But when the call came again from Beijing for Liu Ming-chuan's services, it was his military talents the empire wanted. In 1884 France was making Taiwan a major theater in its war with China over Indochina. Liu was appointed governor of Fujian with express responsibility for trying to stop the French from grabbing Taiwan, then still administered as part of the mainland province. He arrived at Keelung on July 16, but decided to make his headquarters at Taipei, the hub of the island's north. When the French attacked Keelung early in August, Liu led reinforcements to the port and checked the assault. A second French attack in October was also blocked, and although the French did eventually manage to capture Keelung, they were never able to control a secure land base. They were equally unsuccessful in their attempt to take Tamsui, Taiwan's northwestern port, where European residents commented on the extraordinary boost that Liu's presence on the battlefield gave to the Chinese defenders' morale. Liu's personal leadership was equally decisive when the French did finally manage to get a force through to attack Taipei. The six hundred French marines and Foreign Legionnaires were unable to mount a serious assault on Taipei's defenses and retreated.

The Sino-French war petered out in July 1885 but it was a significant victory for Liu and his defenders. They had shown that properly armed, trained, and motivated Chinese troops could match the best infantry soldiers that Europe had to offer. This was heartening news in Beijing, which for a decade had been mulling over what to do about Taiwan. The Japanese punitive expedition to southern Taiwan in 1874 had given Beijing a warning that despite its dismissal of the island as a barbaric outpost fit only as a place of exile for the empire's most useless officials, others saw it differently. The Japanese and now the French perceived Taiwan's strategic position not only on the trade route of Asia, but as a base from which to be able to project power in the region. Shen Pao-chen had, after the Japanese invasion, recommended that greater attention be paid to Taiwan. He continued making his arguments for a decade, and in the aftermath of the French incursion his words began to gather a sympathetic response in Beijing. In 1887 Taiwan was separated from Fujian and made a province in its own right, with Liu Ming-chuan as its first governor.

The appointment gave Liu, for most practical purposes, his own principality. The sea was wide. The mountains were high. The emperor and the numbing hand of the Beijing court were far away. Liu was now free to try to put into effect the ideas of a modernized Confucian state he had marshaled during his years of scholarly exile on his Anhui estate. He began by making an imperial progression through his domain to see for himself the state of affairs on Taiwan, to meet and measure the leaders of the island's clans and families, and to show himself to his subjects. Then, like many reformers before and since, he let everyone know that a new era had dawned with a whirlwind of name changes.

Liu had decided during his months of campaigning against the French that the island's capital was in the wrong place. Since the days of the Dutch the island's administrative capital had been in the far south at Fort Zeelandia, renamed Tung-tu by Koxinga and, in Liu's day, known as Taiwanfu. This made sense in the centuries when the main route to the island for trade or invasion was across the stepping-stones of the Penghu Islands from Xiamen in Fujian or up the Taiwan Strait from Southeast Asia. The emergence of Japan as a regional power together with increasing trans-Pacific trade and the development of the treaty ports such as Shanghai on China's east coast required a change in the center of defensive and administrative gravity on Taiwan.

For a while Liu contemplated moving the capital to present-day Taichung, close to the center of Taiwan's western plains. A town site was laid out with streets on a grid system, walls and gates were built, and the imperial office buildings, the *yamen,* were constructed. The new capital was even garrisoned for a while. The cost overruns were huge, however. Liu felt forced to abandon the project after it had cost a quarter of a million *taels* of silver and there was no end in sight. He decided it would be more economic to adopt and expand the existing small city and commercial center of Taipei, midway between the two ports of Tamsui and Keelung. Taiwan became the name of the whole island and, to avoid confusion, the southern city was renamed Tainan. The prefecture around the city was called Anping.

These clear signs that a new and energetic hand was on the island's tiller were not welcomed immediately by the Taiwanese. They and their forebears had come to Taiwan for the very purpose of escaping imperial officialdom. During the two hundred years of Qing rule the corrupt and inefficient officials dispatched by Beijing to Taiwan had often been a nuisance and sometimes a menace. But they could usually be bought off or otherwise suborned. The society that had evolved in this climate was, in the rural areas, a patchwork of large landholdings controlled by extended families under the rule of warlords and their household militias. Clashes between these clans over landholdings or crucial water rights were frequent and sometimes developed into feuds that went on for generations. In the towns special interests were just as firmly entrenched through trading guilds or other commerce monopolies. Throughout Taiwanese society ran the influence of the triads, hovering on the cusp between political, Ming dynasty loyalist secret societies and simple criminal gangs. There was no significant transportation network on the island beyond some basic footpaths, and there was little industry worthy of the name. The education system and standards were well below those of the mainland, and administrative officialdom was, of course, rotten to the core. Even this slipshod administration reached less than half the island. The mountainous east remained the domain of the aborigines who, when provoked, as frequently happened, would come swooping out of their hills to attack farmsteads and villages in search of plunder and trophy heads.

The primary task handed Liu by Beijing was to bolster the defense of the island against any further encroachments by the foreign powers bent on nibbling away at China's sovereignty. Strengthening Taiwan's military capacity was necessary not only to meet outside threats. The Taiwanese had an earned and established reputation for being a rebellious lot, ready to rise up in arms against authority at the slightest provocation. Liu's task, then, was as much to bring the islanders under effective authority as it was to deter invaders. The island's garrison had been cut almost in half, down to about 17,000 men, after the Sino-French war. Liu immediately supplemented this force by recruiting a 4,000-strong aborigine militia. This and the regular force were both equipped with modern firearms, and foreign army officers were hired to train them. In past emergencies, whether domestic or from outside, troops and munitions had always had to be rushed from the mainland and often arrived too late. Soon after his arrival in 1885 Liu ordered the construction of two munitions factories, one to make artillery shells and the other rifle cartridges, as well as a gunpowder mill. These were all built and managed by foreign engineers. There were five fortresses on Taiwan when Liu assumed control. All were improved soon after Liu's appointment and modern artillery bought from two of the leading gun makers of the time: Krupp of Germany and Armstrong of Britain. The defenses of Keelung, Tainan, and Tamsui were strengthened with the construction of two concrete gun batteries at each city. Four batteries were built to protect the southern port of Takao, now Kaohsiung, and three were constructed on Penghu. Liu wanted to develop a small navy for the defense of Taiwan and its associated islands. He petitioned Beijing to be allowed to buy four warships and six torpedo gunboats but was turned down. The new capital, Taipei, was built within formidable defensive walls mounted with heavy guns. Behind this medieval aspect, however, Liu indulged his passion for modernity. Taipei was set out as a functional capital without all the frippery of imperial decoration common to government establishments on the mainland. Liu's ideas of imperial display turned in other directions. As a symbol of his modernizing enlightenment Liu in 1887 turned on in Taipei the first electric street lights anywhere in China. This was, though, one example of Liu's enthusiasm exceeding his grasp. The street lights were found to be too expensive to run and after a while were disconnected, though electric lights continued to burn brightly outside the main government *yamen.* Liu insisted that most of Taipei's streets should be paved. Those that were not fully surfaced were given several parallel tracks of long stones laid end to end. These were to allow the easy use of another Liu innovation, rickshaws, the two-wheeled, two-seater elegant buggies pulled by a struggling coolie peasant that were until very recently ubiquitous in Asia. For the first few years Liu paid for this, Taipei's first taxicab service, out of his own pocket. Then he turned the rickshaws over to the coolies who pulled them, perhaps Taiwan's first service industry privatization.

Even the best troops and guns are largely useless without effective means of transportation and communications. Liu swiftly began applying the recommendations he had made after 1871 for the defense of Xinjiang. In an unusual burst of foresight among Qing officialdom, in 1876 the then governor of the island and Fujian province, Ting Jih-ch'ang, had authorized the laying of a telegraph cable from the then capital, Taiwanfu, north to Changhua in the central plain. Liu Ming-chuan ordered the cable extended to his new capital, Taipei, where a training center for telegraph operators was opened. This line was completed in 1888. This link was then extended to the port of Keelung. A cable-laying steam ship, the *Feicheu,* was bought and in 1887 a submarine telegraph line was laid from Tainan to the Penghu Islands. Under the direction of a Danish engineer, Emanuel Hansen, the Penghu Islands were then linked to Sharp Peak at the mouth of the Min River on the mainland in 1888. Instant communication was possible between Taiwan and China for the first time.

Rough cart tracks and footpaths were the only roads around western Taiwan when Liu became governor. They made for arduous travel at the best of times. During the monsoons or typhoons the tracks became impassable. The difficulties of communication within the island did much to foster the isolation in which the power of district family warlords and clan groups flourished. The lack of easy contact and intercourse among neighbors tended to sharpen communal suspicions and frictions as well as diminish the effectiveness of central authority. Liu, the modern Confucian, was determined to jerk the island into the nineteenth century by building the most modern means of transportation, railways, an innovation as yet unknown on the mainland, let alone on Taiwan.

Liu's plans for railways on Taiwan first had to overcome skepticism in Beijing. He did this by pointing out that the moving of the capital to the interior at Taipei necessitated a swift and reliable means of transportation. Beijing's agreement was grudging, but Liu got the approval he wanted. More difficult to surmount was the strong devotion among islanders to *feng shui,* the belief that the will of Heaven and its implications for humankind can be divined from the Earth's physical features and phenomena. Under these concepts, any disruption of the Earth by humans, from the siting of a house to the placing of a grave, has an effect on the good fortune of the people involved. These notions of harmony extend to the positioning of furniture within the home and sometimes to convictions that can astonish non-Chinese. At Repulse Bay on the south coast of Hong Kong's Victoria Island is a large, upmarket block of apartments some 30 stories high and built in the early 1990s. But in the middle of the block, which looks out over the South China Sea, is a large hole in the building some four stories high and three apartments wide. This is so that the dragon that lives in the hill behind the building can fly out unimpeded on his regular sorties over the sea.

Liu would have been well aware that his plans to build a railway from Taipei to the island's most efficient port, Keelung, by carving through hills, burrowing through mountains, and brushing aside the grave sites of ancestors would arouse resentment. But he pressed ahead and even demonstrated his determination to the islanders by accompanying the German engineer, a certain Mr. Becker, as he pegged out the first four miles of the railway route to the northeast of Taipei. The pegs proved to be the first problem for the foreign surveyors and engineers, who had no authority over the soldiers and their officers delegated by the governor to do the work of plotting the course of the railway. The soldiers, who had not had their task fully explained to them, found the pegs handy fuel for the campfires to cook their evening meals. Each evening soldiers gathered up many pegs for their fires, which meant that much of the day's work had to be repeated the following morning. The soldier's officers were open to bribes from landholders unhappy at finding themselves in the railway's path. For the right payoff the officers would change the route of the track with never a thought to the demands of engineering. The officers took the moneymaking opportunities of this concept one step further and found they could do excellent business by diverting the intended line of the railway toward the land or family graves of a rich landlord. The landlord could then be induced to pay for the line to turn away in another direction. This led to some alarming twists and turns on the intended path of the railway. As the soldiers had no concept of what it was they were building—that the sweep of curves and slope of gradients are critically important in railway construction—but thought of the enterprise as simply a better kind of footpath, there was much frustration among the foreign engineers. The foreigners' only recourse was to the soldiers' generals, but they were inclined to side with their own men and were undoubtedly taking a rake-off from the various rackets anyway. The result was that work proceeded very slowly and was of poor quality. By the spring of 1889 only 11 miles of the railway had been finished, and this was over the easiest terrain. The engineers then began to address the hills that surround Keelung, and relations with the soldier laborers that had been merely frustrating became tense in the extreme. There were constant arguments about whether to negotiate hills with cheaper cuttings or more expensive tunnels. The Chinese disliked using valuable timber to shore up excavations, with the result that the cutting walls or tunnel roofs were constantly collapsing. Drainage was a luxury that seemed superfluous to the Chinese, so there were many wash-outs of the roadbed and then outbreaks of tropical diseases spawned in stagnant water. Finally civilian laborers had to be brought in to replace dead or otherwise incapacitated soldiers. To excavate one tunnel through a hill, teams started digging toward each other from either side. When both got to the middle they found that one leg of the tunnel was 14 feet higher than the other. Much of the roadbed work had to be redone when engineers found curves and grades so sharp that no train could negotiate them. Liu, to save money, insisted that only the minimum corrections be made. When the Japanese took over Taiwan they rebuilt much of the line from scratch, but despite its imperfections in October 1891 the first train ran the 20 miles from Keelung to Taipei. By the end of the same year there was 20 miles of track running south from Taipei and two years later another 20 miles had been added down to Hsinchu.

At Keelung the line ended, logically enough, at a new wharf in the harbor. The trouble was that for some reason the dock and the railhead were at a point where there was only three feet of water in the harbor at high tide. It would need constant dredging of the harbor bottom to make the wharf functional. A small dredger was bought and it puffed away ineffectually for a few years. Meanwhile in Beijing an anxiety attack about the implications of modernization had taken hold of senior officials at court. They argued that all these expensive improvements on Taiwan and especially at Keelung with its port, railway, and nearby coal mines were likely to make the island even more attractive to foreigners and thus more likely to inspire invasion than before. So when the dredger expired of overwork and poor maintenance it was not replaced. No further work on Keelung was approved. Shipping dropped off so that by 1894 months went by without a foreign trader calling at the port. Liu's railway became a passenger service only as there was no freight to haul, and even then few people entrusted themselves to the hair-raising journey and unreliable timetable.

Liu Ming-chuan's ambitions for Taiwan required revenue to support the capital projects he undertook and the large number of mandarins and their retinues involved in administering the island as a province. Liu also co-opted several local gentry family clans who were not only the de facto local governments but also controllers of household militias. Senior members of families such as the Lins of Wu-feng and the Lins of Panch'iao were appointed to quasi-governmental boards overseeing Liu projects for railway construction, tax reform, and mining. Liu was now in a position too to dispense the kind of patronage from which he had benefited in his youth. Several of the household militias—the "braves" mustered by extended families in times of crisis—were taken onto the public payroll as auxiliaries to the garrison.

While Taiwan had been a prefecture of Fujian it had received a grant of 660,000 Mexican dollars each year as a subsidy and there had been reasonable and avoidable taxes on tea, camphor, opium, and salt. Mexican dollars, introduced as the currency of Spain's trans-Pacific trade, were much favored by Chinese because of the purity of the silver. There were also land taxes, but large landowners easily evaded these by passing them on to tenant farmers. Soon after his arrival in 1885 Liu ordered a reassessment of land and the tax regime. Many major landowners were gathered into the revenue net so that money from this source increased more than two and a half times. Liu ordered the tightening up of collection of import, export, and transit taxes on goods known as *likin.* Tea and camphor, which were the main products in the north, had been subject to *likin* before, and even though Taiwanese didn't like the new efficiency in tax collection, their unhappiness went no further than grumbling. The northerners did come close to the breaking point, however, when Liu attempted to impose the *likin* on goods leaving the treaty ports open to foreign traders, like Keelung and Tamsui, and destined for other island, nontreaty ports. Opposition was so intense that Liu withdrew the measure for a while but managed to reintroduce it without incident when tempers had cooled.

Hardest hit by the new regime of efficient tax collection were the southern sugar producers, on whose exports the *likin* was imposed for the first time. As was their habit, the central and southern Taiwanese did not take this quietly. Much of this region of Taiwan became an area where Liu traveled with some trepidation and only when necessary. On one occasion in Tainan an angry mob kept Liu a virtual prisoner in his *yamen* government office for several days. After his release he never went back to Tainan again.

In the past such incidents would have led to violent government reprisals, the capture and execution of the riot leaders, and probably the leaders' family suffering for several generations the stigma of being traitors or rebels. That didn't happen after the Tainan incident, and, in general, Liu showed unusual tolerance for the criticism that was leveled at him. He was the constant target of satirical poems on wall posters, but he took no notice. Some dissenters were not content to just paste up acid rhymes. On one occasion, when Liu threw a party to mark his mother's birthday, protestors gathered at the gate of his house and gave guests handbills on which was written a poem decrying the extravagance. But more than any other governor of Taiwan before and most of them since, Liu understood the benefit of allowing Taiwanese to vent their strongly held views.

Liu's tolerance of dissent and his vigorous pursuit of modernization on Taiwan caught the attention of many devotees of the self-strengthening movement among the literati-gentry on the mainland. There was a steady trickle of such intellectuals to the hospitable atmosphere of Taiwan and away from the stultifying and often dangerous attitudes toward free thinkers on the mainland. This intellectual accumulation was to become significant a few years later when it provided the impetus for the short-lived Taiwan Republic.

During the six years of Liu Ming-chuan's tenure there were no serious outbreaks of violent unrest among the island's Chinese colonists, one of the few periods in Taiwanese history of which that can be said. It was not, though, a period of peace and repose. James Davidson, an eyewitness, says that after Liu was made governor in 1885, his determination to gain "control over the savages" led to "greater bloodshed during those few years than there had been for a considerable period of time."[2]

There is some dissent among historians about this aspect of Liu's rule. Davidson, who was there, is uncompromising in his criticism. Johanna Menzel Meskill in her history of the Lin family of Wu-feng tends toward Davidson's view, but without his sense of outrage.[3] Some authors adopt the gilded view that Liu set out in his memoriam to the Beijing court: His campaigns resulted in 478 aboriginal villages, 88,000 people—out of a total island population at the time of 200,000 aborigines—coming under provincial authority.[4] Liu also claimed that as a result 250,000 *mou* of land, nearly 38,000 acres, were brought under rice cultivation both by subdued aborigines and Chinese settlers. It is highly debatable whether this was true. Liu's greatest fans, such as William Goddard, make the ultimate act of generosity by omitting any mention of the governor's campaigns against Taiwan's indigenous peoples.[5]

Liu began his drive against the aborigines in the autumn of 1885, soon after his arrival as governor. There were several reasons why Liu saw suppression of the tribes as a pressing matter. The presence of the unassimilated indigenous people was undoubtedly a hindrance to development. Their control of large tracts of the fertile but uncultivated western plains limited the expansion of rice and sugar production. The scarcity of land was a constant cause of fighting and skirmish wars between family clans. Opening up more land for Chinese settlement would relieve these pressures and lessen the reasons for internal strife. Tense relations on the frontier in the foothills between Chinese and the indigenous tribes, together with the aborigines' habit of swooping down on Chinese villages to gather trophy heads when passions boiled over, made harvesting of the camphor forests a perilous occupation. Beyond these considerations, the existence of these wild, untamed peoples offended Liu's sense of order and modernity.

The first campaign against the aborigines, lasting six months over the winter of 1885–86, gave Liu a spirit of false optimism. Liu advanced into plains and low hill country southeast of Taipei while family militia led by Lin Ch'ao-tung, current strongman of the Lins of Wu-feng in the upper valley of the Ta-tu River inland from Changhua, marched northeast in a pincer movement. The tribes encountered by the converging Chinese forces mostly had a long history of living in close proximity to the settlers. When Liu offered them an arrangement whereby they would receive a monthly retainer of rice worth a Mexican silver dollar for every aborigine who engaged in agricultural work, they readily agreed. In return the tribes would stop killing Chinese. Several accounts say most of the tribes submitted en masse and the pacification campaign rapidly became more of a triumphal procession. This was deceptive, however. The less amenable braves fled up into the higher hills and mountains, where they nursed and instilled in the local tribes great animosity against the traitorous actions of their brethren. The aborigines who had surrendered to Liu, "cooked savages" as the Chinese described them at the time, found themselves caught between the ever-encroaching settlers and their own bitter relatives, who took every opportunity for murderous retribution.

Later in 1886 another expedition was sent inland from Changhua to try to pacify aborigines who had been disrupting the camphor industry in the hill forests. This campaign by 1,500 Chinese troops and militia lasted two months and was only a series of skirmishes that in no way achieved the objective of making the forests safe. Even so, the Chinese lost 500 men, a third of their force.

Lin Ch'ao-tung led a contingent of his family militia on this campaign. The tribal warriors became adept at silently and invisibly surrounding Chinese detachments in the mountain forests and then rushing out to fight at close quarters where the advantage of the Chinese firearms was minimized. In one such maneuver Lin and his men were besieged on a mountaintop for ten days. They managed to get word of their predicament out to the family enclave at Wu-feng, where Ch'ao-tung's feisty wife levied fresh troops. She led the mission herself, broke the siege, and rescued her husband. The dashing young woman, wearing a white dress and galloping through the hills on a white stallion to save her threatened lover, has, understandably, become an indelible image in the island's story.

While these expeditions were under way in 1886, a large military force was sent to Ilan on the island's east coast with the intention of attacking the aborigine problem from both sides. There were setbacks from the start. Early in 1887 about 400 soldiers, including a general, were killed in battles with tribal warriors and reinforcements had to be sent. There were months of skirmishes and battles. Among the dead in these engagements was the nephew of Liu Ming-chuan. The nephew, named Lau, led a party of 180 Chinese soldiers into the aboriginal district south of Ilan. One night while Lau's contingent was camped, about 1,000 aborigines surrounded the Chinese. All the Chinese were killed except three soldiers who managed to escape and tell the story.

Liu Ming-chuan conducted the campaigns against Taiwan's indigenous peoples with his customary dedication and enthusiasm. His troops were equipped with the most modern weapons he could acquire, including land mines, mortars, and the precursor of the machine gun, the Gatling gun. But even with this superiority in weapons, Liu's troops never came close to achieving their objective. With the costs of his pacification expeditions rising and pressing demands on the provincial revenue for development projects on the western, ethnic Chinese, portion of Taiwan, Liu quietly abandoned the forays into the hills. As has been mentioned, he took the precaution of first declaring victory in a memorandum to Beijing, but all he had really achieved was inflaming anti-Chinese sentiments among the indigenous peoples.

After 1887, when Liu abandoned his forward policy, warfare in the border areas between the aborigines and the Chinese settlers was more or less continuous. There were atrocities on both sides, though the aborigines usually restricted their butchery to the time-honored custom of collecting heads. The Taiwanese also took to collecting heads, according to Davidson, and displaying them in their villages.[6] Taiwanese despoliation of aboriginal bodies, however, went well beyond that. Writing soon after the events he describes, Davidson said the bodies of slain aborigines were cut up and eaten by the Chinese. "The kidney, liver, heart and soles of the feet were considered the most desirable portions, and were ordinarily cut up into very small pieces, boiled and eaten somewhat in the form of soup," he wrote. "The Chinese profess to believe, in accordance with an old superstition, that the eating of savage flesh will give them strength and courage." He says the flesh of aborigines was sold openly in markets on Taiwan and even sent for sale to Xiamen on the mainland. Davidson was appalled and he concluded: "The Chinese ordinarily deserved all the punishment they received from the savages. Their treatment of these children of the forest was always cruel in the extreme. Contracts were made which were never intended to be fulfilled, and all the deceitful tricks that cunning Chinese could contrive to deprive them, not only of property but even of life, were played upon the ignorant savages."[7]

Liu's unsuccessful campaigns against the indigenous Taiwanese were a bounty to his enemies in Beijing. They mistrusted his tolerant attitude toward his Taiwanese subjects and his passion for the benefits of western industrialization. Liu found dealing with the court more and more frustrating. When in 1889 Beijing objected to a contract he had signed with a British company to improve coal production near Keelung, he was censured and had his title of governor removed by the Board of Punishment, though he was allowed to remain in his post on probation. Liu at this time was suffering increasingly from recurrent malaria and in 1891 was ordered to return to the mainland. He appears to have regarded the order as a relief. He applied to be allowed to retire, which was approved, and he spent his last years at his house in Anhui. He died in January 1896 soon after Taiwan had been ceded to the Japanese under the Treaty of Shimonoseki, which ended the Sino-Japanese war.

Liu Ming-chuan was replaced as governor of Taiwan in 1891 by Shao Yu-lien, a man about whom no historians have much to say and what they do say is not to his credit. He is typically dismissed as a weak man more attracted to the comforts of office than continuing Liu's reform agenda. Those were undoubtedly the qualities that attracted Shao to the men who appointed him in Beijing. Shao held the governorship for only three years and when ordered, in the summer of 1894 and on the eve of his departure, to reinforce the defenses of the island in preparation for war with Japan, he acted true to character. He bought old and substantially useless weapons at knock-down prices. He did request and was sent from the mainland two highly regarded military commanders. One was the naval commodore of Fujian province, Yang Chi-chen. The other was Liu Yung-fu, the hero of Chinese battles in 1884 against the French in Annam, now northern Vietnam, and brigade general of the renowned Black Flag militia.

Liu Yung-fu was another warlord who had successfully made the transition from renegade to imperial servant when Beijing needed his troops to fight the French. Liu was ordered to prepare to defend southern Taiwan, where he was destined to play a pivotal role in the short-lived Taiwan Republic. Lin Ch'ao-tung, of the Panch'iao Lins, with his family militia that had distinguished itself against the French, was put in charge of defending the hills above Keelung on the route to Taipei. Keelung port itself was guarded by 13 battalions of regular soldiers, and another 7 battalions guarded Tamsui. The defenses of the Penghu Islands were reinforced.

This emphasis by Governor Shao on the defense of northern Taiwan was continued by his successor, T'ang Ching-sung. T'ang arrived in Taiwan with a solid reputation built on the part he played defending Annam against the French. It was in preparation for this war that T'ang persuaded Liu Yung-fu, Black Flag Liu, to join the imperial cause. Perhaps unfortunately for the future of Taiwan, each of the two men was suspicious of the other's ambitions. T'ang in particular did all he could to minimize Liu's effectiveness, with chaotic consequences when the Japanese invaded Taiwan in 1895 to claim their rights to ownership of the island under the Treaty of Shimonoseki.

Chapter Twelve

THE TAIWAN REPUBLIC

A good deal of romanticism and self-serving political reinterpretation surrounds assessments of the Taiwan Republic, which survived for a scant five months from May 23 until October 21, 1895. Modern enthusiasts say this interlude demonstrates the deep-seated desire of Taiwanese people for independence and a representative government. The island's brief republic, they contend, was an inspiration to the revolutionary movement on the mainland. It provided the philosophical seeds for the reform movement in China that ousted the Qing dynasty in 1911. Detractors of the significance of the 1895 Taiwan Republic say it was intrinsically inconsequential. Its objectives were muddled and propelled by momentary expediency. Its leaders, with one or two exceptions, had no loyalty to the enterprise and fled the island even before the going got tough. It was never a true republic, and the evidence is contradictory that the aim was to establish Taiwan as an independent state. Moreover it was doomed from the start. There was never any real prospect of the Taiwanese being able to defeat the modern Japanese army that arrived to take possession of its spoils from the 1894 Sino-Japanese war and the Treaty of Shimonoseki.

There is truth in both assessments and the many others that fall between those extremes. What is common to all views, though, is that the five months of the Taiwan Republic and the events surrounding them were a formative period in the island's story. It is an important part of the creation of the island's individuality and distinctive history. Perhaps most significant in the long term, that experience told Taiwanese their fate was in their own hands. When their future was in the balance, not only China but the great powers, too, deserted them. In the end in 1895 they had no choice but to submit to Japanese colonialism. Yet even in that situation the islanders found benefits that remain facets of modern Taiwan. After much resistance many Taiwanese came to appreciate and even embrace what Japan had to offer the island. There was never much affection between the Taiwanese and their Japanese overlords, but the islanders came to adopt a pragmatic attitude toward the relationship.

Japan's desire to become a regional imperial power went hand-in-hand with the restoration of the Meiji emperor after 1853, the country's opening up to the outside world, and its rapid industrialization along western lines. In the late nineteenth century the sure sign of having achieved the status of an imperial power was the acquisition of colonies. Tokyo had acquired the northern Kurile Islands in 1875 from Russia in exchange for the island of Sakhalin. In 1879 Japan annexed the southern Ryukyu Islands. High on Tokyo's list for further imperial expansion were Korea, a former vassal state, and Taiwan, which the Japanese military had scouted in force during its punitive action against island aborigines in the 1870s. These represented a quantum leap in Japan's ambitions. The Kuriles and Ryukyu Islands were populated by people who were ethnic cousins of the Japanese. This was not true of Korea or Taiwan, and both these territories were within Chinese rule or influence. Tokyo waited and watched for opportunities to use its new military muscle in the pursuit of these objectives.

The chance to take on China came in 1894, when a secret society in Korea, the Tong Hake, attempted to seize power. Korea was a tributary state of China and the rulers asked Beijing for aid. China sent troops to help put down the rebellion, but so did Japan. Japanese and Chinese soldiers were soon facing each other, and it was a fairly simple matter to stir these confrontations into war in August 1894. The conflict carried on into the following year, but it was soon evident the victory would go to the Japanese. China had the numbers, but Japan had disciplined forces with modern weapons.

Even before the fighting ended rumors began to spread that Japan wanted possession of Taiwan and the Penghu Islands as prizes of victory. The rumors raised such apprehension on Taiwan that a group of officials and literati went to Beijing to petition the court not to hand over the island. Beijing and its negotiator, Li Hung-chang, played for time, hoping that one of the European powers or even the United States would come to its aid. The British were even asked if they would take temporary guardianship of the island to protect it from Japan's clutches. The British government refused. By mid-April negotiator Li had run out of excuses and diversionary tactics to delay the treaty agreement. On April 17 the Treaty of Shimonoseki was signed, giving Japan sovereignty over Taiwan and the Penghu Islands "in perpetuity."

Official notification of the terms of the treaty were sent to Taiwan's governor, T'ang Ching-sung, two days later. The cable to T'ang told him that the island was to be handed over to Japan within two months. However, those islanders who did not wish to come under Japanese rule would have up to two years to move themselves and their possessions to China. Those remaining on Taiwan must be prepared to become Japanese subjects. T'ang was instructed to issue a proclamation making these facts known. When he did so, there was a sustained outpouring of public indignation. T'ang's office was besieged by petitioners brandishing messages they wanted sent to Beijing demanding that the court not ratify the treaty.

In those early days after the signing of the treaty one man came to dominate the campaign of public outrage at Beijing's cavalier abandonment of Taiwan and the imminent arrival of the Japanese. He was Ch'iu Feng-chia, a Hakka and leading member of the landed gentry from Changhua, whose family had arrived on Taiwan from Guangdong around 1680. Ch'iu had strong links to the island's literati as well. He was involved with Taipei's leading poetry and philosophical discussion group, the Mu-tan Shih-she (Peony Poets' Club), which became the political hub of reaction to the treaty with Japan.

As a young man of exceptional academic credentials, Ch'iu had been brought into the island's civil service by his mentor, Governor T'ang. The relationship between T'ang and Ch'iu became clouded by mutual suspicion and descended into rivalry, however. Ch'iu was not only from the landed class and an intellectual, but he was articulate and personable. He attracted supporters from among both Hakka and the ethnic Fujianese Hoklo elements in Taiwan society. To cap it all, his status as a local landlord brought with it a significant army of Hakka warriors. Governor T'ang's initial response to Ch'iu's growing influence was to play along with it. When Ch'iu announced that under international law the Taiwanese should be offered a plebiscite on self-determination, T'ang passed the memorandum along the Beijing. But toward the end of April the governor began to think that Ch'iu's popularity as a leader of Taiwanese opposition to the Japanese takeover was growing beyond control and threatened his own authority.

T'ang decided on a course frequently adopted by politicians who see the parade of public opinion leaving them behind. He jumped to the head of the cavalcade by becoming as radical as his rival was. T'ang joined Ch'iu in advocating self-rule, independence, for Taiwan, but was clearly uneasy about the move and felt out of his depth in these unfamiliar radical political waters. One of the notions behind declaring self-rule for Taiwan was that one or more of the European powers would come to the beleaguered little island's aid against Japan if it was seen as a small and vulnerable independent state. In a foretaste of frustrations to come in the twentieth century, not one of the major powers ever recognized the Taiwan Republic.

On May 16 matters on the island came to a head when Ch'iu appeared at T'ang's office, the *yamen,* with a delegation of local notables from his home area of central Taiwan. They demanded that T'ang declare Taiwan an independent state and they pressed him to accept the presidency. T'ang accepted the idea of a declaration of independence, but he refused the presidency, apparently fearing it would be a figurehead post with Ch'iu wielding the real power. Ch'iu and his followers took command. They used the telegraph in T'ang's office to send a brief message to Beijing. "The literati and people of Taiwan are resolved to resist subjection to Japan. They have declared Taiwan an independent republic, under the suzerainty of the Sacred Qing dynasty," the message said.[1]

The message was only 16 characters in Chinese, and the one usually rendered into English as "suzerainty" is interesting. It does not mean or imply the same things as sovereignty but conveys a much looser relationship with China. It suggests the republicans imagined Taiwan as a semi-independent or internally autonomous state acknowledging only a general overlordship by Beijing. One country, two systems, perhaps.

Ch'iu and his entourage followed up their first message with a more detailed manifesto saying that by popular insistence T'ang would remain as the island's chief administrator and the brigand-turned-general, "Black Flag" Liu Yung-fu, would stay in command of the defense forces in the south of the island.

Beijing was not pleased with these telegraph cables. Its main concern was that this nascent insurrection on Taiwan would encourage Japan to step back from the only bit of the Treaty of Shimonoseki from which China gained. Tokyo had promised to return the occupied Liaoning peninsula in northeastern China, but might well refuse to do so if Taiwan was not handed over. On May 18 an official was sent from Beijing to oversee the formal handing over of Taiwan to Japan. When he arrived in the region, it was too dangerous for him to go ashore. The handover ceremony had to be performed on a Japanese warship.

T'ang meanwhile was giving careful thought to the implications of the independence declaration and the possibilities for aggrandizement that accepting the presidency might offer. On May 21 he decided to accept the post of the new republic's chief executive. Ch'iu agreed, largely in the belief that France would protect the island state from the Japanese. Two days later, May 23, the Taiwan Republic was formally declared in Taipei. The declaration said:

> The Japanese have insulted China by annexing our territory of Taiwan. The People of Taiwan, in vain, have appealed to the Throne. Now the Japanese are about to arrive.
>
> If we, the People of Taiwan, permit them to land, Taiwan will become a land of savages and barbarians. If, on the other hand, we resist, our state of weakness will not be for long, as foreign powers have assured us that Taiwan must establish its independence before they will assist us.
>
> Therefore, we, the People of Taiwan, are determined to die rather than be subdued by the Japanese. This decision is irrevocable.
>
> The leaders of the People of Taiwan, in council, have decided to constitute Taiwan, a republic state, and all administration, henceforth, will be in the hands of officials elected by the People of Taiwan.
>
> T'ang Ching-sung, Governor of Taiwan, has been appointed President of the Republic of Taiwan.
>
> The official ceremony of inauguration of the Republic will take place on the second day of the fifth moon [May 25] at the *ssu* hour [noon], at which, all persons, those of rank, merchants, farmers, artisans, and tradesmen, will assemble at the *Tuan Fang* [militia] hall.
>
> This is a declaration of the People of Taiwan.[2]

In messages to mainland officials after the declaration, T'ang reiterated that the new republic would be "suzerain" to China with the status of a vassal state. At the inauguration on May 25, a national flag showing a tiger on a blue background was unfurled. This has remained a potent symbol for Taiwanese independentists ever since.

Over the next few days there was a significant exodus to the mainland of Qing officials as well as most of the imperial troops that had been sent to Taiwan to bolster its defense during the Sino-Japanese war. To try to shore up the defenses, T'ang appointed Black Flag Liu grand marshal of the republic while Ch'iu was commander of the volunteer militias defending central and northern Taiwan. T'ang also cobbled together a makeshift administration that concentrated power in his own hands. A parliament of members of the gentry, merchant class, and literati was appointed, but it only met a couple of times.

The Japanese, led by Major General Kawashima Kageaki with a brigade of the Imperial Guard, landed at Aoli, some 20 miles southeast of Keelung, on

May 29. Resistance by the Taiwanese was sporadic or nonexistent. On June 1 the Japanese reached Keelung and after a day's hard fighting with the Taiwanese garrison the city fell on June 3. The basic problem for the defenders was that in training and equipment they were no match for the well-armed and disciplined Japanese. But the Taiwanese also missed many opportunities to delay the advance of the Japanese or harass their supply lines with guerrilla attacks in the mountains around Keelung. The reason for the shambolic defense was that most of the militia units were under the command of gentry warlords who were unwilling to accept outside orders. Thus no broad strategic defensive plan could be implemented and the tactical, local actions by the militias were ineffective. Within a few days of landing the road to Taipei was open to the Japanese.

At this point several senior officials began urging T'ang to take personal command of the militia forces in the mountain passes, impose a strategic plan, and rally the defense. T'ang refused and even while officials were still remonstrating with him on June 5 left with his family for Tamsui, where he boarded a German passenger ship. Shore batteries fired at the ship, the *Arthur,* as it steamed out of the harbor, bound for Fuzhou, with Taiwan's first president safely aboard.

Ch'iu Feng-chia, the architect of the Taiwan Republic, left the island at about the same time. He said he was going to the mainland to seek fresh troops, but by the time he reached Nanjing the Japanese had captured northern Taiwan. He never returned to Taiwan, though he did play a role in the founding of the Republic of China and his son was a member of Chiang Kaishek's government in exile on Taiwan.

T'ang's flight destroyed the little resolution left among the defenders of the capital to confront the Japanese. Guangdong warriors assigned to hold Taipei went on a rampage. They burned and looted T'ang's offices and were soon joined by the city's underworld. The mayhem lasted two days and at least five hundred people were killed. Merchants with much to lose in the looting came to the conclusion that anything was better than this chaos. They sent a deputation to the Japanese asking them to come quickly and told them there would be little resistance. The Japanese entered Taipei unopposed on June 7, captured northern Taiwan by June 11, and inaugurated their own administration in the capital on June 17.

South of Taipei the going proved much harder for the Japanese as resistance by the Taiwanese stiffened. The Japanese took Hsinchu on June 22, but then their advance stalled for a month and a half in the face of constant guerrilla attacks. Some writers have attributed this invigorated defense to a desire to protect the spiritual heartland of the island, Tainan, from the Japanese.[3] There are accounts of people flocking to the main temple devoted to the worship of the great ancestor, Koxinga, in Tainan and seeking his divine intervention to save the island.

On September 17 about one hundred local literati and gentry met at the Kaiyuan Temple on the outskirts of Tainan. They decided to form themselves into a government and to ask Black Flag Liu to become president of the republic. He did not accept, but circumstances pressed him into becoming the effective civilian and military commander of the withering republic despite the lack of title. Liu fashioned a kind of administration that was even able to issue its own money and postage stamps, now much prized by collectors. But it was always a rearguard action. The guerrilla attacks against the Japanese, who were constantly being reinforced until their army numbered about 50,000, could only forestall the inevitable. Early in October the Japanese army finally approached Tainan. As the last assault was being prepared, Black Flag Liu sent a message to the Japanese commander offering to surrender. His offer was refused, so Liu took the same course as T'ang and Ch'iu before him. He disguised himself as a refugee and boarded a British ship, the *Thales,* which took him to the mainland.

With Liu gone two Presbyterian ministers led a delegation of Tainan city worthies to negotiate with the Japanese. On October 21 Tainan was handed over to the Japanese without any fighting. Major General Kabayama, the Japanese commander, announced a week later that Taiwan had been pacified.

That wasn't true, as George H. Kerr in his 1974 book *Formosa: 1895–1945* and several other authors have described.[4] Taiwan was never fully pacified from the day the Japanese arrived in 1895 until well into the twentieth century. Japanese records from its period of colonial rule of Taiwan show a persistent insurrection for which the authorities frequently used the euphemism "banditry." Between 1895 and 1920 at least 8,200 Taiwanese were arrested each year for alleged attempts to overthrow Japanese rule. The numbers began to decline as many Taiwanese benefited from the administrative, social, agricultural, and industrial advances promoted by the Japanese. Even so, between 1921 and 1930 never fewer than 6,500 people were detained for insurrection in any year. From 1931 to 1940 the number declined further but was still never less than 3,450. There were 19 major uprisings during the period of Japanese rule, including 2 attempts to take the capital, Taipei. In the first seven years of Japanese administration there were 94 guerrilla attacks by Taiwanese. The Japanese lost many more soldiers to partisan attacks in the first few months after their mission to occupy Taiwan was accomplished than they did during the invasion and the quelling of the Taiwan Republic. The Taiwanese guerrillas suffered similarly. At least 12,000 died in the guerrilla war, about double the number thought to have been killed during the five months of resistance to the arrival of the Japanese.

The quiet subversion that developed throughout the period of Japanese occupation was ultimately more significant for the political development of Taiwan than the violent uprisings were. The subversion began as pressure for Taiwanese representation on various colonial institutions but grew into demands for island "home rule" within the Japanese empire. From there it was a short step to the evolution of the Taiwanese independence movement, which is a bequest from the island's Japanese colonial period to modern times.

Chapter Thirteen

BECOMING JAPANESE

Japan expected many benefits from the acquisition of its Taiwan colony. Foremost was acknowledgment from America and the European powers that an Asian nation could merit admission to their club of imperialists. Beyond kudos, Japan expected immediate and long-term advantages from the possession of Taiwan. The agricultural and resource potential of the fertile island was alluring for Japan, where there were too many people and not enough productive land or raw materials on the home archipelago. Looking further ahead to Japan's as-yet undefined hopes for future power in Asia, Taiwan was not only a fine stepping-stone toward Southeast Asia, but it was and remains a choke and control point for maritime traffic in the Yellow Sea, the East China Sea, and the South China Sea.

The early years of Japanese rule on Taiwan were, of necessity, military in nature, and the governors were military men. The first administrators were preoccupied with stamping out the brushfires of insurrection that continued to spring up from the embers of the Taiwan Republic. Some efforts were made to establish an efficient model for civil administration and some preliminary assessments of the economic potential of the island were made. But the enforcement of an acceptable degree of peace and order was the priority, and it was a slow process. This did not sit well with the government in Tokyo, which was having to massively subsidize the Taiwan imperial adventure and had hoped by now to see some return on its money. There were even some mutterings that perhaps getting into this business of acquiring colonies had been a mistake. Selling Taiwan to the French was even considered by the Japanese parliament at one point. The eventual decision, however, was to send to Taiwan officials who would concentrate on the economic and administrative development of the island. Another army officer, Lieutenant General Kodama Gentaro, was appointed governor in 1898, but he was a man of many official positions and maintained only a distant, supervisory authority over his fiefdom. He did, though, appoint as his chief civil administrator a man who indelibly marked the course of Japanese endeavors on Taiwan.

Goto Shimpei was a doctor by profession and a scientist by inclination. He devised an approach to ruling Taiwan that he called "biological colonial management."[1] His thought was a fairly simple, pragmatic, and obvious one. "Just as you don't move the eyes of a flounder [on the top of its head] to create a bream [with the eyes on either side], so you don't automatically move one country's rules and policies to its colony."[2] Japan's colonial enterprise on Taiwan would have to begin by working with the culture, customs, and economy of the Taiwanese. Only after these were understood could Japan start to make good and loyal Japanese out of the islanders, Goto decided. He authorized a spate of investigations of everything from agricultural methods to "ancient Chinese customs."

It should not be taken from this that Goto was sympathetic or indulgent toward Japan's Taiwanese colonial subjects. Far from it. His notion was that by understanding Taiwan and its heritage the Japanese would be able to construct a more efficient and solid form of authoritarianism. The American writer George H. Kerr, who worked in Taiwan as a teacher during Japanese rule in the 1930s and returned as one of Washington's diplomats to Chiang Kai-shek's court after the Second World War, has written that Goto's style was "a natural expression of the samurai's command-and-obey tradition."

> Goto proposed to produce obedient Formosan farmers and semi-skilled laborers trained for light industrial employment; there was to be compulsory education, so that every child in the island could read and write at an elementary level—enough to improve his economic productivity and no more. On completing primary school he should be able to read orders, patriotic slogans, and simple technical information—the directions on a bag of fertilizer, for example, or directions for simple technical operations, but he would not be encouraged to think for himself.[3]

Maintaining civil order and security remained a problem in spite of the shift of Japanese emphasis toward development. Goto moved the prime responsibility for maintaining order from the army to a new and enlarged police force. The force numbered about 12,000 with another 5,000 operating in the aboriginal areas. All candidates were carefully selected and trained for their particular functions. The police were omnipresent and became the front-line face of Japanese rule. In addition to normal police duties the officers were expected to act as tax collectors, enforcers of public health regulations, agricultural advisers, promoters of local industries, and much else besides. To enable the police to keep close watch on their charges, a Japanese version of the old Chinese administrative tool of district and family mutual responsibility, *pao-chia,* was introduced. The difference was that while the demands of Chinese *pao-chia* could usually be ameliorated by greasing the palm of compliant officials, the Japanese ran a largely corruption-free police state. Called by the Japanese *ho-ko,* this system led to the creation of a network of informants and collaborators, but was also used to raise manpower for communal tasks. As in China, the *ho-ko* system held responsible the head of a family or leader of a district for any breaches of law or regulations in his area. If the true culprit was not promptly handed over to police, the family or district elder would be detained, sometimes tortured, or publicly whipped. Taiwan, then, became a very thorough police state with the local people left in no doubt as to who were the rulers and who the ruled.

Though the police were given broad responsibilities that might suggest they were more community officers than law enforcers, this was not the case. The police were widely detested by the Taiwanese. Members of the Japanese force, especially in isolated areas, were under a constant state of siege by local people ever on the lookout for an opportunity to murder an officer or burn down his station. When such attacks did occur, as happened frequently in the first decades of Japanese rule, the reaction was usually brutal reprisals out of all proportion to the offense. This was a purposeful policy to impress on the Taiwanese the futility of violent defiance of their masters.

The *ho-ko* system was designed in part to break down traditional Chinese family hierarchies and respect for elders. On mainland China the Communists utilized a similar system for the same purpose after they came to power in 1949. The system also aimed to break down trust among family members and between friends so that everyone felt themselves a hostage under the ever-present eyes and ears of Japanese authority. To this end Goto took a further step and created a Youth Corps, which every Taiwanese boy was required to join at age 16. The corps, whose membership numbered 55,000 by 1903, was a forum for indoctrinating young Taiwanese with patriotic fervor for the Japanese empire. Corps members were used in community work such as rat catching, census taking, riverbank repair, and road maintenance. A daily function of the teenagers, though, was to act as police scouts and informants. They were required to report to the police any unusual happenings in the community and to pass on rumors or information about individuals, all of which went into the copious files kept on every Taiwanese.

This infrastructure of control was of great assistance to the paramilitary police in attempting to eradicate the remaining Taiwanese guerrilla "bandits." Many of these partisans had taken to the hills but depended for survival on supplies from villages under Japanese control. Japan's spy and informant network made it more and more difficult and dangerous for villages to maintain this liaison with the guerrillas. In 1901 military and police launched a sweep through southern Taiwan, where Hakka partisans remained a serious problem to the authorities. After the drive it was announced that over 3,000 "bandits" had been killed. But rumors quickly started circulating in Tokyo that most of the deaths had been of villagers suspected of supporting the partisans.

In 1902 Goto offered an amnesty to the rebels, and hundreds of Taiwanese came out of the hills in response. At Taichung the local authorities lavished praise on the former guerrillas and announced there would be a banquet to celebrate the event, followed by an allegiance ceremony. The celebrations were to be held in an assembly hall and the former guerrillas were asked to wear a white rosette as a symbol of their honored status. When 360 of the partisans were in the hall the doors were bolted and everyone wearing a white flower was killed. The massacre caused more dismay in Tokyo and Goto was censured by the parliament for "disgracing the nation."[4] Goto didn't account for the incident until several years later when he wrote that "although they presented themselves, they all proved so unmanageable that they were all killed in the hall where the ceremony was held."[5]

There was a greater community of interest between the Japanese and their three million islander subjects on economic development than on Taiwan's power structure. Japan's population at home was rising rapidly and there were real fears that despite improvements in agriculture the country could not long remain self-sufficient in food. A land survey in Taiwan in 1902—the first for over two hundred years—found nearly twice as much land available for rice cultivation as the last Qing records estimated. After being catalogued, the additional land was rented out to either Japanese or compliant Taiwanese. An immediate benefit for the colonial administration of the land survey and redistribution was a tripling of revenues from tax.

Japan at the time was a major importer of sugar, which required large outlays of hard currency and played havoc with the country's balance of trade. Goto addressed this issue early on and pushed a program to increase sugarcane production. From 1905, when the program gathered momentum, until 1938 the land producing sugarcane increased four times, the total cane produced on that land multiplied by 12, and the yield per hectare almost tripled.

By 1905 Taiwan was making a profit and no longer drawing subsidies from Tokyo. Indeed, it was putting money in Tokyo's pocket. It then became possible for the Japanese to extend Taiwan's social development as well as to invest in road, rail, and power generation construction to further boost the economy. As a medical doctor, Goto had soon after his arrival put some emphasis on public health and the eradication of the many tropical diseases that had given Taiwan such a bad name for centuries. He was remarkably successful with the result that Taiwan's population grew steadily, not so much because of an increasing birth rate but because fewer people died young.

There arose the difficult subject of education. The Japanese wanted their colonial subjects to be educated, especially in the Japanese language and cultural values. But they did not want Taiwanese educated to the point where they developed ideas of their own, especially about their status as colonial subjects. Six-year primary education was made available to the Taiwanese around the turn of the twentieth century. These schools concentrated on teaching Japanese, basic mathematics, as well as history and geography from a Japanese viewpoint. There was a good deal of Japanese nationalism in the curriculum, and the aim was to make the Taiwanese into useful, but loyal, subjects. Some historians have noted that an unintended consequence of the school system was that it brought together Taiwanese children who would otherwise have been educated, if at all, in the seclusion of their homes. The school system thus began to break down many of the clan and family divisions that plagued Taiwanese society during the Qing period and began to create a sense of island national identity.

The Japanese colonial administrators, making up about six percent of the island's population, operated a strict system of ethnic apartheid. The Japanese had their own residential areas and reserved jobs. Their children also went to their own segregated schools. Taiwanese children were initially prohibited from attending Japanese schools—where standards were much higher than at the colonial schools—colleges, or the university built in Taipei. This policy began to change in the early 1920s when facility with the Japanese language rather than ethnicity was made the qualification for entry. This still discriminated against the Taiwanese students who were operating in a second language, but an increasing number managed to negotiate the hurdles to advancement. Those who did get accepted for higher education usually found themselves being steered toward technical subjects rather than the arts and humanities, which might stimulate a political career.

Japan was painstaking in its efforts to eradicate Taiwanese culture and to create an island of dutiful, second-class Japanese citizens. The Kuomintang was equally persistent to its own ends in the second half of the twentieth century, but was equally unsuccessful. The Japanese destroyed many Taoist temples and tried to legally enforce adherence to Shintoism. In contrast, the authorities restored the main temple to Koxinga in Tainan, a reminder that the founding father of Taiwan was half Japanese. Chinese-language newspapers were banned, and the use of the Taiwanese dialect, Minnan, heavily discouraged. The colonial administrators also took aim at social customs they felt were corrosive or wasteful, such as lavish expenditures on marriages or funeral rites and what they considered unnecessarily plentiful holidays.

Very many Taiwanese took the path of least resistance in their dealings with their Japanese overlords. There were substantial benefits for those who acquiesced to Japanese rule and even more for those who actively collaborated. Some Taiwanese took full advantage of the favoritism in business that was available to those who showed enthusiastic support and became very rich. Ku Hsien-yung, who is credited with telling the Japanese army in June 1895 that Taipei was undefended and urging the officers to make haste to restore order in the capital, profited mightily from his decision. In 1899 he was put in charge of the salt monopoly—always a swift path to wealth in traditional Chinese society—with the power to organize and regulate the trade throughout the island. Another Taiwanese to profit from his cooperation with the Japanese was Yen Yun-nien, whose minor mining interests near Keelung blossomed under Japanese patronage into a mighty industry employing thousands. Other Taiwanese, mostly from the landowning gentry class, invested in trading companies or started banks. Many became public advocates of support for Japanese rule, arguing that Beijing had forfeited the right to Taiwan's allegiance by giving the island to Japan.

The main danger of collaboration was becoming a target for the partisans who operated throughout the Japanese colonial period. The Japanese, though, were well aware that their authoritarian approach to governing Taiwan was expensive and inefficient. They put much effort into courting Taiwan's gentry and intellectual classes. For all its constraints, life and opportunities under Japanese rule seemed much more secure and hopeful than the chaos that was again engulfing China after the fall of the Qing dynasty. Workers' wages doubled within the first five years after the arrival of the Japanese. Farmers received twice as much for their crops as before. Public health was immeasurably improved by campaigns against infectious diseases. But these very advances, the access to education, and the spirit of the age, stemming in part from United States' president Woodrow Wilson's declarations about the rights to self-determination of peoples during the Treaty of Versailles negotiations in 1919, bred a new line of resistance on Taiwan.

The question of the political relationship between Japan and its colony was an issue among the island's elite from soon after the arrival of the Japanese. Some of the landowning gentry and the literati accepted without question the benefits of associating with the new masters. Others took a more Taiwanese nationalist stance, but without openly challenging Japanese authority. One such was Lin Hsien-t'ang of the Wu-feng Lin family. Lin had been an impressionable teenager at the time of Ch'iu Feng-chia's ill-starred attempts to inspire the Taiwan Republic in 1895 and was moved by these nationalist sentiments. Lin's initial aim was to moderate the harsh Japanese administration of Taiwan. In 1913 he visited Japan and met liberals there, most notably Count Itagaki Taisuke, founder of the Japanese Liberal Party. Itagaki's view of liberalism was what might be expected from an aristocrat. He favored representative parliaments but was equally adamant that Japan should be the leader and inspiration of Asian peoples in their resistance to western colonialism. The count therefore advised Lin to establish a Taiwanese "Assimilation Society," advocating full absorption of the islanders into Japanese political culture. He offered to act as patron of the new society. Itagaki went to Taiwan late in 1914 and oversaw the formation of the organization, which enrolled over three thousand members during its first month in existence. The count was too notable a figure in Japan for the then governor of Taiwan, Sakuma Samata, to react while Itagaki remained on the island. But Sakuma believed the society would threaten colonial rule and in January 1915 he charged the organization with "illegal acts." Some of the second-tier members of the society were given heavy sentences while Lin Hsien-t'ang was attacked in official speeches and newspapers. Lin abandoned the idea of Taiwan becoming a fully assimilated part of Japan and began thinking in terms of home rule within the Japanese empire.

By the end of the First World War, out of which Japan and Taiwan had profited by supplying Britain and her allies, there were over three thousand Taiwanese students at Japanese universities. The tolerance of and opportunities for political activity were much greater in Japan than in the island colony. The students formed an "Enlightenment Society" whose objective was to describe to influential Japanese the harsh authoritarianism of the administration on Taiwan. They also pressed for Taiwanese representation in the Japanese parliament, the Diet. The students soon ran up against conservative elements in the Japanese bureaucracy and the organization had its permits withdrawn. The effect was to radicalize the attitudes among young Taiwanese in Japan. If assimilation was unacceptable and home rule not in the cards, then their task as they saw it was to preserve Taiwanese nationalism and culture until a more auspicious time.

The political landscape changed late in 1919 when Tokyo appointed Baron Den Kojiro the first civilian governor-general of Taiwan. Den came to office as newspapers in Japan were publishing, with information and views supplied by the Taiwanese students, stories about discontent on the island. Early in 1920 a petition was put before the lower house of the Diet asking for a parliament in Taipei through which islanders could have a voice in major issues of policy. This official attention to the island prompted Taiwanese students in Tokyo to try once more to form an organization. With the financial backing of Lin Hsien-t'ang and other wealthy Taiwanese, they formed the Taiwan Cultural Society in March 1920. The organization's purpose was to preserve Taiwan's identity, distinct from both Japan and China, and to campaign for an assembly on the island as well as elected representatives at the Diet in Tokyo.

Taiwan's individuality was at the heart of the concept for the society. There was never any idea of the organization urging a reunification with China. That was an extremely unattractive proposition at the time, with China in the throes of a contest between regional warlords. And the quarter century under Japanese rule had left the parents of many of the students with the view that as unpleasant as some of Tokyo's actions on Taiwan were, life in general had improved and the rapacity of the Qing had been much worse.

The founding of the Taiwan Cultural Society and its influential publication, *Taiwan Youth Magazine,* thus marks the beginning of the island's independence movement, now nearly a century old. In later years, when Taiwanese students and political refugees from Kuomintang persecution started going to North America and Europe in the 1950s, 1960s, and 1970s, new branches and spin-off organizations of the Taiwan Cultural Society were formed. But the formative link with Japan remained and remains. Very many of the surviving elders of Taiwan's independence movement today spring from the island's student movements in Tokyo in the prewar years, and elements of the political culture of Japan still weave their way through Taiwanese public affairs.

The society and its magazine were banned on Taiwan. But when students returned to the island for holidays they frequently held meetings and spoke to public gatherings about their aspirations for Taiwan. The vast majority of the students came from the island's leading families and commanded respect in their communities. The police subjected them and their families to as much harassment as they could without actually setting the island's elite firmly against Japanese rule. In Tokyo, meanwhile, the petitions to the Diet continued and in 1921 the Japanese government decided that to appease Taiwanese sentiments, an advisory council to the governor would be set up on the island. It was minimalist appeasement. The majority of the council members were Japanese, and the Taiwanese members were often the most avid collaborators. Among the Taiwanese appointees, however, was Lin Hsieh-t'ang. There was a mistaken assumption among the Japanese colonial officials that Lin would become more amenable as a council member. He did not and on several occasions in the following years was detained while still a council member.

In 1924 Lin sent the governor a list of 12 demands for reform of the colonial administration. He suggested there be more opportunities for Taiwanese to take part in local government and a formal end to pro-Japanese discrimination in these appointments. Lin advocated curtailing police abuse of their power and the outlawing of opium smoking, which the Japanese quietly allowed as a means of social control. Lin felt that the *ho-ko* system of communal responsibility should be abolished and that Taiwanese should have a greater say in the gestation of economic policies. Taiwanese should be allowed to travel to Japan without passports, he said, and the administration should stop prosecuting all criticism of the government as though it was sedition. Lin's proposals were not directly taken up by the Japanese, but they slowly filtered the recommendations into the system and they influenced the political reform that began in the mid-1930s. In the early 1940s Lin was one of the few Taiwanese appointed to the upper house of the Japanese parliament shortly before the end of the Second World War.

Lin remained a moderate throughout his political career, and when he was eventually challenged in the 1930s by younger, more radical elements in the Taiwan home-rule movement it did not dent his status as the unofficial leader of the island's people. Lin welcomed the return of Taiwan to China in 1945 but was quickly disillusioned with the Kuomintang. He was outraged at the slaughter of demonstrators by Kuomintang soldiers on and after February 28, 1947. In 1950 Lin went into self-imposed exile in Tokyo, where he died six years later.

More radical elements began surfacing in the Taiwan Cultural Association in the 1920s. The association had its roots among landowners and rural peasants, but the boom after the First World War and increasing industrialization of Taiwan created an urban working class and a labor movement. Politically left-wing Taiwan independentists began to gain more influence in the Taiwan Cultural Association and in 1930 many of the more moderate members quit the organization. They formed their own Taiwan Local Autonomy Association, which spoke up for the welfare of Taiwanese while continuing to acknowledge Japan's contributions to the island's development. The result was that while the Japanese authorities mounted a crackdown on local left-wing elements, the Local Autonomy Association was able to carry on undisturbed until the outbreak of war with China in 1937.

It was in the early 1930s that Japan's efforts to subjugate Taiwan's aborigines and bring the mountain districts under administrative control came to a dark and bloody conclusion. Japan's interest in Taiwan was to create a profitable colony. From that point of view it made no sense that about 70 percent of the island's territory, the forested mountains of the eastern and central regions, was beyond the control of the administration and in the hands of the aboriginal tribes. Most of the world's known stands of camphor trees were in those mountains. As well as having medicinal properties, camphor had been discovered to be a necessary ingredient for making smokeless gunpowder for rifles and artillery. But taming the mountain tribes with their headhunting habits and always vigorous defense of their territories had proved to be beyond the courage or tenacity of all previous rulers of Taiwan. Goto Shimpei, as civilian administrator from 1898 to 1905, took another approach and sought to tempt native Taiwanese out of the hills. Aborigines were offered subsidies to give up their hunter-gatherer lifestyle and to become farmers. Schools were built and a special branch of the police force trained to work in the hills. Officers were even encouraged to marry aboriginal women, a mode of integration and assimilation first adopted on Taiwan by the Dutch missionaries more than three hundred years before. Goto's policy was reasonably successful with the Ami and Paiwan tribes. But elsewhere Goto was reduced to repeating Qing dynasty policy. He attempted to reduce friction between the aborigines and the settlers by creating a no-man's land between them and building guardhouses to enforce the separation.

Goto's successor, army general Sakuma Samata, was a less patient man. He decided on direct action and dispatched four thousand troops into the forests, targeting one region at a time. The tribal warriors proved more difficult to subdue, despite their simple weapons, than Sakuma had anticipated. Casualties among the Japanese were unacceptably high. Sakuma increased the number of troops involved to 12,000 and introduced bomber aircraft to the fight. Villages that were within range of naval guns were bombarded from the sea by

Japanese warships. It was immaterial to Sakuma's plan whether the aborigines submitted or were exterminated. There were atrocities of the worst kind and entire villages were obliterated. The campaign was crudely successful and by the time Sakuma returned to Japan in 1915 most of the island's aborigines had submitted to the authorities.

Resentment among the aborigines festered despite their submission, however. On October 27, 1930, the provincial governor in the hill region behind Taichung gathered with several hundred Japanese local officials and their wives at the aboriginal village of Musha. They were there to dedicate a new administrative building at the terminus of a road and pushcar rail line constructed to boost the camphor trade. No one noticed there were no aboriginal women or children in the village or that the Taiwanese porters had disappeared. As Japan's rising sun flag was raised hundreds of tribal warriors leapt on the Japanese and killed 197 of them, including the provincial governor. Local Japanese policemen in outlying stations, it was soon found, had been murdered the previous evening.

Army units were quickly sent into the hills and after a three-week campaign announced they had dealt with a majority of the rebels. There was a good deal of suspicion both in Tokyo and Taiwan, though, when the statement went on to say that the wives and children of the rebels had committed suicide by hanging themselves in their huts, which had therefore had to be burned. There was then and remains a belief that the Japanese used chemical or biological weapons against the villages.

Subsequent investigations produced the story, well publicized in Japanese newspapers, that the attack on the Japanese in Musha had been instigated by an educated aborigine whose sister had been raped by a local policeman.

The incident was deeply troubling for the Japanese, especially because of the hints that the Taiwanese porters at least knew of the plans and slipped away from the scene. An alliance between Taiwanese and the aborigines would have been a severe threat to Japanese rule. The savage response by the military to the incident forced both the governor-general of Taiwan and the civil administrator to resign in January 1931. As the matter became a domestic issue in Japan the government appointed a new governor, Ota Masahiro, a specialist in the management and deployment of police. Ota approached the situation by using a tactic that has been deployed many times before and just as many since. He commissioned a survey of the feuds and rivalries among the tribes. Then he classified some as "allied tribes" and others as "protected tribes." The villages and homes of the "protected tribes" were invaded and searched for any kind of weapons. Then military arms were issued to the "allied tribes" and Ota and his police looked the other way while thousands of the "protected" tribes' men, women, and children were slaughtered. Shades of Rwanda, East Timor, and Darfur.

In March 1932 Ota was recalled and the government in Tokyo quietly decided to extend some democratic privileges to the Taiwanese. There would be elective government in Taiwan in 1935. The province, counties, and towns would have assemblies, with half the members elected by popular vote and half appointed by provincial governor. The system was rigged. In the first elections about 187,000 Taiwanese men met the age, sex, and property ownership qualifications to earn a vote. By all accounts at least 96.7 percent of them voted. Yet when everything was tallied it was found that of the 172 people chosen to take assembly seats, 109 were Japanese and only 63 Taiwanese. Further delving into the figures showed that only 37 Taiwanese actually owed their council seats to the voters. The rest were Taiwanese collaborators who had been engineered into office by Japanese manipulation of the vote. Over the next four years the Japanese were persuaded by the home-rule movement to substantially dilute this racial gerrymandering and to dramatically increase the number of elected city, county, and provincial councils. In the 1939 elections 286,700 Taiwanese were registered as eligible to vote and 3,104 Taiwanese were elected to the various assemblies.

By this time Japan had already instigated the "Marco Polo Bridge Incident" near Beijing on July 7, 1937, as an excuse to invade northern China, which led ultimately to the War in the Pacific in the 1940s. War with China inevitably made Japan apprehensive about the loyalty and dependability of its ethnic Chinese subjects on Taiwan. An even more intense program of Japanization was implemented on the island. Taiwanese were pressed into adopting Japanese names, wearing Japanese-style clothes, and were even required to maintain Shinto shrines in their homes. At the same time foreign missionaries, teachers, and businessmen were forced off the island. There was a sustained campaign of persecuting Christians. Industry and agriculture were goaded into ever greater feats of productivity to feed the war effort.

There are several views recorded of the mood and attitudes of the Taiwanese at that time. George Kerr, the American teacher and diplomat, differentiates sharply between three generations of Taiwanese.[6] Elderly people with memories of Qing rule and affection for their ancestral homeland regretted war between Japan and China, he says. Those of middle age who had battled to retain Taiwanese identity saw Japan's Asian crusade as just another hoax masking imperial ambitions. The young, raised under the full force of Japan's patriotic indoctrination, eagerly supported the war. These divisions are undoubtedly too clear cut. But Kerr was a painstaking, thoughtful, and usually reliable observer of what he saw and heard going on around him. So his view should not be dismissed out of hand. In contrast, the author Hung Chien-chao leans toward a "one China" view of Taiwanese history and judges the islanders were dragooned by their colonial masters into supporting Japan's war.[7] Denny Roy, an American academic, concludes that Taiwanese "responded enthusiastically to the opportunity to serve in the Japanese armed forces."[8]

Doubtless there were as many personal motivations as there were Taiwanese who enlisted under the rising sun ensign. The numbers were substantial. About 80,000 islanders served in the Japanese army and navy. A further 126,000 worked for the Japanese in civilian roles such as coolie porters, nurses, interpreters, and agricultural advisers to local farmers in occupied areas of China and Southeast Asia. Despite the then recent animosities and antagonisms, aboriginal Taiwanese volunteered in some numbers for both fighting and noncombatant roles. About 30,300 Taiwanese were killed during the war in the service of Japan.

The Japanese legacy on Taiwan is as ambiguous and subject to partial interpretations as all other aspects of the island's history. It remains pertinent today because so many Taiwanese of the older generation are inclined to view that period as, on balance, beneficial to the island. This judgment is in marked contrast to the abiding hatred of Japan in other colonial territories such as Korea and Manchuria. This is in part because Japanese rule was a good deal more brutal in those territories than on Taiwan. But Beijing remains outraged that Taiwanese retain a mild affection toward Japan. It is seen as ethnic and spiritual corruption. This reaction certainly prompts some Taiwanese to espouse a gentler view of the Japanese colonial experience than they truly feel or is justified. Many island nationalists are willing to see merit in any stance that enrages Beijing.

There is a wider and less provocative strand of thought among islanders that sees the period of Japanese rule as an essential element in Taiwan's story, for both good and ill. The regimentation and cultural indoctrination of the Taiwanese as well as the ever-present, insufferable demonstrations of racial superiority by the Japanese made aspects of life grim. But there was the benefit of dramatic social and economic development of the island in the half century of rule by Japan. It brought the island standards of efficient and clean government against which the Qing administration before and the Kuomintang after compared poorly. In their battles for some voice in their own government, Taiwanese developed a sense of their own identity and their island's distinction as a community. This experience formed the base for today's attitudes toward independence and mainland China.

And it made the Taiwanese, alongside their colonial masters, the most highly educated people in Asia. This sense of self-worth came into powerful play when in 1945 the largely illiterate and ignorant scruffs of Chiang Kai-shek's Kuomintang army got off their ships to take possession of Taiwan. The Kuomintang were only one demonstration of how much the world had changed while Taiwan was secreted in the Japanese empire. Behind Chiang was a new player, the United States of America, whose interests were about to become a dominant influence on Taiwanese life.

Chapter Fourteen

MISSIONARIES AND FILIBUSTERS

The United States had marched into China in the 1840s amid the pack of ravening western countries led by Britain. After its defeat by Britain in the First Opium War, China thought it might dilute British power by extending to other countries the concessions demanded by London. Thus on July 3, 1844, Caleb Cushing signed the Treaty of Wanghsia on behalf of the United States. This guaranteed American merchants access to the five treaty ports of Canton (Guangzhou), Amoy (Xiamen), Foochow (Fuzhou), Ningpo (Ningbo), and Shanghai. It gave the U.S. most-favored-nation rights to low tariffs, allowed the Americans to establish churches and hospitals in the treaty ports, and excluded American citizens from the authority of the Chinese courts. In an early example of moral rapport between Beijing and Washington the treaty prohibited opium as an object or currency of trade between the two countries. America was equally quick to take advantage of British military labors after the Second Opium War and actually signed its own Treaty of Tientsin with China in 1858, two weeks before the British did. The Tientsin treaty opened up ten additional ports, allowed for diplomatic representation in Beijing, permitted travel by foreigners throughout China, and gave freedom of movement throughout the country for Christian missionaries.

From the start Americans in China were beguiled by the country, its culture, and possibilities well beyond the mere opportunity to make money. China became an emotional fixation for Americans in much the same way that

India did for the British. That half-suppressed passion remains and always throbs just below the surface in America's dealings with China.

There was a moment in the 1850s when American passion for China, much of it stemming from fundamentalist Christian missionary zeal, might have changed the course of Chinese history and wedded the two countries in ways that can now only be the stuff of fantasy. In the early 1840s a young man from a Hakka farming family in Guangdong province, Hung Hsiu-ch'uan, resentful at his lack of success in the onerous imperial civil service examinations, turned to Christianity. He became convinced he was the younger brother of Jesus Christ. Hung formulated a highly selective and self-centered version of Christianity tinged with Confucianism that, despite its heretical content, attracted an American Southern Baptist missionary, the Reverend Issachar J. Roberts. Roberts, however, developed doubts about the authenticity of Hung's Christianity, especially after Hung demanded to be paid to be baptized. The American missionary refused, and this final rejection turned Hung into a crusading Christian revolutionary leading the Taiping Rebellion. Within a few years Hung had raised an army that had captured much of the lower Chang Jiang (Yangtze) River valley, including the imperial southern capital Nanjing, and threatened Shanghai. The Taiping rebels became a focus for popular discontent with the enfeebled and corrupt Qing dynasty. Peasants flocked to Hung's colors and in areas that the Taiping controlled, a series of puritanical reforms were instituted. The mutilation of young girls by foot binding was outlawed and so were opium and tobacco smoking. Land was held in common and allocated according to a family's needs. There are parallels between the Taiping rebels and the Taliban rule of Afghanistan in the 1990s. People were initially willing to put up with stern government if it meant an end to chaos. Modern Beijing sees a more troubling comparison, from the viewpoint of the Communist Party, with the spiritual sect Falun Gong. China has been beset with civil unrest since economic reforms began to bite in the mid-1980s. The end of collectivized agriculture, the smashing of the "iron rice bowl" of Communist centrally planned social support, and the asset stripping of privatized state-owned industries by corrupt party officials left some 250 million people out of work by the early twenty-first century. In 1989 the Tiananmen Square student demonstrators became the focus for nationwide dissent, and there were violent uprisings all over China. It took the institution of martial law to restore order. In the late 1990s, with hopes of quick political reform removed from the national agenda by the army, Falun Gong began attracting millions of disenchanted Chinese. The sect's advocacy of seeking bodily and spiritual well-being through meditation and traditional stylized exercises was particularly attractive to middle-aged Chinese whose lives had centered on faith in the Communist Party. In April 1999 Falun Gong showed it was a national organization with a communications network beyond official control. Falun Gong mounted a demonstration of some 12,000 people outside the walled Zhongnanhai leaders' compound in Beijing containing the main Communist Party offices and the homes of several leaders, without the security services getting any forewarning. It was especially troubling for the party that so many people were able to gather at the Zhongnanhai, originally the gardens of the imperial palace next door, when security was meant to be at its tightest because of the upcoming tenth anniversary of the Tiananmen massacre. The organization was banned and a sustained campaign of persecution begun. Communist leaders' suspicion that Falun Gong was a direct threat to the party's hold on power was compounded by the fact that the sect's leader, Li Hongzhi, lives in exile in New York. Americans had also been more sympathetic than the other foreign powers toward the Taiping rebels.

All the foreign powers active in China were initially well disposed toward the Taiping rebels because of their professed Christianity, but the Americans particularly so. That sympathy eroded when deputations to the Hung court in Nanjing were treated like emissaries from vassal states. Despite this rebuff the foreign powers decided not to turn against the rebels and support the court. After all, the Taiping rebels might win, in which case it would be important to be able to negotiate protection for foreign interests. It was therefore decided to remain studiously aloof and neutral in China's internal conflict. But in 1860, when the Taiping army was threatening Shanghai, the merchants in the city organized a defensive militia. They hired to lead their army an American ship's captain and soldier of fortune from Massachusetts, Frederick Ward, who trained some 5,000 Chinese along European lines and scored the first major victories against the rebels. The emperor bestowed the title "Ever Victorious Army" on Ward's legion, though it didn't always win and the ultimate collapse of the Taiping Rebellion stemmed more from internal dissent than external military force. When Ward died of wounds in 1862, command was given to another American, Henry Burgevine, but he was an adventurer of a different stripe. Burgevine helped himself to 40,000 silver dollars from the imperial coffers. He was sacked and replaced by British officer, Charles "Chinese" Gordon, killed later by Dervishes at the defense of Khartoum. Ward and Gordon taught the imperial court an important lesson. When properly trained and armed the Chinese could fight as effectively as European troops.

Not all the Americans in China at this time were filibusters like Ward and Burgevine, rabid Christian evangelical missionaries, or merchants. Yale University extended a hand to China when the "Self-Strengthening Movement" looked for assistance from the industrialized nations to aid modernization. The first Chinese graduate from Yale was Yung Wing in 1854, but when he returned conservative factions at court regarded him with suspicion. It was not until 1872 that he was allowed to lead 120 Chinese students to Yale. They were accompanied by an elderly scholar whose job was to see the students' Confucian morals were not corrupted by life in America. This project was abandoned in 1881, but the United States continued to be a favorite destination for young Chinese seeking a modern education. Between 1903 and 1919 nearly 34 percent of Chinese students studying abroad were at American colleges. Most, 42 percent, went to Japan for reasons of proximity and cost as much as anything.

China's transition to a frail republic after 1911 and America's emergence as a major power—if not yet visibly a superpower—at the close of the First World War only strengthened the sympathy in the United States for China. The failure of the negotiations at Versailles in 1919 and early 1920 to resolve the question of foreign enclaves in China led to the Washington Conference of 1921–22, aimed at reasserting China's territorial integrity and political independence. As an expression of goodwill by the eight powers with footholds in China—Britain, the United States, France, Italy, Japan, Belgium, the Netherlands, and Portugal—the conference was a success. The resulting treaty lacked enforcement power, however, and foreigners continued to hold high positions in the Chinese civil service. Their trading enclaves carried on as quasi-colonial concessions beyond the power of Chinese law or administration. Britain continued to dominate the trade of southern China through its Hong Kong colony and Japan carried on colony building in northeastern China through its control of the Southern Manchurian Railway. These encroachments pushed the tide of Chinese nationalism, which in May 1925 burst forth in Shanghai in violent student demonstrations protesting the treatment of striking workers at a Japanese-owned cotton mill. The shooting of a dozen of the students by British police led to soul-searching by the foreign powers. By the end of the 1920s many of the municipal and tariff privileges enjoyed by the foreign powers had been relinquished voluntarily.

The tapestry of Chinese political progress into which this small victory over foreign depredations was woven did not make a pretty picture. By the mid-1930s the ostensible government of China was the Kuomintang inheritors of the republican revolution of Sun Yat-sen. In reality this was an uneasy alliance of local warlords held together by the guile and graft of the biggest warlord of them all, Chiang Kai-shek. Chiang's attempt to eradicate the Communist movement had failed. The Communists, led off and on by Mao Zedong, had broken out of Jiangxi in southern China and completed the Long March to Pao An in the far northwest and later Yenan. Japan had conquered Manchuria in 1931 and in 1937 engineered an incident with Chinese troops at Marco Polo Bridge near Beijing with the intention of taking over northern China.

Into this melee strode two Americans whose impressions and beliefs continue to characterize the divided views and approaches toward China and Taiwan in the United States. One was a young journalist named Edgar Snow. He was a left-wing activist who learned Chinese and was thus able to freely associate with the young nationalists and intellectuals in the university area of Beijing where he lived. With these credentials and a letter of introduction from the widow of Sun Yat-sen, Soong Ch'ing-ling, Snow spent four months with the Communists at Pao An in 1936. From this intense period of investigation of the Communists, then a largely unknown quantity in the outside world, Snow produced his highly influential book, *Red Star over China.*[1] How far the Communists hoodwinked Snow or his own sympathies colored his reporting remains a matter of intense debate. In any event, Snow's writing and that of other American correspondents convinced many influential politicians and officials in the United States that Mao and his followers were not Communists in the way Joseph Stalin in Russia was a Communist. They could better be described, it was thought, as agrarian reformers intent on ending the feudal power of the landlord class—a purpose embedded in the foundations of the United States and which therefore found considerable sympathy.

The other early influence on U.S. public opinion toward China during the Second World War and after was retired American Air Corps captain Claire Chennault. He was hired by Chiang Kai-shek in 1937 to build a Chinese air force. By 1938 Chennault had overseen the construction of several airfields and an effective radio network to give early warning of Japanese raids. But he was less successful in training Chinese pilots and instead recruited American mercenaries, the Flying Tigers. Chennault and his pilots brought their own brand of romanticism to America's view of China that was no less potent than Snow's and often at odds with it. Chennault remained a close and trusted confidant of Chiang Kai-shek and his American-schooled wife, Soong Mae-ling, sister of Soong Ch'ing-ling. Much of the overly glossy view of Chiang held by President Franklin D. Roosevelt and American postwar support for the Kuomintang stems from Chennault's public relations offensives. He was also instrumental in promoting Soong Mae-ling, who remained a darling of audiences in the United States right up to her death in 2003 at the age of 106. Mae-ling and her brother, T.V. Soong, were so successful at boosting Chiang Kai-shek in the United States that one disenchanted American diplomat in China, John Paton Davies, once wrote ruefully to a superior: "The Generalissimo is probably the only Chinese who shares the popular misconception that Chiang Kai-shek is China."[2]

Davies was one of a coterie of American "China hands," many of whom had grown up in China as the children of missionaries, who came to believe Chiang was corrupt, a despot, and willing to fight the Japanese to the last American. This group of career diplomats came to believe the Communists would ultimately win any conflict with the Kuomintang unless Washington took a "hardboiled" attitude toward Chiang. Their urgings went unheeded and many were forced out of government service during the McCarthy purges of the 1950s. They were accused of being soft on communism and of having "lost China." Their ousting left a significant gap in knowledge and experience of China in the State Department. That vacuum played some role in the vacillations in American policy toward Chiang and the Kuomintang following their flight to Taiwan after 1949.

Coming from a different route than the China hands, General Joseph "Vinegar Joe" Stilwell, who commanded American and some Chinese troops in Southeast Asia under the daily frustrations of the Generalissimo's cautious and kleptomaniac ultimate veto, arrived at the same conclusion as the China hands. Stilwell soldiered on nonetheless. He retained great faith in the fighting ability of the Chinese soldier if properly trained and armed. With the backing of massive U.S. gifts of weapons and supplies, much of which Chiang hoarded for the coming fight with the Communists, Stilwell used about 1,000 American instructors and advisers to train and equip 39 divisions.

Turning the Kuomintang army into an effective fighting force to deploy against the Japanese was one of three elements of America's China policy in the war years of the early 1940s. Another was to broker a rapprochement between the Communists and the Kuomintang. This was frustrated by both sides being more intent on fighting each other to win power in China than in confronting the Japanese.

The third element in American policy, flowing primarily from Roosevelt and his political seduction by Chiang and Soong Mae-ling, was to make China appear a great power on the world stage even if there was little substance to the image. It was in this endeavor that the seeds of confusion over Taiwan's postwar status were sown.

At Roosevelt's insistence Chiang and his wife were invited to Cairo in November 1943 for a summit with Winston Churchill. The British prime minister objected strenuously to China's inclusion as a "great power" with the prospect of equal status with the other allies in the future United Nations, then being contemplated as a postwar guarantor of world peace. Roosevelt, however, wanted to make a generous gesture to the Chinese people and to flatter Chiang into exerting himself more fulsomely against the Japanese. Churchill reluctantly went along with the charade. Despite his warm intentions, Roosevelt found his first encounter with "the first real Oriental I have met" very trying.[3] Most of Roosevelt's previous firsthand contacts with Chinese had been with Soong Mae-ling and her brother, both of whom were highly Americanized Chinese. At Cairo Madame Chiang interpreted for her husband, who spoke no English and who didn't much care for the company of non-Chinese unless it was necessary to charm them. Roosevelt convinced himself that Chiang must be placated and that all the reports he had had of Chiang's corruption and dictatorial instincts simply reflected the exigencies of wartime leadership. The American president did later reconsider his verdict. Roosevelt came to a view of Chiang that was closer to that of Stilwell, who usually called the Chinese leader "the rattlesnake" or "peanut," rather than the more flowery characterizations of Chennault. In 1945 Roosevelt told Edgar Snow, "I was never able to form any opinion of Chiang at Cairo. When I thought about it later I realized that all I knew was what Madame Chiang told me about her husband and what he thought."[4]

The Cairo talks were complicated by Chiang's refusal to meet Joseph Stalin. Chiang was incensed at the Soviet-Japan Neutrality Pact of 1941, and he believed, with good reason, that the Russians were supplying the Chinese Communists with weapons. So when Roosevelt, Churchill, and Chiang agreed on the Cairo Declaration in November 1943, its contents were not announced until the American and British leaders had met Stalin in Tehran a few days later in December and obtained the Russian's approval. The declaration was not a treaty or a binding document. None of the leaders even signed it. The document was merely issued as a press release setting out the policy intent of the leaders.

The key segment of the Cairo Declaration referring to Taiwan said: "It is [the three powers'] purpose that Japan shall be stripped of all the islands in the Pacific which she has seized or occupied since the beginning of the First World War in 1914, and that all the territories Japan has stolen from the Chinese, such as Manchuria, Formosa [Taiwan] and the Pescadores [the Penghu Islands], shall be restored to the Republic of China."[5]

After Roosevelt's death in April 1945, the new president, Harry Truman, reaffirmed at the Potsdam summit the following July the policies set out in the Cairo Declaration. On August 6 and 9 atomic bombs were dropped on Hiroshima and Nagasaki. On August 15 Japanese emperor Hirohito broadcast to his people—the first time any had heard the sacred voice—and told them the war was over. The Japanese surrender document signed on board the U.S.S. *Missouri* in Tokyo Bay on September 2, 1945, accepted the provisions of the Potsdam Proclamation.

The swift end of the War in the Pacific brought about by the use of the atomic bombs caught almost everyone by surprise. There was no slow attrition of the enemy forces as had happened to the armies of Nazi Germany, battered by the Soviets from the east and the North Atlantic allies from the west. Instead the Japanese army of some 2.3 million men, half of them in China and about 150,000 on Taiwan, remained potent and intact.

One man who did see the opportunities presented by the chaos that would follow the Japanese surrender was Mao Zedong. On August 9, the day the second atom bomb was dropped, he loosed his three million–strong Communist forces with orders to occupy as much of northern and rural China as possible. Mao's move also came a day after the Soviet Union entered the Pacific war, apparently with the aim of picking up what spoils it could from Japan's collapsing empire. There followed a mad scramble for territory between the Communist and Kuomintang armies. In this race the Communists were better positioned to occupy the Chinese heartland from the north. Chiang, isolated behind the natural barriers of western China, even ordered the surrendered Japanese forces to fight off the Communists until Kuomintang forces could arrive to administer their disarming and repatriation to Japan.

The United States did not want to see the Communists take control of China, which seemed likely unless immediate aid was given to Chiang. Some fifty thousand American marines were sent to hold key ports and communications centers while three Kuomintang armies were airlifted to Beijing, Tianjin, and Shanghai. In the following weeks the Americans moved about half a million Kuomintang troops to various cities around the country. This massive effort stemmed the Communist advance for a while, but the picture that swiftly emerged was of the Kuomintang bottled up in the cities while Mao and his army controlled the countryside. The Communists were in an even better position in Manchuria in the northeast. After declaring war on Japan on August 8, the Soviet forces swept into Manchuria and carried on well to the south, even after Japan's surrender. The Soviets then assisted the entry of the Chinese Communists into this region and even handed over to Mao's army large quantities of captured Japanese weaponry. American diplomats led by Washington's envoy Patrick Hurley and later by General George Marshall attempted to broker an alliance between Mao and Chiang aimed at the emergence of a "strong, united, and democratic China," but in reality neither leader was prepared to compromise and China's civil war was already under way.

Chapter Fifteen

NEW BEGINNING, NEW BETRAYAL

On August 15, 1945, the thin and wavering voice of Emperor Hirohito was heard on radios across the Japanese empire announcing defeat and that the War in the Pacific was over. On Taiwan emotions ranged from relief at the ending of the war through excited anticipation that Japanese colonial rule was over to anxiety about the fate of their island. On balance, though, the mood was of eager expectation as the islanders waited for the victorious allies to arrive. And waited. And waited. Nothing happened. The nearly 150,000 Japanese troops on Taiwan kept mostly to their barracks. The Japanese police continued their daily rounds and patrols. Taiwanese people went about their lives as normal. The Japanese organized a massive clean-up operation to remove wreckage left by American bombing raids in the final weeks of the war. There was no breakdown of law and order, though retribution was taken against a few individual policemen. These were all in revenge for personal abuses and not unfocused uprisings against Japanese authority.

Finally, two weeks later, on September 1, a Japanese warship, a submarine chaser, appeared in Keelung harbor. It had been commandeered in Xiamen by three young American servicemen and two Chinese who claimed to be colonels. They introduced themselves to the Japanese commanders as a team sent to assess the situation of allied prisoners of war on Taiwan. The Japanese were happy to see them, thinking this was the first indication they might be going home soon. But the Americans and the Chinese showed very little interest in allied prisoners of war. They showed much more enthusiasm when offered $200,000 in public funds to cover their expenses while in Taiwan. Most of that money disappeared within two days.

Japanese intelligence officers and the ever-curious Taiwanese quickly discovered the Chinese "colonels" were actually officers from Chiang Kai-shek's internal security operation, the Bureau of Investigation and Statistics, better known among Americans as "Chiang's Gestapo." The three accompanying Americans, later joined by a fourth, were from one of Washington's intelligence agencies and had been assigned to liaise with the Chinese. The true purpose of the team was to make an assessment of the political situation on Taiwan. They were especially interested in noting the names of people on the island who had been pressing the Japanese for home rule. Political activism of any kind was a dangerous quality to be watched in the future. The team also documented which Taiwanese had got rich under Japanese rule. The assets of collaborators were fair game now that the war was over.

On September 5 an American naval flotilla arrived off Keelung with more genuine interest in allied prisoners held on Taiwan. Within two days 1,300 allied prisoners were taken off the island. Another five days went by and then a group from the U.S. Office of Strategic Services (OSS) flew in from Kunming in western China. Their job was to hunt for Communists, of which there were precious few on Taiwan after 50 years of a Japanese police state. The OSS men were followed by an American graves' registration unit with the task of listing allied airmen who had died on the island.

None of these groups had the authority to accept the surrender of the Japanese, who were increasingly impatient to get home but still operating as a disciplined army. On September 30, six weeks after Japan's surrender, a Chinese survey group made a brief reconnoiter of Taipei and on October 5 a Chinese general, Keh King-en, arrived.

In his first address to the Taiwanese people the general set the tone for several decades to come. The island, he told them, had been "degraded" by Japanese occupation and the islanders were a "degraded people" outside the bounds of pure Chinese civilization. The implication of General Keh's observations got lost, however, in the very genuine atmosphere of happy anticipation that overtook Taiwan as the truth sank in that 50 years of Japanese colonialism was over.

Some of the truths of Taiwan's new status began to be suspected ten days later on October 15, when American transport ships brought 12,000 Kuomintang troops to Keelung. Many were mere boys, illiterate, unkempt, undisciplined, and fearful. They refused to leave the ships unless American troops agreed to march ahead of them for fear of ambushes by the Japanese. General

Chen Yi, appointed governor of Taiwan by Chiang Kai-shek, arrived on October 25 with his Japanese "geisha" wife, a description that most contemporary accounts strongly hint is a euphemism for a more sordid history. A motor parade into Taipei was arranged and tens of thousands of people turned out to watch the arrival of their new lord into the capital.

General Chen received the Japanese surrender the same day and went on to proclaim that this act constituted the reincorporation of Taiwan into China under the sovereign administration of the Kuomintang. This assumption went too far for the Americans and other allies. They objected to Chen's act, pointing out that despite the wording of the Cairo Declaration that Taiwan and the Penghu Islands "shall" be restored to the Republic of China, the legal resolution of what to do with the territories regained from Japan awaited the signing of a formal peace treaty. In the meantime the Kuomintang was merely administering Taiwan on behalf of the allies.

This objection was put to Chiang, but not forcefully because few Americans in Washington or the field wanted to address the issue of Taiwan sovereignty and no one imagined the headache it would become. Among the diplomats of the State Department, the so-called China Firsters, the acceptance of China's "historic claims" had been part of their specialist education. There was no willingness to question whether that claim was just. Military men in the field were consumed by the daily nightmare of managing the chaos of peace and China's drift toward civil war. There were plenty of problems to deal with without looking for more on Taiwan.

Taiwanese enthusiasm for their liberation was already restrained. The schoolchildren marshaled to line Chen's parade route shouted the traditional Japanese greeting "banzai" as he passed, but the greatest applause was for the American liaison troops riding at the back of the cavalcade. The islanders began to react as it became more and more apparent the Kuomintang troops considered Taiwan conquered territory to be looted and its people Japanese collaborators worthy only of contempt. Wall posters began to appear making fun of the Kuomintang troops. Comments such as "The dogs have gone and the pigs have arrived" and "At least the Japanese dogs protected property" were scrawled everywhere.

Chen Yi had been appointed Taiwan's governor-in-waiting a year before. He was a close personal friend and ally of Chiang Kai-shek. They both came from Zhejiang province south of Shanghai. When Chiang was preparing to capture Shanghai in the late 1920s, Chen had used their mutual links with the great commercial city's triad underworld to ensure the Kuomintang troops entered unopposed. One of Chen's rewards was to be appointed governor of Fujian province, where he had had a peaceful war because hostilities with the Japanese had been kept to a minimum to avoid interference with the trade across the front line that Chen encouraged. Chen's amicable relations with the Japanese were such that he was invited to Taiwan in 1935 to take part in the celebrations marking 40 years of Tokyo's colonial rule on the island. When in an unusual bout of warfare in 1942 the Japanese took over the Fujian provincial capital, Fuzhou, they gave Chen advance notice so he could get his family and his large accumulation of possessions to safety before the invading troops arrived.

Chen's history gave fair warning of the way he would administer Taiwan. He did not attempt to set up a true civilian administration in keeping with the island's purported status as a reclaimed Chinese province. Instead Chen established a military administration staffed exclusively by mainlanders and his relatives. Then the systematic acquisition of all Japanese-owned assets and the looting of anything of value began. The looting proceeded at several levels. Ordinary Kuomintang soldiers were notoriously badly paid, if at all, and were expected to live by plunder. This they did with the thoroughness of locusts. But even as the Taiwanese were being robbed to the walls they couldn't help but be amused at the antics of the ignorant mainland country boys. There are many stories from those days of soldiers stealing bicycles and then carrying them off on their backs because they didn't know what a bicycle was or how to ride it. At the officer level the plunder was more grandiose. All Japanese military establishments were taken over by the Kuomintang army and navy, which then shipped all the stores to the mainland to be sold for great profits. Chen's own coterie of administrators took control of all the industries, businesses, enterprises, and even the housing districts that had been Japanese. This amounted, according to some estimates, to 90 percent of the island's economy. They all disappeared into monopolies and what Chen described as "necessary state socialism."

The industries and businesses quickly atrophied because the mainlanders put in charge were incompetent. But the Chen administration made large profits by sending stored goods to be sold in China and even dismantling and shipping out entire industrial production plants. The administration also ended up with a vast real estate empire of land that had been held by Japanese and that remains the basis of the Kuomintang political empire. Not all Taiwanese were innocent victims or bystanders to this frenzied rapine. Many old scores were settled by informing the authorities that a rival had collaborated with the Japanese. But mostly it was the carpetbagger mainlanders who accused usually innocent Taiwanese of being collaborators to justify seizure of whatever property they wanted from the islanders, including people's homes.

Not surprisingly the economy collapsed. Between November 1945 and January 1947 the consumer price index spiraled out of control. The price of food rose by over 21,000 points in that period and clothing by nearly 25,000 points. There were even greater increases in the prices of seed and fertilizer as well as scarcity of supply. As a result the rice crop in the early postwar years was only half what it had been in the 1930s and the general agricultural production fell to the level of 1910. The public health programs and regulations so assiduously followed by the Japanese were abandoned. The bubonic plague and cholera became endemic again. Malaria reappeared as a serious problem when stores of quinine medicines left by the Japanese were sold to the mainland and replacements sent by foreign donors were diverted to the same destination.

In 1946 Chen Yi announced that young male islanders would be conscripted to serve in China fighting the Communists. There was a public outcry and the governor had to abandon the idea. He was not always so responsive to criticism or public opinion. The detention or harassment of journalists or administration critics became systematic in mid-1946 and gathered pace over the following months.

America's deep ambivalence about Chiang and the Kuomintang intensified as the civil war in China progressed. On one hand Washington wanted Chiang to win and check any further Communist expansion. To that end Chiang was lavishly supplied with American weapons and instructors. But America, and especially the State Department, was increasingly troubled by Chiang's corruption, dictatorial tendencies, and evident incompetence as a civil and military leader. This ambivalent attitude included Taiwan. Washington did not want the island at the strategic crossroads of the Far East to fall into Communist hands. Equally unappetizing was the idea of continued Kuomintang rule there. The questionable morality of allowing Chiang to have sovereignty over the island and its people became more concerning as reports arrived about the rapacious colonial rule of General Chen Yi on Taiwan.

By early 1947, then, a dangerous and unstable cauldron of public resentment was reaching a boiling point on Taiwan. Any incident could have toppled the cauldron. In the event it was what happened to a widow, Lin Chiang-mai, who was selling cigarettes in a Taipei park on February 27, 1947, that transformed resentment into open rebellion. Lin was accosted by six agents from the Monopoly Commission who accused her of selling contraband cigarettes. They grabbed the woman and her money. She resisted, was hit on the head with a pistol butt, and called out to passersby for help. An angry crowd gathered quickly. One of the commission agents fired his pistol into the crowd to force an escape route and killed one man. The agents escaped, but the crowd went on a rampage and burned the commission truck.

The next morning several thousand people gathered at the park and marched to the Monopoly Commission offices with a petition demanding the prosecution of the agents. They found the bureau locked and guarded so the crowd turned to Chen Yi's office. They arrived at about noon and were fired on by soldiers with a machine gun. Two people died and several others were wounded. News spread quickly and by late afternoon the streets were full of angry crowds. Two Monopoly Commission agents were caught and beaten to death. Within two days the uprising had spread to cities throughout the island.

Martial law was declared on the evening of February 28, and military patrols began roaring through Taipei firing from their vehicles at anyone they saw. This indiscriminate use of force revealed a real problem faced by Governor Chen. The demands of the civil war on the mainland had shrunk the forces available to Chen from 48,000 at their height to only 11,000 in March 1947. Chen played for time.

On March 1 a group of civic leaders led by the speaker of the Taiwan Provincial People's Political Council, Huang Ch'ao-ch'in, went to see Chen and demanded that martial law be lifted. The governor agreed to do so, but even as the meeting was being held more and more troops were spreading through Taipei, gunning down anyone they saw. The next day Chen made a radio broadcast saying a generous restitution payment was being made to widow Lin to settle the February 27 incident and that he had agreed to form a joint settlement committee with civic leaders. While he was speaking there was one of the most serious clashes thus far, at the Taiwan Railway Administration building, in which over 120 people were killed by army machine gun fire.

On March 7 the settlement committee presented Chen with a list of 32 demands. It was a broad-based prescription for reform starting with an end to military rule and the establishment of Taiwan as an autonomous province of China. There were items dealing with the lack of Taiwanese people in the administration and requirements for free and fair elections. Some demands dealt with the independent and notoriously corrupt police forces attached to some government departments. Others urged the release of political prisoners. Still more addressed economic issues such as abuses of the tax system. An irate Chen rejected the demands and the committee retreated to soften its proposals.

The insurrection was continuing throughout the island, and many towns and cities were under the effective control of the local people. In Taipei the civic leaders of the settlement committee believed that despite Chen's initial rejection, a reworking of the 32 demands could create a compromise that would restore order. What they didn't know was that on March 5 Chen had sent a message to China asking for reinforcements. On March 8, 10,000 troops landed at Keelung in the north and another 3,000 at Kaohsiung in the south. The following morning the new forces began a campaign of indiscriminate shooting, raping, and bayoneting as they moved to reestablish Chen's control over the island. By March 13 most of the insurgents in the towns and cities had been suppressed, but fighting continued in the mountain regions for at least another week.

Then the troops and Chen's security operatives began a hunt for dissidents. About one thousand middle school students in their early teens were detained and close to one hundred arbitrarily executed. Lawyers, leading businessmen, and newspaper editors were rounded up. So were members of the settlement committee. Several of them were killed. The reaction to the popular uprising became an orgy of killing by government forces of anyone considered a leader of Taiwanese society. Many were tortured and mutilated before being killed and their bodies left in the streets as a warning to others. The Kuomintang's own records say that at least 28,000 people were killed.

The Two-Two-Eight Incident, as it became known from the date of the outbreak of hostilities on February 28, was a turning point in the American view of and policy toward Chiang Kai-shek and Taiwan. Six weeks after the outbreak on Taiwan the U.S. ambassador to China, John Leighton Stuart, wrote a long memorandum to Chiang based on eyewitness accounts by American diplomats and highly critical of General Chen's style of government. Chiang Kai-shek, then in Nanjing, professed to know nothing about what was happening on Taiwan. In August Lieutenant General Albert Wedermeyer, the commander of American forces in Asia, wrote an equally critical message to the U.S. secretary of state. "Chen Yi and his henchmen ruthlessly, corruptly and avariciously imposed their regime upon a happy and amenable population. The army conducted themselves as conquerors. Secret police operated freely to intimidate and to facilitate exploitation by Central Government [Kuomintang] officials."[1] Wedermeyer went on to proffer an alternative to Kuomintang rule over Taiwan. "There were indications that Formosans would be receptive toward United States guardianship and United Nations trusteeship. They fear that the Central Government contemplates bleeding their island to support the tottering and corrupt Nanjing regime, and I think their fears are well founded."

Chen Yi was recalled from Taiwan on March 22. Chiang, however, was not going to undermine internal discipline in the Kuomintang by appearing to be Washington's poodle. Chen was promoted to be governor of his and Chiang's native province of Zhejiang, a larger and more important place than Taiwan.

Chen brought about his own downfall two years later by acting true to his corrupt form. In 1949, as it appeared the Communists were going to win the civil war, Chen began making arrangements to change sides. Chiang Kai-shek got wind of it. Chen was arrested and sent to Taiwan, where he was executed by firing squad in June 1950. When news of the death became public knowledge, it sparked a day of celebration throughout Taiwan.

American officials began soon after the Two-Two-Eight Incident discussing ideas for resolving the island's status. They picked up on the notion of a United Nations trusteeship and explored the idea of a referendum, with no one doubting it would lead to the islanders choosing independence. In January 1949 the National Security Council produced a draft report on Taiwan and its future. The report noted the implications of the Cairo Declaration and said America's national interest was that the island be denied to the Communists. While that tended to argue that Taiwan should be left in Kuomintang hands, the report noted that U.S. policy "cannot leave out of account the Formosan people and their strong resentment of Chinese rule arising from Chinese maladministration and repression."[2]

By the autumn of 1949 various branches of the U.S. government had agreed on a plan to take the future of Taiwan to the United Nations. That scheme came to a halt with the Communist victory on the mainland in October 1949 and the flight of the Kuomintang to Taiwan. Washington was overcome by fatalism. It looked as though it would only be a matter of time before the Communists took Taiwan. With that likelihood Washington wanted to be able to deal with the winner. On January 5, 1950, President Truman announced America would have no further involvement in the Chinese civil war and would provide no more weapons or advice to the Kuomintang.

It was not only Chen Yi who made early arrangements to try to survive a Communist victory on the mainland. Chiang Kai-shek had thought about it too. Late in October 1948 an order was issued stopping the export of food and goods from Taiwan. Efforts began to be made to rebuild the island's economy so it could serve as a haven for Chiang, his supporters, and remaining military when—no longer if—the Communists triumphed. Mainlanders and their assets—among them almost the entire contents of the National Palace Museum—began moving to Taiwan in large numbers. By the time Chiang formally moved the capital of the Republic of China to Taipei in December 1949 there were about two million mainlanders on the island, among them 600,000 surviving members of the Kuomintang army.

Chapter Sixteen

THE UNSINKABLE AIRCRAFT CARRIER

Washington managed to wash its hands of Taiwan and Chiang Kai-shek's exiled army for only six months. On June 25, 1950, North Korean forces attacked the South across the thirty-eighth parallel, the line along which the peninsula had been divided at the end of the Second World War. Taiwan was suddenly on the front line of a conflict that directly affected American interests and prestige in Asia. Two days later President Truman ordered the 7th Fleet to patrol the Taiwan Strait. His main intention was to prevent China from using the cover of the Korean War to invade the "unsinkable aircraft carrier" of Taiwan. "In these circumstances," he said in a statement, "the occupation of Formosa [Taiwan] by Communist forces would be a direct threat to the security of the Pacific area and to the United States performing their lawful and necessary function in that area."[1] The deployment of the 7th Fleet was, however, just as firmly aimed against Chiang using the opportunity to invade the mainland and drag the United States into a war with China, which might well escalate into a nuclear war with the Soviet Union. It was at this moment that Truman uttered the still-unfulfilled promise that "The determination of the future status of Formosa must await the restoration of security in the Pacific, a peace settlement with Japan, or consideration by the United Nations."[2] No attempt was made to settle the question of Taiwan's status when the Japanese Peace Treaty was negotiated and signed in 1951. Japan merely formally relinquished its empire without saying in whose benefit it gave up its conquered territories.

One of the few occasions when there has been a formal legal consideration of Taiwan's status was in 1959, when District of Columbia federal judge Alexander Holtzoff ruled that two Chinese liable for deportation could not be sent to Taiwan. "Formosa may be said to be a territory or an area occupied or administered by the Government of the Republic of China, but it is not officially recognized as being part of the Republic of China," Judge Holtzoff said. "Expressions of the State Department are drawn with care and circumspection to refrain from such recognition." He went on to accept lawyers' arguments that neither the Japanese Peace Treaty of 1951 nor any subsequent agreement had given China sovereignty over Taiwan. "The situation is, then, one where the Allied Powers still have to come to some agreement or treaty with respect to the status of Formosa."[3] The people of Taiwan are still waiting for that resolution.

As late as 1971 the American official position remained that Taiwan's status was "undetermined" because the conditions set out by Truman in 1950 had not been met.

Once Washington had decided that occupation of Taiwan by the Chinese Communists would be a direct threat to U.S. interests in the Pacific region, military and civilian aid began flowing in ever-increasing amounts to Taipei. Chiang and the Kuomintang began to hope that they would soon be in a position to invade the mainland and oust Mao and the Communists. Hope blossomed into rejoicing in 1952 when former general Dwight Eisenhower was elected president. The Republican campaign had lambasted Truman for "losing China" and not doing enough to support Chiang either on the mainland or on Taiwan. So Chiang was full of confidence that Eisenhower would remove the 7th Fleet and support unfettered action by the Kuomintang army against the mainland. There is an institutional Washington that quickly shackles a new president, whatever he may have said on the campaign trail. Entry into the Oval Office involves indoctrination into a cultural view of America's national interests that changes remarkably little from administration to administration. That's what happened with Eisenhower. He did theoretically "deneutralize" Taiwan, but the reality was that the United States continued to oppose any large-scale invasion of the mainland by Chiang's forces. This prohibition was spelled out clearly when America and Chiang's Republic of China government signed a defense treaty in 1954. "Offensive military operations by either party from the territories held by the Republic of China would be undertaken only as a matter of joint agreement," the document said.[4]

This prohibition on lone action by the Chiang regime contained the elements of a "two China" or "one China, one Taiwan" policy by the United

States. Chiang may still have believed Taiwan was only a temporary resting place before a return to the mainland, where the populous would rise up in his support, eager to throw off the slavery of communism. The Americans do not appear to have had any such illusions. That division of view first surfaced in 1958 when the Communists began shelling the offshore mainland islands of Kinmen and Mazu. Eisenhower and his secretary of state, John Foster Dulles, thought it made no sense for Chiang to maintain large garrisons on these islands, which could be given up without causing any strategic threat to Taiwan and the Penghu Islands. Abandonment of some of the offshore islands might even lead to a ceasefire across the Taiwan Strait. But the Kuomintang were attached to the offshore island clusters. These islands were the only part of mainland China the Kuomintang controlled. Their possession gave some legitimacy, however slender, to the Chiang regime's claim to be the government of the Republic of China, especially when Chiang's status on Taiwan and the question of whether Taiwan was indeed part of China remained unresolved. Washington did manage to persuade Chiang to abandon some of the most far removed and least defensible northerly islands in the Mazu group, but the rest remain part of the territory administered by Taipei.

Chiang Kai-shek's claim to represent the true government of China grew increasingly tiresome for Washington administrations, especially as the United Nations blossomed. Various tenants of the White House also found it irksome and irritating that Taipei had developed a strong lobby of support for "Free China" in the Congress and among influential Americans such as the publisher Henry Luce. Chiang and the Kuomintang were always ready to make China a domestic American political issue when they had troubles with the administration.

President John F. Kennedy toyed with confronting the problem during his first year in office in 1961, but thought better of it. The Republic of China was threatening to use its veto on the UN Security Council to bar the entry into the organization of Outer Mongolia, a supposedly independent state within the Soviet Union that had been a Chinese colony until 1921 and over which Taipei still claimed sovereignty. Kennedy's secretary of state, Dean Rusk, suggested to the president that Washington might defang Taipei by quietly suggesting to other UN members that Mao's People's Republic of China also be admitted to the organization. Kennedy liked the "two China" idea. "It really doesn't make any sense—the idea that Taiwan represents China," he said.[5] But he warned Rusk that backing Communist China for a UN seat would raise a huge domestic political storm that could see his administration run out of office. Instead Kennedy pursued unofficial talks with Beijing through the two countries' embassies in Warsaw to try to lessen tensions. This channel of contact was primarily concerned with testing the solidarity of China's loyalty to Moscow in the red-hot days of the cold war and the Cuban missile crisis. Washington was picking up hints of an ideological divide among the Moscow and Beijing Communists as well as a good deal of anger and mistrust over border territory disputes. The information was correct and the Warsaw talks were early steps on the road to Sino-U.S. diplomatic recognition a decade later. As part of these confidence-building discussions, the American ambassador told his counterpart that the United States would not support any invasion of the mainland by Chiang but was equally determined to defend Taiwan should China make the mistake of trying to take the island. That message, with some variations, remained substantially the same for over 40 years.

An American war in Korea saved Chiang and the Kuomintang from abandonment by Washington in 1950. In the mid-1960s another American conflict came along to remind Washington of Taiwan's strategic importance at a moment when the administration was again tiring of its Taiwan entanglement. The war in Vietnam showed American military planners that Taiwan was just as convenient a staging point for action in Southeast Asia as it was for the Far East. Taiwan became a base for American bombing raids on North Vietnam and a rest and recreation center for troops. The Taipei government relished its renewed importance in Washington, and Chiang did what he could to consolidate "Free China's" position as a bastion against Communist incursion into Southeast Asia by cementing ties with the sundry local dictators whom America felt forced to adopt as allies in the great crusade.

Behind the scenes, however, institutional Washington had become convinced that for America's immediate strategic interests in the cold war with the Soviet Union and for the long-term stability of Asia, mainland China should be coaxed in from the cold of its self-imposed isolation. China quietly encouraged this mind-set by taking a minimal role in the Vietnam War. This was not difficult for Beijing. It mistrusted Ho Chi-minh and the North Vietnamese almost as much as did Washington, as China's 1979 border war with Vietnam was to show.

On Taiwan the Kuomintang government was aware that Washington was drifting purposefully toward an accord with the People's Republic of China. Taipei's efforts to reenergize its support among U.S. policymakers by reminding them of the island's strategic significance were not successful. Taiwan had no real alternatives but to try to maintain as sound relations as possible with the United States, with whose economy its own was now inexorably interwoven, and to hope its interests would not be abandoned in Washington's strategic shuffle. Taipei began to appreciate that perhaps undertaking a process of democratic reform along the lines suggested by Washington was the surest guarantee available of the island's strategic security. It also agreed to abandon and dismantle the advanced program to build nuclear weapons it started on Chiang Kai-shek's orders in 1969 using a small research reactor it had bought from Canada, similar to another Canadian model that India used to manufacture a nuclear bomb. Taiwan's admission that it was on the path to making a bomb was in itself a significant act of deterrence toward China. The fact that Taiwan had come close to building nuclear warheads demonstrated a capacity that China must still take into account when threatening to invade the island.

Chapter Seventeen

REFORM AND TERROR

Chiang Kai-shek and the Kuomintang retreated to Taiwan in December 1949, insisting this was only a temporary setback. They would restore their strength while on the island and when they returned to the mainland the Chinese people, having suffered the "slavery" of communism, would rise up as one in joyous welcome. To that end it was necessary for the Kuomintang to attempt to retain some semblance of still holding the mandate of Heaven. It was therefore important to govern Taiwan as though it was China and to begin implementing the doctrine on which Sun Yat-sen had founded the party. That doctrine said that before democracy there must be a period of popular tutelage when there would be a benevolent one-party dictatorship. During this transition period the party would concentrate on establishing economic, social, and political conditions suitable for the flowering of democracy.

The economy was the most pressing concern. Inflation continued to run out of control in large part because the administration kept printing money to finance the restoration of publicly owned—in reality Kuomintang-owned—enterprises. It was not until 1953 that the authorities managed to curb inflation by trimming the money supply and encourage saving by paying high interest on short-term deposits.

An essential element in Taiwan's economic reconstruction and its later emergence as one of the industrial "miracle" states of Asia was land reform. Taiwan in 1949 still had a largely feudal landholding system under which large tracts were owned by wealthy families, and most farmers were tenants paying rents worth from 50 percent of their crops to as high as 70 percent in the more fertile areas. These rents were often fixed to what a piece of land should theoretically produce and not the actual value of the crop in a bad year. Tackling land ownership was a task relatively free of political risk for the Kuomintang, much more so than earlier attempts on the mainland had been. Kuomintang party members did not own agricultural land and the native Taiwanese landowning class was without influence. The program started in 1949 with a required reduction of rents to a maximum of 37.5 percent of the crop value. In 1951 the government sold off all the farmland, but not the urban or industrial plots that had been seized from the Japanese. This amounted to about one-fifth of the island's arable land. To forestall grabs by the rich, the land was sold off in lots of a suitable size to support a family of six. The cost was two and a half times the value of the land's expected annual yield, and buyers, of which there were over 150,000, were allowed to pay the debt off over ten years from their crops. The final step in land reform was the 1953 law requiring landlords to sell to the government their holdings beyond what they could farm themselves. They were paid in land bonds and in shares in the major government-owned industries. The government then resold the land to family farmers under the same terms as the 1951 program.

The program was astonishingly successful. At least two million Taiwanese became landowners, farmers' incomes doubled, and productivity had increased by 50 percent by 1963. It was the acquisition of equity through land ownership that prepared Taiwan for its light industrial revolution in the 1960s and 1970s. Enterprising farmers who wanted to start factories had the land and collateral with which to go to the bank for backing.

The social outcome of the land reform program was equally profound. It removed at a stroke the traditional privileges of the gentry class and created a far more equitable society. Not everyone was happy. One former landowner, talking to author Douglas Mendel in the 1960s, said, "The regime will never give its real reason for stealing our land because one was political. They wanted to eliminate the power of the landowners because we were the social elite in every community, looked up to by the peasants, and we were known to have been active in the 1947 revolt."[1]

The political implications of land reform were not all beneficial for the Kuomintang. Independent farmers and, later, small business owners quickly became independent thinkers, especially in matters of local political interest. And the disinheriting of the young offspring of the landowning class, who were among the island's best-educated and articulate people, tended to make them into radical Taiwanese nationalists.

U.S. aid played an important part in Taiwan's economic revival. This aid started to flow after Washington decided the island was worth saving from communism when the Korean War started in 1950. American advisers helped frame the land reform program as well as infrastructure developments and industrial policy. Through the 1950s Taiwan received $100 million a year from the United States, up to 80 percent in the form of nonrepayable grants. This money represented a third of all capital investment. Washington finally shut off the tap in 1963, when Taiwan was clearly a going concern no longer needing support.

The light at the end of the political tunnel was not so bright or so close. The Kuomintang maintained martial law after the February 1947 uprising on the grounds that Taiwan was under constant threat from the mainland Communists. The same logic dictated the keeping of a large standing army and the spending of up to 12 percent of the island's gross domestic product on the military.

From the start the Kuomintang allowed contested elections at the district level. This entailed little threat to the Kuomintang's supremacy as opposition parties were banned and opponents of the administration had to run as independents. Kuomintang candidates had the advantage of the backing of a dominant and wealthy party machine. And the intense security operation run by the main secret police force, the Taiwan Garrison Command, was well able to ferret out any aspiring politician who represented a real threat to political stability.

This token pluralism amounted to a very minor respect for democracy, but it was seen as important in maintaining international support for the Republic of China, especially in Washington. The Kuomintang justification for the deplorably low representation of native Taiwanese in major institutions on the island was simple. These institutions represented the government of the Republic of China, of which Taiwan was only one province. It would have been wrong to have people from only one province overrepresented in national institutions. This rationale became more bizarre as the years passed, aging members of the national institutions like the parliament died off, and mainlanders became increasingly integrated into Taiwanese society.

The tokens of democracy at the district level did little to comfort many native Taiwanese, who took up the cause of island autonomy as they had with the Japanese. They began to take aim at the ban on opposition political parties in the late 1950s. A petition from a group of prominent native Taiwanese asking for the right to form a political party was sent to the administration in 1958. It was refused and the full weight of the government security and propaganda machine was leveled at the authors. Some of Chiang's mainlanders began joining the fray in the 1960s with demands for greater respect for human and political rights. The government's usual tactic was to label reform advocates as Communist sympathizers and to throw the full authority of the martial law regulations at them.

The responsibility for overseeing state security and dealing with people held to be a threat to the Republic of China was with the Taiwan Garrison Command. Its powers were almost boundless. People could be arrested for real or imagined Communist tendencies, for advocating insurrection, criticizing the Chiang family, or questioning sacred Kuomintang doctrines like Taiwan's status as a province of China. Arrests were made by military personnel and detainees were tried in military courts. These trials were held in secret, and for several years the accused were not allowed legal representation or contact with their families.

There was a threat to Kuomintang supremacy, of course, but it didn't come from Communists or agents of Mao Zedong's government in China. It came from Taiwanese, who wanted to be masters of their own house. To the Garrison Command this was treason against their version of China. The command's campaign against Taiwanese advocates of reform or independence became known as the White Terror and lasted from after the 1947 uprising into the 1980s. Some analysts estimate that as many as 90,000 people were arrested during the White Terror years. About 10,000 of those were actually tried in military courts, but about 45,000 were executed summarily.

Behind the Garrison Command lurked a network of often competing intelligence and security organizations under the direction of the Generalissimo's son, Chiang Ching-kuo. The younger Chiang is an elusive figure. He is adored beyond comprehension by some people and hated by others with a deep loathing that is equally extreme. Both views have some merit. Chiang Ching-kuo carries the ultimate responsibility for the deaths of tens of thousands of Taiwanese and there is good reason to think his involvement was more direct in many of those deaths. At the same time it was the younger Chiang who finally saw that Taiwan's long-term security lay in political reform. While it remained a one-party military dictatorship, the United States and other allies would always have reason to abandon the island. A functioning democracy would attract more loyalty. Chiang took this path even though he knew it meant abandoning his father's dreams of a victorious return to the mainland. Chiang Ching-kuo knew also that reform meant putting Taiwan's future in the hands of the islanders, most of whom did not see the island as a province of China and who had no interest in any kind of unification with the mainland.

Chiang Ching-kuo was born in 1910 in his father's home village, Xikou, south of Shanghai. His mother was Chiang Kai-shek's first wife, Mao Fu-mei. Fu-mei was an illiterate young woman from a neighboring village who had been betrothed to Chiang Kai-shek when he was 14 years old. The couple drifted apart as Chiang became more and more involved in the politics and underworld of Shanghai. They were to all intents and purposes separated in 1909 when Chiang Kai-shek's mother took the young woman to Shanghai and insisted her son make Fu-mei pregnant. Chiang Ching-kuo was born on April 27 the following year.

Chiang Kai-shek was seldom present as Ching-kuo grew up, but his influence was all around. The father oversaw his son's schooling and wrote copious letters commenting on the boy's progress, many of them harshly critical. In 1921 Chiang Kai-shek divorced Fu-mei and married a 14-year-old girl, Ch'en Chieh-ju, in Shanghai. When he was 12 Ching-kuo was enrolled at a school in Shanghai and went to live with his stepmother, who was only four years older than he was. He completed his schooling in Beijing, where he came under the influence of Communist teachers and thought of himself as a "progressive revolutionary," as Jay Taylor records in his book *The Generalissimo's Son.*[2] The Kuomintang was strongly supported by the Soviet Union at that time and much of the party's doctrine was adopted from Moscow. In 1925 the Soviet Communist Party opened in Moscow the Sun Yat-sen University of the Toilers of China. Chiang Ching-kuo was determined to go to the Moscow university, but his father, who, according to Taylor, regarded his son as "a block of wood," took much persuading that the cost would be worth it.[3]

Chiang Ching-kuo left China by ship from Shanghai in October 1925 with 90 other students. He would not return for 12 years. The students arrived in Moscow in bleak, frigid November and were taken to the dour and austere university. The first thing that happened to Ching-kuo was that he was given a Russian name, Nikolai Vladimirovich Elizarov. He joined the Chinese Communist Youth Corps and the Soviet Komsomol. Early in 1926 a new student moved into the university dormitory, a bubbly, solidly build small young man who had been living in Paris. It was Deng Xiaoping, who quickly became known among fellow students as the Little Cannon. The same year Ching-kuo, then 16 years old, married a fellow student, Feng Fu-neng, the daughter of a Chinese warlord.

Chiang Ching-kuo's inclinations were very much to the left-wing, Trotskyite faction of the Communist Party. When his father in 1927 slaughtered the Shanghai Communists with the help of his triad brothers in the Green Gang, Chiang Ching-kuo's life was thrown into crisis. At a student meeting he denounced his father as a "traitor and a murderer." The young man then issued a written statement along the same lines. This was reprinted by several Soviet newspapers. To cap the political breach with Chiang Kai-shek, Ching-kuo wrote an article for the newspaper *Izvestia* that ended "Revolution is the only thing I know, and I don't know you as my father anymore."

When the Soviet leader Joseph Stalin ousted the Trotskyites, Chiang Ching-kuo had his first confrontation with the conflict between ideology and survival. He chose survival and abandoned his pro-Trotsky views.

Ching-kuo was selected for military training in Leningrad, now St. Petersburg again, late in 1927. The curriculum included guerrilla warfare, basic military logistics, and the political control of armed forces. He graduated top of his class in 1930 and returned to Moscow, where he suffered his first bout of diabetes, which was to plague his later life. He wanted to join the Soviet Red Army but was sent instead to study engineering at the Dynamo Electric Plant in Moscow.

At this time, 1931, Chiang Ching-kuo's status in Moscow changed because of events in China. He became, in effect, Stalin's hostage as relations between Moscow and Chiang Kai-shek declined. At the same time Chiang Kai-shek was beginning to show signs of missing his son, despite Ching-kuo's renunciation of his father. The father's feelings were made more poignant because his latest wife—four years before he had established the groundwork for the Kuomintang family dynasty by marrying the American-educated Soong Mae-ling—had borne no children, apparently because Chiang Kai-shek had become infertile after contracting venereal disease from Shanghai prostitutes. Messages were passed to Stalin suggesting Ching-kuo return to China, but the Soviet leader decided the young man was a useful card to keep in Russia. Ching-kuo was sent to work on a collective farm.

In 1935 Chiang Ching-kuo married for a second time. Faina Epatcheva Vahaleva was "a good looking average girl" of 17 with "slightly Japanese eyes."[4] In December that year the couple had a son named Ai-lian.

By 1937 relations between the Kuomintang and Moscow had improved, and Stalin decided to send Ching-kuo back to his father. This was not an entirely friendly or altruistic move by the Soviet leader. To Stalin it seemed a good moment to insert the young committed Communist in the heart of the Chinese party, where he might later work Moscow's will. The father and son reunited in Hanzhou in April 1937. Ching-kuo told his father he wanted an assignment where he could test his "progressive ideas," but Chiang Kai-shek said he must first relearn the writing of Chinese characters and steep himself in Chinese classical literature. This Ching-kuo did, and the following year, 1938, he was brought into the mid-levels of the Kuomintang hierarchy as head of a regional branch of a new youth corps.

Chiang Kai-shek clearly had affection for his son but did not yet trust his politics. Ching-kuo saw out the war against Japan in a variety of posts where he gradually gained the confidence of his father by working with ruthless efficiency. The Generalissimo finally showed faith in his son in 1948, when Ching-kuo was delegated to try to bring order to chaotic Shanghai. It was a thankless task as the Communists closed in on the Kuomintang, but Ching-kuo's efforts drew further confidence from his father. In August 1949 he was put in charge of sorting out the party's intelligence organizations and cleaning up the messy and corrupt Kuomintang administration left on Taiwan by Chen Yi.

On Taiwan Chiang Ching-kuo purged the top levels of the Central Bureau of Investigation and Statistics and its rival, the Military Bureau of Investigation and Statistics. He merged them into the Reference Group of the Presidential Palace's Confidential Office. This became Ching-kuo's power base from which he assured his right to succeed his father and worked to undermine rivals. The Reference Group spawned five junior intelligence agencies working not only on Taiwan but overseas in the United States and China, and anywhere there was an expatriate Chinese community.

The immediate task for Ching-kuo's agents in 1949 was to eradicate supposed Communist sympathizers on Taiwan. This was done with excessive enthusiasm. Thousands of people were detained, tortured, and killed or sent indefinitely to the infamous prison camp on Green Island off Taiwan's southeast coast.

The reputation of Ching-kuo's agents for gross brutality outraged even loyal Kuomintang members. In 1952 the governor of Taiwan province, K. C. Wu, cornered Chiang Kai-shek and said, "If you love your son, do not have him head of the secret police. He will become the target of people's hatred." The Generalissimo ignored the advice.

When the Korean War changed Washington's view of Taiwan, Chiang Ching-kuo established a close working relationship with the Central Intelligence Agency that served him well in later life. At one point there were more than six hundred CIA agents based in Taiwan. They cooperated on guerrilla and spying operations in China, but also in Burma, which was to secure Ching-kuo's links to Washington during the Vietnam War. Two Kuomintang divisions had been left in China's southwestern Yunnan province in 1949.

They were driven out by the Communists into Burma's Shan state, where the soldiers turned to opium and heroin trading to sustain themselves. The CIA saw the two divisions as a useful asset for intelligence on China and raids across the border. Langley adopted the Kuomintang soldiers as its first secret army. But the glue in the deal was CIA help, through its offshoot, Air America airline, in trafficking the Kuomintang's drugs. The relationship intensified with the war in Vietnam and the CIA's patronage of local hill tribes in Burma's Golden Triangle. Heroin remained the currency of these relationships, and the CIA continued playing its facilitating role despite being fully aware that the drug was eventually traded on the streets of America and among U.S. soldiers in Vietnam.

Chiang Ching-kuo stepped out of the shadows, where secret policemen live, in 1969 when his father named him deputy premier. As Chiang Kai-shek's health declined in the 1970s his son took an increasingly prominent role. In 1970 Ching-kuo made an official visit to Washington as President Richard Nixon and Henry Kissinger were beginning to contemplate U.S. relations with China. From their questions Ching-kuo got an idea of what was in the wind and began thinking about how Taiwan should react. He went on to New York after his Washington meetings and was to give a speech to a business council. As Ching-kuo entered the Plaza Hotel two men with guns jumped out from behind a pillar. One, Peter Huang Wen Hsiung, fired a shot that narrowly missed Ching-kuo's head.

Chiang Ching-kuo became Taiwan's premier in 1972 and began promoting some moderate reforms, such as cracking down on corrupt officials and even, for the first time, making public most provisions of the national budget. His attitude toward political opponents of the Kuomintang was still as vitriolic as ever, though, and his spy network in the United States was becoming so pervasive as to be dangerous to U.S.-Taiwan relations. Only Ching-kuo's long relations with the CIA prevented, for example, his spies' pursuit of U.S. nuclear weapons knowledge from becoming conclusively damaging incidents.

Chiang Kai-shek died in April 1975, and two years later, March 1978, Ching-kuo assumed the presidency of the Republic of China. Washington's shift of formal diplomatic relations from Taipei to Beijing later that year was not unexpected, but it focused Ching-kuo's mind on how best to ensure Taiwan's security. The coming to power in Beijing of Ching-kuo's old dormitory companion from Moscow days, Deng Xiaoping, and China's evident turn toward opening up and economic change made change on Taiwan more important yet. Chiang Ching-kuo began aligning himself with a more liberal wing of the Kuomintang, much to the alarm of party hard-liners, most of them mainlanders.

When Chiang Ching-kuo was told in December 1979 that opposition politicians planned a rally in Kaohsiung to mark International Human Rights Day, he insisted troops must not be used to quell the demonstrators. If attacked, police must not retaliate, he said. Those orders were largely followed, but government agents in the crowd played a role in instigating violence. Many people were injured, among them several policemen whose injuries were played up by government media. There was an outraged backlash from conservative elements within the Kuomintang. They argued the Kaohsiung Incident showed the kind of strife that might engulf the island if liberalization continued. Ching-kuo decided to launch a major crackdown against the leaders of the Kaohsiung demonstration primarily to try to stop the Kuomintang from splitting into factions. He insisted, though, on open trials, to the annoyance of the conservatives. The Kaohsiung Incident and the subsequent persecution of the leaders of the pro-democracy movement gave birth to the modern Democratic Progressive Party. The Kaohsiung Incident launched the political careers of Annette Lu and Chen Shui-bian, and also fixed harsh attitudes toward the Kuomintang and authoritarianism in general among the current leaders of the DPP. Ching-kuo used his sop to the right wing of the Kuomintang over the Kaohsiung trials to move forward his liberalization agenda. In December 1980 he decreed that the Kuomintang must not deploy its usual palette of dirty tricks in upcoming legislative elections. The election was not fair. It could not be in a one-party state. But it did not have the same overpowering smell of corruption as had previous votes.

Chiang Ching-kuo's presidential term was due to end in 1984. There was no doubt he would be reselected by the National Assembly, but his declining health convinced him to pick a vice-president and successor early. Ching-kuo decided in 1983 that his heir should be a native Taiwanese, but he wanted one dedicated to the ultimate unification of the island with China. He was already considering the Taiwan provincial governor and former mayor of Taipei Lee Teng-hui, when Lee made a speech that sealed the deal. Lee denounced the idea of Taiwan independence and said the island could never forget its China heritage. Lee was invited to repeat his remarks to a meeting of the Kuomintang Standing Committee, the politburo. At the end Ching-kuo remarked, "Lee Teng-hui has performed very well," and everyone understood that the vice president and heir had been chosen. There is, then, great irony that Lee rose to leadership by damning the cause of Taiwan independence, for which he is now one of the most outspoken advocates. This Pauline conversion is a major reason why Lee is so bitterly disliked and mistrusted by devoted elements within the Kuomintang.

By 1987 Chiang Ching-kuo was nearly blind and confined to a wheelchair. The nearing end energized him to push ahead the reform process. He wanted to permit the formation of opposition parties, put an end to martial law, and restructure the Kuomintang so it could operate in a climate of democracy. On July 7, 1987, under pressure from Vice President Lee, the Legislative Yuan unanimously approved an end to martial law. On January 1, 1988, the government announced dates for the submission of applications to register political parties. At the same time restrictions were lifted on the number of newspapers allowed to publish on the island. Soon after, Ching-kuo ordered the lifting of the 40-year ban on visits to the mainland by people living on Taiwan.

On January 12, 1988, one of the young Turks of the Kuomintang, Harvard-trained Ma Ying-jeou, had just completed drafting a task force report on parliamentary reform. He planned to see Chiang Ching-kuo the next day to discuss the document. But that afternoon Ching-kuo died of a stomach hemorrhage while taking a nap.

After news of the death was announced Soong Mae-ling, Chiang Kai-shek's widow, made a pointed attempt to dictate the succession. She called the most senior party members and insisted to them that leadership of the Kuomintang could not possibly go to a native Taiwanese, in direct contradiction to what her stepson wanted. The party leaders realized they must act swiftly or risk internal conflict in the Kuomintang. On January 27, 1988, Lee Teng-hui was chosen to be interim president and party leader.

And that was the end of four hundred years of prologue and the moment of birth of a new Taiwan.

Chapter Eighteen

STRATEGIC AMBIGUITY

President Richard Nixon grasped the challenge of securing a productive relationship with mainland China, both as an adjunct to extricating America from the Vietnam War on the basis of a new security alliance in Asia and as a counterbalance to the Soviet Union. Nixon's national security adviser, Henry Kissinger, traveled to Beijing in July 1971, and he met both Premier Zhou Enlai and Communist Party chairman Mao Zedong. There is a frequently recounted story from those groundbreaking meetings that Kissinger does not mention in his memoirs and whose provenance is beyond discovery. It is said that during initial getting-to-know-you talks with Zhou, Kissinger asked what the premier thought were the last repercussions of the 1789 French Revolution. Zhou, the story goes, thought for awhile and then replied: "It is too early to tell." This message to Kissinger that he was dealing with a culture that viewed objectives in a very different time frame from that of the United States was reinforced in the meeting with Mao. Kissinger tried to get from the Chinese leader a commitment that the Taiwan issue would be dealt with peacefully. Mao said it was difficult to give such a commitment on a matter of "internal" Chinese politics, but Beijing would agree to work for that objective. Later Mao added that he believed China could "do without" Taiwan for a hundred years, but he thought that in the end the matter would have to be dealt with by force.

In the run-up to Nixon's visit to China in 1972 and the concluding Shanghai Communiqué, Beijing established the framework in which it wanted

Washington to deal with Taiwan. Beijing refused to contemplate any reference to "two Chinas," "one China, one Taiwan," an "independent Taiwan," or that "the status of Taiwan remains to be determined." It is still uncertain whether Beijing could have been moved on any of these matters had Nixon and Kissinger had a mind to press firmly. Their overriding concern was U.S. interests in promoting strategic security in Asia. Taiwan figured in the Shanghai Communiqué only to the extent that it impinged on that aim. The salient section of that statement said: "The United States acknowledges that all Chinese on either side of the Taiwan Strait maintain there is but one China and Taiwan is a part of China. The United States government does not challenge that position. It reaffirms its interest in a peaceful settlement of the Taiwan question by the Chinese themselves."[1]

It is worth noting that Chinese versions of the communiqué have rendered the word "acknowledges" into characters more accurately translated as "accepts." This implies that Washington agrees with and supports the concept that Taiwan is part of China. The English wording says only that America observes that others accept that Taiwan is part of one China. On many occasions Beijing has pulled its translation out of the desk drawer to criticize Washington for going back on its word. The true import of the communiqué is fairly simple. America said it has no national interest in either helping Taiwan remain independent or in fostering unification. That is up to the people of the island and the mainland. The United States does have a strategic national interest, however, and one that it would maintain, in ensuring that whatever resolution is achieved on the Taiwan issue is arrived at peacefully.

This was the moment when the United States could have set down its marker and stood by the position that Taiwan's legal position had remained unresolved since the end of the Second World War. Implicit in the Shanghai Communiqué is that the Republic of China had sovereignty over Taiwan. In the context of China's incomplete civil war, this supported Beijing's view that Taiwan was a "rebel province." Kissinger and Nixon could have insisted the matter of Taiwan's status be dealt with by the United Nations and a plebiscite of the island's people, as had been considered by previous administrations. They did not do so in part because their approach to China was dominated by thoughts of the cold war and Vietnam. The Taiwan issue appeared a relatively small matter in comparison with the titanic struggle with the Soviet Union. At the same time, there was no unavoidable moral necessity to side with the people of Taiwan. The regimes in both Beijing and Taipei insisted Taiwan was part of China. The Taiwanese people had no voice and the island's independence movement was evident only among exiles and expatriates because of the Kuomintang's repression at home. The Taiwanese were thus never heard from at this critical moment. Nevertheless, this was the lost opportunity when the current standoff could have been averted or forestalled by more rigorous adherence by Nixon and Kissinger to the dictates of Taiwan's unresolved legal status.

The immediate result of Nixon's visit to China was the establishment of diplomatic liaison offices by each country in the other's capital. The United States still recognized the Republic of China in Taipei as the government of China and kept its embassy there. Mao and Zhou pushed Nixon to switch Washington's recognition of the government of China from Taipei to Beijing, but this was too far for the president to go in one step without risking serious domestic political repercussions. Nixon and Kissinger said they would consider such a move during Nixon's second term as president when future political considerations did not weigh so heavily. The Watergate scandal and Nixon's resignation in mid-1974 intervened.

Between Kissinger's secret July 1971 visit to Beijing and Nixon's grand tour the following year Taiwan received another jolt. In October 1971, after many years of staving off the inevitable, Taiwan left the United Nations on the eve of being expelled when Beijing gained enough votes in the General Assembly to take over the China seat. In Taipei there was a belief that the elevation of Gerald Ford to the Oval Office after Nixon's resignation would stall for a while the disgraced president's project to switch diplomatic recognition of "China" from Taiwan to Beijing. But the continued presence of Henry Kissinger in the administration, now as secretary of state, left the Kuomintang regime uneasy. In an attempt to retain power and influence in the United States, Taipei advanced on two fronts. The first was a massive charm offensive aimed at anyone in American politics, administration, academia, business, sport, or anywhere else of influence who could be enticed into accepting Taipei's lavish hospitality. All kinds of civic, cultural, scientific, and other organizations were established to give the illusion of a strong web of connections between Taiwan and the United States. The second initiative by the Kuomintang was extraordinary and, in retrospect, foolish and counterproductive. The United States became the target of an extensive espionage operation by Taiwan sanctioned by Chiang Kai-shek's son and the boss of Taipei's security apparatus, Chiang Ching-kuo, who took over the island's leadership after his father's death in 1975. There were three main aims. One was to infiltrate the administration so as to be able to influence and, it was hoped, frustrate moves to shift diplomatic recognition to Beijing. Another was to gather intelligence on and counter Beijing's growing influence among the immigrant and expatriate ethnic Chinese communities in America. The third was to keep tabs on and when necessary act against the Taiwan independence movement in the United States. A number of such organizations were strongly supported in the communities of native Taiwanese exiles in the United States, most of whom had fled Kuomintang repression, and among students.

It took U.S. authorities a surprisingly long time to realize it was the target of a huge spy operation by an allied government. Taipei kept pressing Washington to be allowed to open more and more consulates, which acted as hubs for this network. Washington agreed, in part as an apology to the Chiang government for America's moves toward Beijing. By 1975 Taipei had 15 consulates in the United States, far more than any other nation.

Taipei's espionage efforts in the United States began to unravel in 1975 when the Federal Bureau of Investigation discovered Taiwan's senior defense attaché in Washington, Rear Admiral Chiu Hau-ku, trying to buy state-of-the-art Mark 37 torpedoes through a mafia contact in San Francisco. The collapse came in 1977 when another admiral, Wang Hsi-ling, the former head of Taiwan's National Security Bureau and posted as a "counselor" in Taipei's Washington embassy, was found to have riddled the American administration with spies and informants. In June 1977 Taiwan became the first Washington ally to be put on a secret list of nations considered "hostile" to U.S. national security. As such, Taiwan's diplomats and contacts in America became targets for FBI surveillance. This severely damaged Taiwan's reputation in official circles in Washington, especially as the full extent of the Kuomintang's corruption at home was becoming well known. Not only was it evident that the Kuomintang regime feasted on bribery, but the island had acquired the image of a refuge for criminals and triad gang bosses as well as a hub of opium and heroin trafficking. Had the FBI looked further than the Kuomintang's attempts to infiltrate Washington's corridors of power and seen the pressure and violence the island's spies directed at Taiwanese in America, especially members of the pro-independence movement, that reputation would have been sullied even further.

Jimmy Carter, who won the American presidency in 1976, needed no lessons on the iniquities of the Kuomintang. Carter first came across Chiang Kai-shek's style of administration as a young submarine officer in 1949. He later recalled berthing at ports along the China coast as the Communist armies closed in on the Kuomintang and seeing young boys and old men being dragooned into the Chiang Kai-shek's forces at bayonet point. When Carter surfaced as the Democrats' rival to Gerald Ford in 1976, the Kuomintang's efforts to suborn him were less brutal but just as inept. Carter wrote later:

> Taiwanese influence [in Washington] was very strong. Taiwanese lobbyists seemed able to prevail in shaping United States policy on this fundamental issue in the Far East. I began to see how effective they could be after I won a few primaries in 1976. A flood of invitations came to my relatives and neighbors around Plains [his hometown in Georgia] for expense-paid vacation trips to Taipei. Those who succumbed to these blandishments were wined and dined by the Taiwan leaders, offered attractive gifts, and urged to influence me to forget about fulfilling American commitments to China. I was able to prevent embarrassing favors to my closest family members, but my opposition to the trips and entertainment endangered my relationships with some of my hometown friends.[2]

Carter's disdain for the Kuomintang, bordering on contempt, shines through his words. Yet on the matter of normalizing U.S. diplomatic relations with China he had to move by stealth. The true nature of the Kuomintang regime was not evident to the American public, which only saw an underdog threatened with life under a Communist dictatorship. And Taiwan's supporters—both those with genuine sentiments for the island and those who had been bought and paid for—were vocal and persistent in denouncing the commitment to give full diplomatic recognition to Beijing. A public opinion poll done for the *U.S. News and World Report* in 1978, and representative of several made at the time, showed 58 percent of respondents were opposed to recognizing Beijing as the government of China and abandoning Taipei.[3] Only 20 percent supported such a change, and the remaining 22 percent had no opinion.

Carter anticipated a strong public reaction to the recognition of Beijing, so the deed was done swiftly and in the dead of night. The terms with Beijing were agreed during the course of several visits to China by Carter's national security adviser, Zbigniew Brzezinski, in 1978.

On the night of December 16 the American ambassador in Taipei, Leonard Unger, was pulled out of a pre-Christmas ball at the American Officers' Club by a phone call from Washington. He was told to arrange an immediate audience with Chiang Ching-kuo. Unger was to tell the Taiwanese president that the United States would establish diplomatic relations with Beijing on January 1, 1979, and that recognition would be withdrawn from Taipei. More than that, the Carter administration would in 1979 abrogate the mutual defense treaty with Taiwan. Chiang was roused from his bed about

2:30 in the morning and given the news. It was not a surprise, but the manner of its delivery irked.

In Beijing the new Chinese paramount leader, Deng Xiaoping, celebrated with a glass of California champagne. He had got almost all he could have hoped for. Washington's switch of diplomatic recognition was a major victory in itself, with Carter's commitment to end the military alliance with Taiwan and the prospect of decreased arms sales to the island encouraging bonuses. Carter had stuck on only one point. The ambiguous wording on Washington's view of the "one China" question that had been conjured up by Henry Kissinger in 1971 remained. But Deng, in an elaborate toast, was moved to say: "I feel certain that the far-reaching influence the establishment of diplomatic relations between our two countries exerts upon defense of world peace will become more and more evident with the passage of time."[4]

Strong elements among the American public and in the Congress were less certain that the future was so bright, especially for the people of Taiwan. Carter's statement that the deal with Beijing "will not jeopardize the well-being of the people of Taiwan" appeared to ring hollow. Attention focused on Carter's abandonment of the mutual defense treaty with Taiwan and early in 1979 work began in Congress to fashion a replacement. The Taiwan Relations Act was approved by both houses of Congress on April 10. Support was bipartisan and overwhelming. The act passed by 339 votes to 50 in the House of Representatives and by 85 to 4 in the Senate. The tone of the act in many respects followed the thoughts of the governor of California, Ronald Reagan, who would become president a few months later. In a speech early in 1979 Reagan warned Beijing:

> We wish to live in peace with you, and we shall not interfere in your affairs if you do not interfere in ours. We can help you to modernize and update your economy, and we will do so, consistent with our national security objectives. But, when it comes to those 17 million people on Taiwan, we emphatically state that so long as they wish to retain their independence in the world, so long as they declare their unwillingness to be either "liberated" by you or unilaterally "reunited" with you—then so long will they also have the specific and clear support of the United States of America.[5]

The Taiwan Relations Act did two things. It attempted to assure that American support for the island's defense would continue and that diplomatic links would be retained with Taiwan at a high though superficially informal level. Congress required the United States to make available to Taiwan defensive weapons in quality and quantities "necessary to enable Taiwan to maintain sufficient self-defense capabilities." What was necessary and appropriate was to be decided jointly by the administration and Congress. This is significant. What aid should or should not be given to Taiwan is not to be decided at the whim of the president, who, like Jimmy Carter, might have scant regard for the island and its people. The president was required to inform Congress promptly of any threat from China to Taiwan. Should that happen, the United States would take "appropriate action" to protect Taiwan's independence. To maintain diplomatic relations with Taipei, the act mandated the establishment of the American Institute in Taiwan, which functions as an embassy in all but name.

The act was welcomed in Taipei. It is in many ways more firmly worded that the mutual defense treaty it replaced. There were quibbles, however, stemming from the Kuomintang's own "one China" culture. Chiang Ching-kuo and his officials didn't like the constant references to "Taiwan," which suggested the island was a separate state. And they were unhappy that the act excluded the offshore islands of Kinmen and Mazu for similar reasons.

The reaction in Beijing was more intense and adverse. Deng Xiaoping told visiting members of the Senate Foreign Relations Committee, "The inference of the U.S. act was to negate the political basis for normalization [of relations] and the thrust of the act was support for Taiwan and inconsistent with the idea of one China."

Policy toward China and Taiwan in the early years of the Reagan administration was complicated by the presence of Alexander Haig as secretary of state. Haig's only concern was developing a strategic alliance with China that would keep as many Soviet divisions as possible tied up in the Russian Far East and away from the European theater. He saw Taiwan as a pointless irritant in this equation. In May 1982 Haig went so far as to recommend that arms sales to Taiwan be terminated as they only aggravated Beijing and deflected attention from the main objective of confronting the Soviet Union. That view infected the State Department, even after Haig's resignation a few weeks later. These sensitivities were reflected, though not as brutally, in the now-notorious Sino-U.S. Joint Communiqué issued on August 17, 1982, and known as the Shanghai II Communiqué. This document said:

> The United States government . . . does not seek to carry out a long-term policy of arms sales to Taiwan—that is, arms sales to Taiwan will not exceed either in qualitative or in quantitative terms the level of those supplied in recent years since the establishment of diplomatic relations between the United

> States and China, and that it intends to reduce gradually its sales of arms to Taiwan, leading over a period of time to a final resolution.[6]

To Taiwan's American friends, such as Senator Barry Goldwater, this looked like yet another betrayal of the island and its people. "It's one more little country we have double-crossed," said the senator. Reagan and his officials emphasized again and again that there was a caveat, a condition, on the U.S. reduction of arms sales to Taiwan. It was predicated on Beijing pursuing a fundamentally peaceful policy toward an agreement with Taiwan. Should Beijing fail in this regard, then Washington would pursue a more vigorous and activist definition of the Taiwan Relations Act.

Beijing, then as now, continued to refuse to make a commitment not to use force against Taiwan, arguing no state could make such a promise on a matter of "internal" security. The Chinese government regularly complains, though, that Washington has failed to live up to its pledge to phase out weapons sales to Taiwan.

Often ignored or consigned to a footnote is that while the United States was negotiating the 1982 joint communiqué with Beijing, Washington also established with Taipei what has become known as the six assurances. These are:

- The United States will not set a date for ending arms sales to Taiwan.
- Washington sees no mediation role for the United States between the two sides of the Strait. Since the election of Chen Shui-bian, however, Beijing has tried with some success to involve Washington as a restraining influence on the Taiwanese president.
- The United States will not exert pressure on Taiwan to enter negotiations with Beijing.
- There is no change in the United States' position on the sovereignty of Taiwan. That is, Washington acknowledges the existence of China's claim without specifying its own view.
- The United States plans no revisions to or withdrawal of the Taiwan Relations Act.
- The United States will not agree to any prior consultations with Beijing before making arms sales to Taiwan.[7]

By the end of Ronald Reagan's presidency in 1988 the ever-turbulent three-cornered relationship of the United States, China, and Taiwan was beginning to change again. The death of Chiang Ching-kuo in January 1988 opened the doors to full-scale political reform on Taiwan.

While Deng Xiaoping and Jiang Zemin had been preoccupied with overseeing China's return to capitalism in the 1980s and 1990s, a process brutally interrupted by the national uprising spurred by the Tiananmen Square student demonstrations in 1989, the whole political construction of Taiwan had changed, and with it the essential ingredients of future cross-straits relations. When the Kuomintang ruled Taiwan as a colonial elite managing a one-party military dictatorship, there was a degree of confidence in Beijing that unification would be ultimately achieved. The Communists and the Kuomintang hated each other, but it was the hatred of rival brothers. The two parties knew each other well and shared the same objectives. They were the opposite sides of the same Stalinist coin. Deng Xiaoping and Chiang Ching-kuo had, after all, been classmates in Moscow. They had learned the trade of governing from the same masters. And while the unreconstructed, mainlander-dominated Kuomintang remained in power on Taiwan, it was just as dedicated to the island's unification with China as were the Communists in Beijing. The only question was the terms, not the intent. Indeed, the Kuomintang as one-party dictators reacted even more violently and repressively against Taiwanese independentists than they did against Communist infiltrators or fellow travelers.

Fundamental political change on Taiwan began in the late 1970s. Chiang Ching-kuo was forced, very reluctantly, to concede that the Kuomintang's dream of regaining power on the mainland had become a fantasy. The events that forced home this message started with Taiwan's withdrawal from the United Nations in 1971—a few hours in advance of being expelled—and became fixed when the United States shifted diplomatic recognition from Taipei to Beijing at the beginning of 1979. From that flowed the acceptance, as unappetizing as it was, that Taiwan was now the home of the exiled mainlanders. Colonial rule could not therefore be sustained, and the younger Chiang, egged on by Washington, began a slow process of reform. It started with native Taiwanese being appointed in increasing numbers to senior positions in the governing network, though for many years ultimate power remained with mainlanders. Pro-democracy demonstrations by native Taiwanese in the late 1970s, and especially the Kaohsiung Incident in 1979, gave impetus to the reform imperative. Before his death Chiang Ching-kuo lifted the ban on opposition parties in 1986, and martial law was ended in 1987. Just as important, in 1988 he chose as his successor Lee Teng-hui, the island's first political leader to be native Taiwanese.

Lee Teng-hui came from that elder generation of Taiwanese who grew up on the island during the most stable and constructive period of Japanese colonial rule in the 1930s and early 1940s. Lee was among the brightest and best of this generation of Japan's subjects, and he benefited from what was probably the best educational system in Asia at the time. Lee, like others—among them Peng Ming-min, who would later oppose him in the 1996 Taiwanese elections—appreciated what Japan had to offer but remained frustrated by the islanders' second-class status in the empire. This generally positive experience of Japanese colonialism colored their views when Taiwan was handed over to the Kuomintang in 1945. Japanese rule may have been stern, but it was efficient and not corrupt. The Kuomintang, in contrast, arrived as a rapacious rabble and proceeded to impose the worst kind of colonial rule on Taiwan. Lee's response was to first toy with communism, but he then swiftly chose a course of hiding his true Taiwanese nationalist sentiments while working his way up through the Kuomintang hierarchy. Peng also could have been a local star of Kuomintang rule. Unlike Lee, however, Peng was temperamentally unable to hide his true feelings. He was tried and imprisoned after producing a manifesto for Taiwan's independence. He managed to escape to Sweden and then became a law professor in the United States. Peng returned to Taiwan only after martial law was lifted and Lee Teng-hui was president.

Lee Teng-hui's accession to the presidency in 1988 was the moment when the chances of a negotiated union between Taiwan and Communist China shrank to near nothingness. It was the end of mainlander colonialism on the island and the beginning of a process, called "Taiwanization," that affected all aspects of life. It was a slow process at first as native Taiwanese found their voice. But the realization that Taiwanese had finally achieved ascendancy in their own home soon infected the arts, the media, schools and universities, and even everyday discourse, where the local dialect, Minnan, began to supplant the Kuomintang-imposed Mandarin.

Lee's revolution was most evident in politics. He accelerated the reform process and established a timetable for full democracy. In 1991 he reconstructed the Legislative Yuan, which had become an extraordinary and laughable anachronism. The Chiangs, father and son, had insisted that this body was the true parliament for the whole of China. So it was made up of members elected on the mainland in 1947. When elections and other aspects of democracy were suspended on Taiwan under martial law, the original parliamentarians stayed in office until, after several decades, death inevitably took its toll. When this happened, other people from among the mainland exiles and from the same regions of China were appointed to fill their places. If suitable people from the right districts of China could not be found, legislators were appointed from among the Chinese diaspora in North America, Europe, or Southeast Asia. In December 1991 Lee forced the remaining mainland members of the Legislative Yuan to resign, including the then prime minister. New elections were held for Taiwan constituencies only.

Lee further simplified and localized the Taiwanese political system by doing away with another Qing dynasty relic: the Taiwan province and its administration, which Chiang Kai-shek allowed to continue as part of the mythology that the Kuomintang was the true government of China and the island was merely a province in that nation. Lee argued successfully that with a trimmed down parliament geared only to the governing of Taiwan, the cumbersome and expensive provincial government structure was superfluous. Ending the all-China Legislative Yuan and dismantling the Taiwan provincial structure scandalized Beijing, where these moves were seen as a clear act of separating the island from its history as an appendage to the mainland. The last governor of Taiwan province, James Soong, was also enraged by what he saw as a purposeful and personal political attack by Lee. Soong had built a substantial political following based largely on his ability to dispense patronage as provincial governor. Soong was working toward national leadership and thought, with good reason, that Lee was intent on destroying his political base of support. To try to keep his ambitions alive, Soong later launched his own political organization, the People First Party.

Jiang Zemin and Communist leadership in Beijing began to perceive in the early 1990s that Lee Teng-hui was not only not a Stalinist with familiar and predictable motivations but an out-and-out Taiwanese independentist. Their response, though, was seriously misconceived, perhaps as a result of self-indoctrination by their own propaganda. They maintained, and apparently believed, that "Taiwanese compatriots" were secretly yearning for unification with the mainland. Beijing said on numerous occasions that the islanders had been misled by a few unscrupulous "splittist" politicians like Lee Teng-hui. Without this divisive influence, Taiwanese natural love for the motherland would revive. Beijing also perceived Washington working behind the scenes to forever sever Taiwan from the mainland. Beijing saw secessionist schemes when in June 1995 Lee was invited to visit his alma mater in the United States, Cornell University, and Washington gave him a visa. America's insistence that this was an unofficial visit and that no breech of Washington's pledges to Beijing to downgrade relations with Taiwan had occurred did not convince the Communist Party leaders. They chose to see Lee's visit as a dangerous provocation.

Lee's program of democratic transition culminated with the island's first free and fair presidential elections in 1996. Beijing was perplexed about what to do. Both candidates for the presidency, Lee and Peng, were clear independentists. There was no good election result possible from the point of view of the mainland government. It opted for a demonstration of rage. So in the weeks before the 1996 election Beijing ordered the firing of several unarmed missiles into the sea approaches to the island's main ports, Kaohsiung and Keelung. The purpose was to show how easily Taiwan could be blockaded and the island's trade brought to a halt. At the same time the People's Liberation Army, Navy, and Air Force held an exercise on Dongshan Island off the coast of Fujian province simulating an invasion of Taiwan. The immediate aim was to stop the rot of democratization on Taiwan and show the islanders what awaited them if they allowed the creep toward recognized independence to continue.

Beijing misjudged the timbre of the times on Taiwan and the spirit of self-determination that had infected the island. Lee Teng-hui won the election with 54 percent of the vote in a close contest with the DPP's Peng Ming-min, and became the first freely elected leader of a predominantly Chinese community in China's entire four thousand–year history. The 1996 democratic elections completed the change in the nature of the question of cross-straits relations that started with the death of Chiang Ching-kuo. There was never an appetite among Taiwanese for unification with the mainland, and any thought of union under Communist sovereignty was totally inedible. For newly emancipated Taiwanese, the question was how best to maintain their independence, enhance their extraordinary economic success, and reinforce their aspirations as a distinct people. The majority of Taiwanese in those years translated these desires cautiously into support for the status quo. That meant maintaining the island's opaque legal status and actual independence while keeping Beijing firmly at arm's length and avoiding provocation. Voters therefore looked at leadership candidates with an eye to whether they could be trusted to manage the China file with wisdom and caution. However, as confidence grew, the mood of the islanders began an inexorable shift toward identifying themselves primarily as Taiwanese rather than Chinese and growing increasingly impatient to claim the trappings and legal reality of statehood.

This result perplexed Communist Party leaders in China. They began to be dimly aware that their policy toward Taiwanese unification was failing and that the islanders were drifting ever further away. This was despite China proclaiming since 1979 its preference for peaceful unification and, from Beijing's point of view, generous offers of autonomy as well as economic benefits. And now, in 1996, its threats of invasion had been equally ineffectual. Taiwan had completed the transition to democracy and elected as president a man whom Beijing was convinced would continue to make hopes of a negotiated union less and less realistic.

What might have changed these divergent courses would have been for Beijing to set aside or water down its "one China" principle. But it was unable to do that. Powerful voices in Beijing held that to deal with Taiwan as an equal entity, to negotiate without Taipei first submitting to Beijing's sovereignty, would breech the unity of the state. This would lead inevitably to the dismemberment of China and the collapse of the Communist Party. Following the same logic, the quest to own Taiwan could not be abandoned, even if it meant seizing only the territory of Taiwan and not the hearts of the island's people.

While China was launching missiles into the sea and honing its skills at seaborne invasion in the run-up to Taiwan's 1996 election, something happened that concentrated minds in Beijing on the full scope of the task of capturing the island. U.S. President Bill Clinton saw China's show of force as a test of America's will as much as a threat to the voters among the island's 23 million people. Clinton responded to Beijing's war games by ordering two aircraft carriers, the *Independence* and the *Nimitz,* together with their protective battle groups of destroyers, frigates, and submarines, to show the flag in water close to the island.

There could not have been a more clear statement to either China or the islanders that even an American president like Clinton, less inclined to take military options than others, would honor Washington's commitment to aid the defense of Taiwan. In Beijing this demonstration of intent by Washington clarified what China had to do to assure its future power and influence in Asia, of which its Taiwan ambitions were only a part. The Taiwan question came into focus in Beijing as part of the much larger issue of Washington's "hegemonic" efforts to curb and contain China's rise as a regional and, perhaps, world power. Apart from its Pacific Ocean aircraft carrier battle groups, Washington had upward of 100,000 troops based in Japan and South Korea. It was also beginning to discuss with Japan the development of a theater missile defense system that would include Taiwan under its umbrella. The publicly stated reason for this defense system was protection against any rogue attacks from North Korea. But it was an open secret that the ultimate purpose was to deter Beijing from using its batteries of intercontinental ballistic missiles.

China's military planners had begun to see the difficult road ahead when they, like much of the rest of the world, watched on television the first Gulf War in 1991. They were stunned by the significant battlefield advantage America had developed through precision munitions and with surveillance, information, and command and control technology. China's five million–strong primarily infantry army, most of whose members were by this stage of the country's economic revolution far more involved in entrepreneurial enterprises than military matters, was clearly woefully inadequate and ill prepared.

The political imperative in Beijing to be ready to invade Taiwan became a handy template for the reconstruction of the armed forces.

Washington's intervention in the 1996 saber rattling, however, made it abundantly clear that China could not have freedom of political movement in Asia unless it had the ability to deter or defeat American forces. At first China set out to reform and reequip its armed forces by seeking to match American capabilities. In the mid-1990s China was seeking to acquire its own aircraft carriers. This was in addition to the modern warships and aircraft it bought mostly from Russia in deals that included technology transfer and manufacturing rights. Computer technology with both civilian and military applications was scooped up by Chinese agents. Many useful gadgets could be bought on the open market. What couldn't be bought was often stolen or acquired through bribery. China admits to a military budget of U.S. $20 billion a year in this period, but many western analysts put the true figure at more than double that.

After the failure of its demonstration with rockets and a mock invasion during Taiwan's 1996 election, China reassessed its approach to military upgrading and reform. It decided that at this juncture in the military reconstruction process it didn't need to have its own aircraft carrier battle groups in order to be able to counter this American capacity. Beijing's purchases from Russia began to lean heavily in the direction of state-of-the-art weaponry designed to defeat American battlefield technology as well as to achieve superiority over the powerful, largely American-equipped Taiwanese forces. China bought from Moscow Su–30 fighter-bombers, Kilo-class submarines, anti-ship cruise missiles, and anti-aircraft missiles. "Missiles, aircraft and submarines all are means that can be used to attack aircraft carriers," Major General Huang Bin, a professor at the People's Liberation Army National Defense University, said in May 2002. "We have the ability to deal with an aircraft carrier that dares to get into our range of fire."[8] Chinese plans for invading Taiwan, Huang said, included deterring or defeating any American forces sent to help defend the island. "The United States likes vainglory; if one of its aircraft carriers should be attacked and destroyed, people in the United States would begin to complain and quarrel loudly, and the U.S. president would find the going harder and harder," Huang said.[9]

By the summer of 2005 China's submarine fleet numbered about 50 boats with the expectation by western analysts it would have about 80 vessels by the end of the decade. Many of these boats were elderly diesel-electric conventional submarines, but were being armed with modern missiles and torpedoes that could be fired while submerged. These represented a significant threat to the U.S. Navy, which had allowed its anti-submarine and mine countermeasure abilities to deteriorate after the end cold war and amid immediate pressures of the war on terror and the threats of nuclear weapons proliferation. By the summer of 2005 American military planners were admitting publicly that the Chinese submarine force was already a deterrent to the United States swiftly responding to a threat on Taiwan by dispatching aircraft carrier battle groups, as it had done in 1996. "They [the Chinese] are building their force to deter and delay our ability to intervene in a Taiwan crisis," Eric McVadon, a former military attaché at the U.S. embassy in Beijing, told the *New York Times* in April 2005. "What they have done is cleverly develop some capabilities that have the prospect of attacking our niche vulnerabilities."[10]

American government military analysts were taken by surprise by the speed and extent of China's military buildup. In the mid-1990s they had calculated it would be several decades before the People's Liberation Army could attack Taiwan with any expectation of success. But by 2005 the Pentagon and CIA said in their annual reports to Congress they believed China was not only an immediate threat to Taiwan, but was fast becoming a challenge to U.S. military supremacy in the Asia-Pacific region. These concerns, echoed with increasing frequency by other administration officials, were usually voiced in polite language because of Washington's continued hope that Beijing would put decisive pressure on the North Korean regime of Kim Jong-il to abandon his nuclear weapons program. But Washington's belief that Beijing aimed to refashion the military balance in Asia was expressed in pointed terms on several occasions. In June 2005 U.S. defense secretary Donald Rumsfeld in a speech to a regional security conference in Singapore said China's military buildup threatened the delicate security balance in Asia. "Since no nation threatens China, one wonders: why this growing investment?" Rumsfeld said.[11] Behind the scenes Washington began taking more direct action. Since the Second World War about 60 percent of American naval forces had been oriented toward the Atlantic Ocean and the threat from the Soviet Union while 40 percent were based on Pacific Ocean ports. In 2005 Washington began reversing that deployment so that 60 percent of its navy was in a position to confront China's naval power.

Chapter Nineteen

THE PERILS OF DEMOCRACY

The 1990s were a particularly testing time in Sino-U.S. relations. In Washington there was a profound change of presidential style when Bill Clinton defeated the patrician senior George Bush in 1992. In Beijing there was also new and insecure leadership under Jiang Zemin after a shake-up following the 1989 national uprising spurred by the Tiananmen Square student demonstrations. Public opinion in the United States, as in the rest of the western world, was appalled at the imposition of martial law and the bloody end to the demonstrations. Many politicians and analysts in the West, and especially the United States, believed that political reform would inevitably and speedily follow economic liberalization in China. At Tiananmen Square the Chinese leadership appeared to be saying this was an overly simplistic judgment on a complex and culturally secure society for which western rules do not apply. Only children from privileged families were allowed entry into universities that fed the Tiananmen protest. The Chinese Communist Party was prepared to slaughter its own children rather than contemplate political reform and was confident it could triumph. The western analysis of the Tiananmen Square events was clouded by being narrowly focused. Western television and other journalists only had access to the area in and around the square. They did not get the broad picture that the students had inspired a nationwide uprising in China against Communist Party corruption and abuse of power. China was rushing toward total civic collapse and probably civil war. Deng Xiaoping and other party elders reluctantly emerged from retirement to order the imposition of martial law and the June 4, 1989, crackdown. Outrage in the West at China's abuse of human rights and the Communist Party's evident determination to resist political reform spawned years of trade and diplomatic sanctions. At the same time the opening up of China's economy to outside trade and investment had given substance to the argument for "constructive engagement" as an agent of civic reform in China over the long term. Many western and Asian companies and governments understood that the period of sanctions against China provided a great opportunity. The Chinese government would remember and give advantages to people who had stood by it in tough times. Public disgust in America against the Tiananmen Massacre, as it is known, did not abate for several years. Formal reconstruction of the Beijing-Washington axis did not begin until October 1997 with the visit of Jiang Zemin, untainted by involvement in the Tiananmen crackdown, to Washington, followed by Bill Clinton's visit to China the following June. It was during this latter visit in 1998 that Clinton set out his controversial "Three Nos." These were that the United States would not support the concept of "one China, one Taiwan" or "two Chinas," it would not support "Taiwanese independence," and it would not back Taiwan's membership in international organizations whose prime qualification was representation of a recognized nation-state. Clinton and his officials reiterated, however, America's paramount interest was in the Taiwan dispute being resolved peacefully.

Clinton's Three Nos did not change in any substantial way Washington's policy going back to the early 1970s. The tone and timing, though, seemed to be overly generous toward Beijing. Taiwan had, with the presidential election in 1996, completed its transition to democracy, a style of government the United States says it has a moral duty to promote worldwide. Yet here was Clinton giving aid and comfort to the one-party regime in Beijing that not only rigorously opposed reform in China but that remained adamant that it had the right to invade democratic Taiwan. Washington's perceived long-term interest in promoting sound, functional relations with China had again outweighed the alliance with little Taiwan.

The context of Clinton's three pledges to Beijing was negotiations to allow China's entry into the World Trade Organization. After the 1989 uprising in China, which displayed the fragility of economic reform, the view hardened in Washington, Europe, and the rest of the industrialized world that every encouragement should be given to draw Beijing into the community of nations. Luring China into living by the rules and courtesies of international trade and discourse would, the argument went, begin to make China a reliable partner.

Membership in the WTO and other collegial organizations would also require the entrenchment of the rule of law, at least on matters of international commerce, within China. Inevitably this would infect domestic, civil, and criminal law and with that infection would come pressure for an accountable and representative government.

Hard-liners within the Communist Party in Beijing imagined just the same scenario and didn't like it one bit. They argued that WTO membership would allow foreigners to control strategic aspects of Chinese economic policy and that the authority of the party would be undermined, perhaps irrevocably. The champion of WTO membership, premier and economic policy tsar Zhu Rongji, who never quite fit into the mold of party loyalists, frequently seemed beleaguered and uncertain of victory. Early 1999 was an especially bad time for Zhu. In April he traveled to Washington to try to hammer out an agreed framework for China's entry into the WTO. The deal was not yet to be had, particularly on issues like a timetable for China to remove its subsidies to agriculture. This was of prime concern to Beijing, which was already facing serious problems of rural unemployment and unrest. Zhu returned to China in mid-April cloaked in an aura of failure.

The prospect of Sino-U.S. relations running off the rails increased the following month, May, when an American aircraft involved in action by the North Atlantic Treaty Organization against Serbs in the former Yugoslavia bombed the Chinese embassy in Belgrade. Washington apologized and insisted the bombing had been an accident. The officers selecting targets had been working from an outdated map of Belgrade, said Washington's spokesmen. Chinese public opinion was not convinced. Tens of thousands of people went on a rampage, attacking the American embassy in Beijing and some of its regional consulates. The party leaders hesitated. The vehemence of the anti-Americanism in the crowds both surprised and worried them. They contemplated that if they attempted to suppress the demonstrations the rioters might turn their anger from the U.S. diplomatic missions to the Zhongnanhai Communist Party leader's compound next to the Forbidden City. The alternative was to attempt to control the protests by supporting them. This is what happened. Government buses and marshals were provided for the rioters. Within a few days and after a good deal of damage to the American missions the rage was spent.

On both sides the events of April and May 1999 gave a stark picture of what could be lost in U.S.-China relations. It concentrated minds and re-energized the trade negotiations, and in the following months a deal was concluded that became the key piece in China's negotiations with other

WTO would-be partners. China became a member of the WTO at the beginning of 2000 and thus its Clinton-era relations with Washington ended in an upbeat mood.

As the turn of the century and the new millennium approached, Beijing had some hopes that the second presidential elections on Taiwan in 2000 would produce a much more respectful administration with which it could do business. The need for military action might be avoided. Lee Teng-hui could not run again. In his place the Kuomintang would have as its candidate the vice president, Lien Chan. Lien, a mainlander not infected by Lee's Taiwanese nationalism, looked to Beijing like a man with whom China could do business. Even better, Lien's running mate was likely to be James Soong, the ousted governor of the now-defunct Taiwan province. Soong was also a mainlander, but with a passion for unification and a documented vehement opposition to Taiwanese nationalism. Public opinion polls in Taiwan indicated that a Lien-Soong ticket would handily defeat the Democratic Progressive Party candidate Chen Shui-bian and his running mate, the often unwisely outspoken advocate of Taiwanese independence Annette Lu.

Beijing's dream ticket fell apart because Lien and Soong harbored deep and mutual personal dislikes. Soong believed he should be the Kuomintang's lead candidate, but his intemperate internal lobbying alienated the party's mainstream. He was expelled from the party a year before the election, together with 21 officials who supported him. The Kuomintang then began a campaign to blacken Soong's name. Soong, now running for the presidency as an independent, was accused of siphoning off millions of dollars in Kuomintang party funds while he was the party's secretary general. But the mud being thrown by the Kuomintang probably smeared both camps. It not only besmirched Soong but reinforced in the minds of voters a major domestic issue: the "black gold" corrupt relations between the Kuomintang and criminals.

In the weeks before the island's presidential elections in 2000 Beijing was less overtly aggressive than it had been in 1996 but was equally threatening. China's premier, Zhu Rongji, gave a bellicose speech in which he warned Taiwanese that if they did not soon agree to a timetable for unification with the mainland, Beijing would be forced to invade. "No matter who comes to power in Taiwan in the election, we won't allow the independence of Taiwan to happen," Zhu said in a televised speech. "If the Taiwan independence forces come to power it could trigger a war between the two sides of the strait," he warned.[1] Those threats were as counterproductive as the firing of missiles had been in

1996. On March 20, 2000, election night, Chen Shui-bian of the avowedly pro-independence Democratic Progressive Party became Taiwanese president. His victory with only 39 percent of the vote, though, undoubtedly owed more to the split in the Kuomintang camp between Lien and Soong than to voter revulsion at the threats of the Chinese prime minister.

In his inauguration speech two months after the election, Chen Shui-bian, in an effort to calm Beijing and ease Washington's fears that he was a loose canon, departed significantly from his party's pro-independence policy. Chen was also undoubtedly conscious that as he had won the election with a minority of the vote, he did not have a mandate to pursue the DPP's policy with full vigor. The new president said he would not declare formal independence for Taiwan unless China attacked the island. He pledged not to change the official name of the state from the Republic of China. Chen said he would not initiate a referendum on Taiwan's political status. He promised to keep in place two trappings left over from mainlander domination of the government: the Guidelines for National Unification, which involved a purposefully ambiguous definition of the "one China principle," and the National Unification Council. In some ways Chen adopted a more conciliatory approach to Beijing than had his predecessor, Lee Teng-hui. One of Chen's promises was that he would not include in Taiwan's constitution any requirement that negotiations with China take place on a basis of equality. This stemmed from a remark by Lee to a German radio reporter in 1999 that any substantive talks with Beijing must be on the basis of a "special state-to-state relationship." In other words, there could be no talks while China stuck to the "one China principle."

None of this was enough for the Chinese Communist leaders. They wanted Chen to clearly distance himself from Lee's "state-to-state" pronouncement and affirm the new Taiwan administration's commitment to the "one China principle." Beijing said Taiwan had accepted what is known as the "1992 consensus" on the "one China principle" and should offer a reaffirmation. Chen's officials denied there had been any consensus in 1992. Both sides had merely agreed that there was "one China," but reserved the right to decide for themselves what that included. Chen came under pressure from his supporters, who had no doubt in their own minds that China did not include Taiwan. A few weeks after the inauguration the new chairwoman of Taiwan's Mainland Affairs Council, Tsai Ing-wen, set out clearly that "we never accepted Beijing's 'one China principle.'"[2]

The rosy glow that bathed Beijing-Washington relations as the new millennium dawned did not last long either. In the United States recognition that

Beijing was bent on becoming a militarily significant force with the capacity to project power in Asia agitated the American establishment's always-conflicting views of China. George W. Bush, campaigning for the Republican nomination in 2000, said he saw China as a "strategic competitor" to the United States in the future. This was a purposeful contrast to Bill Clinton's view of China as a "strategic partner." Bush added that not enough had been done by Washington to ensure the security of Taiwan or to reward the island for its transition to democracy and economic achievements. However, institutional Washington began to influence Bush once he gained the Republican nomination and became president. He started to speak more strongly of the need to maintain good relations with Beijing. But an incident in April 2001 swung Bush back toward a more pro-Taiwan line. That month a U.S. reconnaissance plane on a regular flight down the China coast, listening in to PLA communications, was bumped and then forced to land by Chinese fighter jets. China's playing of the incident for publicity gain and its slow return of the detained crew—to say nothing of its acquisition of a plane loaded with American signals intelligence secrets—soured the Bush administration's view of China. Later the same month the administration approved a significant arms package sale to Taiwan. When interviewed about the return of the reconnaissance plane's crew, Bush made his seminal comment that his administration would do "whatever it took" to aid the defense of Taiwan including, it was strongly implied, the sending of U.S. forces if China invaded the island. When Taiwan's equally new President Chen sought to make a transit stop in the United States in May en route to Latin American, the ground rules imposed were far more liberal than those applied to previous Taiwanese official visitors. It was a message to Beijing that America's past promise to have no "official" links with Taiwan would be interpreted in light of the mood of the times. The more belligerence shown by China, the bigger the welcome mat that would be offered to visiting Taiwanese.

Chen in his inaugural speech had promised not to remove the trappings of Taiwan's mainland links brought to the island by the Kuomintang. But it quickly became apparent that he considered everything else fair game. Washington and Beijing both watched with concern as Chen began acting in ways that China characterized as promoting "creeping separatism." There was the increasing use of the local dialect, Minnan, for official purposes, a campaign for the "rectification of names"—essentially using the name "Taiwan" in place of "Republic of China" and promoting the island's own English renderings of Chinese names. There was a general policy of "de-Sinicization" starting with an emphasis on teaching in the schools Taiwanese history divorced from its mainland context.

Beijing became convinced that Washington was complicit in Taiwan's endeavors to give social and cultural depth and breadth to its de facto independence. It saw the ease with which Taiwan's defense minister Tang Yao-ming was able to visit the United States for a "private" conference in Florida in 2001 and then meet with America's deputy defense secretary Paul Wolfowitz and the assistant secretary of state James Kelly. In remarks to the privately sponsored conference both Wolfowitz and Kelly exhibited sentiments that were markedly more pro-Taiwan than had been those of officials of the previous administration. Over the same period several Pentagon assessments surfaced discussing circumstances under which nuclear weapons might be used in the defense of Taiwan and calculating that China's military modernization was aimed at being able to defeat or deter U.S. forces sent to the island's aid.

The terrorist attacks on New York and Washington in September 2001 swiftly altered the attitude toward China among the neoconservative elite in the Bush administration. The dominant drives were for security at home and aid in hunting terrorists or other potential threats from abroad to the United States. Beijing appreciated the opportunity of this crisis more quickly than did the Chen administration in Taipei. The Chinese leaders grasped immediately that the Bush drive against terrorism and the doctrine of "preemptive" strikes against possible enemies gave Beijing greater latitude than previously in dealing with its own minority dissidents. China had been heavily criticized in the United States and elsewhere for its suppression of the Uighers, Muslims of ethnic Turkic origin in China's far northwestern Xinjiang province. Beijing now played on its supposed community of interest with Washington in confronting Islamic terrorism and even got the Bush administration to put some of the Uigher organizations on its list of designated terrorist organizations. When in early 2002 George W. Bush gave his "axis of evil" speech, in which he linked Iraq, Iran, and North Korea as threatening rogue states, he handed China another opportunity. Beijing is thought to be the only outside force with the capacity to persuade or coerce the fraternal socialist regime of Kim Jong-il in Pyongyang. Bush's placing the destruction of North Korea's suspected nuclear weapons development program high on the list of his priorities in the war on terror made China an indispensable partner for Washington. It is a role that Beijing, understandably, has been in no rush to see end.

At the same time, Chen failed to fully appreciate that Washington's preoccupation with homeland security and supposed foreign threats sharply limited his actions. The Bush administration was in a mood to interpret anything that risked diverting its attention from or capacity to respond to its terrorism and axis of evil agenda as amounting to an unfriendly act. The Bush White House wanted China on its side in the campaign to contain North Korea, and it certainly did not want Taipei disturbing the Far East balance to the extent that the United States might be forced to confront China. Washington expected Chen to recognize that he was "under adult supervision" and to govern quietly without doing anything to provoke China. He either didn't understand the message or else was unable to resist the temptations of his own enthusiasm and activist nature.

Soon after Taiwan's presidential elections in 2000, Beijing put its relations with the Chen administration into cold storage. In place of seeking negotiations with the Taipei government it starting courting the Kuomintang, believing that now that the Taiwanese nationalist Lee Teng-hui had retired, the resurgent conservative mainlander elements in the party could be made allies. Beijing believed Lien Chan would see eye-to-eye with them on negotiating Taiwan's unification with the mainland under the "one China principle." Beijing misunderstood what was happening within the Kuomintang. The reemergence of mainlander influence within the party did not signal a revival and return to its historic essence, but the beginnings of the party's disintegration. But buoyed by their misinterpretation the Communist leaders in China began trying to bolster the Kuomintang and undermine the DPP administration. Many Kuomintang members of the Legislative Yuan were invited to China, where they were entertained lavishly. The message to Taiwanese was that favored status and untold financial benefits awaited those who demonstrated patriotic affection for China. Beijing even managed to persuade a few anti-Chen members of the DPP to partake of the Communist Party's largesse. Seductive pressure was also put on the several hundred thousand Taiwanese businessmen and women managing the island's investments in the mainland, at the time totaling some U.S. $100 million.

Yet again Beijing failed to understand the nature of the political transformation on Taiwan. The heartland of DPP support was among the island's native blue-collar industrial workers. There was already growing antipathy among these voters toward the largely Kuomintang-supporting business leaders, who were moving their companies to the mainland in order to take advantage of China's much lower production costs. By feting Taiwanese entrepreneurs, Beijing only managed to reinforce island DPP supporters' beliefs that closer and easier economic ties to the mainland threatened their own job security.

Chen's first few months in power gave Beijing every reason to hope he would be a one-term president. The early weeks of the Chen administration resembled someone's preliminary efforts to ride a two-wheel bicycle. There were several false starts, a lot of wobbling, much overcorrection when the bike didn't steer in the right direction, and one or two tumbles into the ditch. That was not surprising. Even in mature democracies changes of administration are seldom seamless transitions. On Taiwan the task was unusually fraught. It was no easy matter taking over and directing a civil service that had been heavily indoctrinated by the Kuomintang during 50 years in power. Even though Lee Teng-hui had done much to remove the culture of the one-party state from Taiwan's governmental institutions, the old mentality persisted. Many of Taiwan's civil servants in the old propaganda and security departments had not yet adjusted to the unsettling end to the comforts of martial law, let alone a sudden change of political masters. It did not help acclimatization to the new reality that many of the new men and women in the big corner ministerial offices had only a few years before been the targets of repression and disinformation campaigns by the same officials who now served them. Moreover the DPP had little significant experience with administration. Chen's closest supporters were either veteran dissidents imbued with a deep hatred of the Kuomintang, which made relations with officialdom difficult, or they were young idealists. On top of that, the DPP did not have a majority or a controlling alliance in the Legislative Yuan.

Lee Teng-hui, who in retirement remained highly popular among voters, came to Chen's rescue. The former president fell out conclusively with the Kuomintang during 2001. He even called the party he had led an "alien regime." The Kuomintang expelled Lee and he helped establish a new party, the Taiwan Solidarity Union (TSU). This was aimed at conservative nationalist Taiwanese voters who found the DPP's left-wing social policies hard to stomach. At the same time Lee's public endorsement of President Chen helped reverse the DPP's dwindling electoral fortunes. In legislative elections at the end of 2001 the DPP became the party with the largest number of seats and, with the support of Lee's TSU, gained much greater ability to command parliament. But the DPP and its allies still did not have a majority in parliament, and the Kuomintang alliance retained the ability to frustrate the work of government.

The Kuomintang's loss of seats surprised officials in Beijing. China's Taiwan analysts had given Jiang Zemin glowing predictions of a major Kuomintang victory. When the results reached Beijing the analysts were so astonished and scared of the likely reaction from Jiang that it took them many minutes to summon up the courage to tell him the news. Their fear was well founded. Jiang flew into a rage of theatrical proportions. It was at this time that the leaders in Beijing began to fully comprehend that the political transformation on Taiwan was outside their experience and not amenable to the traditional Chinese pressures of flattery and, if that didn't work, threats of force.

The full realization that the Communist Party's approach toward Taiwan had failed came at a sensitive time in Chinese domestic politics. Early in 2002 the party began assessing and preparing for the sixteenth party conference late that year, when Jiang and the most prominent leaders were due to retire. What had not been settled, though, was who would take over and in what positions. Hu Jintao, then a vice president, had been groomed for the top posts in accordance with Deng Xiaoping's edict that the relatively young technocrat should be at the core of the future party leadership. Deng's vote was the only one that counted, even though the old patriarch had been dead for five years at that point. Jiang, having convinced himself if no one else that at 76 he was still a vigorous man, was not prepared to let go. He agreed to let Hu have the presidency, but for months he tried to hold on to the post of party boss, the secretary-general. There were even rumors during that summer that the position of party chairman, which had died with the last holder, Mao Zedong, might be revived to accommodate Jiang.

It would have been unseemly for the internal debate, which even spilled out into public on a few occasions, to be seen as a squabble over power, influence, and position. So it was couched in terms of ideology and political philosophy. It was inevitable in a party with a revolutionary heritage, whose continued justification to hold power was dubious, that the contestants would try to appear to be the most steadfast, uncompromising, and fervently patriotic. That's what Jiang and his supporters did. The most generous interpretation of his actions is that he wanted to insure an orderly transition by keeping the guiding hand of his experience available to the new leaders. That interpretation is difficult to sustain in light of what happened, however. Jiang divided China's leadership, gathering around him a coterie of people mostly, like himself, from Shanghai. Upper echelons of the party found themselves having to take sides with either President Hu or Jiang's Shanghai clique. Jiang could not in the end muster enough support to keep the post of party secretary-general. But that aim may even have been a diversion because he was able to retain without any argument the hub of real power in China: Jiang kept the chairmanship of the Communist Party's Central Military Commission for two years. This position gave Jiang, in effect, command of China's armed forces. From that vantage point Jiang was able to dictate policy to President Hu and Prime Minister Wen Jiabao on many critical issues. He forced the new leaders to take much tougher lines on Taiwan than their own political instincts dictated. It rapidly became party doctrine that a political resolution of the Taiwan issue was increasingly unlikely. China would probably have to resort to military force to get possession of the island. Jiang also successfully pressed for a policy of no compromise with the people of Hong Kong in their desire for reform and an accountable government. He was equally adamant that domestic dissent should be met with unswerving force, obstructed even the most modest political reform, and even meddled in economic policy. When the president and prime minister suggested policies to cool China's overheated economy and moves to boost development of the deprived hinterland, Jiang suspected an attack on the economic supremacy of Shanghai. Jiang put his foot down and the policies of breakneck coastal development remained in place. On military and foreign policy matters, where the Taiwan question dominated, Jiang managed to get President Hu, a vice-chairman of the party's military commission, almost entirely excluded from deliberations. Fundamental decisions on China's military and foreign policies were frequently made by Jiang or his alter ego on the commission, Zeng Qinghong, together with two generals, Guo Boxiong and Cao Gangchuan. Hu often didn't know the meetings had taken place.

Jiang repeatedly stressed the need to have the military prepared and able to attack Taiwan should the island pursue internationally recognized independence. In May 2004 Liu Yazhou, the deputy political commissar of the Chinese Air Force, wrote an essay discussing preparations for an invasion of Taiwan and quoted Jiang as saying: "We must fight a war with Taiwan."[3] In this way Jiang became the chief lobbyist in Beijing for modernization of the military and made himself the darling of the generals. And beyond the Taiwan issue, Jiang managed to make a doctrine of Chinese military preparedness a cornerstone of foreign policy in general. Early in his tenure President Hu began using the phrase "peaceful rise" to describe his vision of China's emergence as a world power. This phrase, conjuring up visions of a benign and neighborly China, may have only been a public relations gambit. Through the 1990s the countries of Southeast Asia especially became increasingly anxious as they saw China bloom and become more assertive in the region. The lesson of history was that at some point China might try to reimpose the status of "vassal states" on surrounding nations. Jiang, however, objected to the "peaceful rise" phrase, even as a diplomatic ploy. It quickly disappeared from Hu's public statements. In its place Hu found himself saying such things as: "from beginning to end, we must place national sovereignty and security in first place, resolutely defend fundamental national interests, and resolutely defend national sovereignty and territorial integrity."[4]

Even so, Beijing approached Taiwan's presidential elections in 2004 with some confidence. Lien Chan and James Soong had managed to patch up their differences enough to run as joint candidates for the presidential and vice presidential posts. Polls indicated their joint vote should be similar to the sum of their separate votes in 2000. They should defeat Chen and Annette Lu with a lead of about 10 percent of the vote. But in the background Beijing's military moves were just as threatening as in the past. Beijing built up an arsenal of nearly five hundred missiles aimed at the island, a battery that by mid-2005 had grown to about seven hundred missiles. Some of these are missiles designed to knock out Taiwan's well-planned defensive installations. Others are anti-aircraft missiles aimed at countering Taiwan's air superiority over the strait and its significant bomber force that would take the battle into China. Still others are shore-based antiship missiles that would target Taiwanese or American naval vessels. In Washington and Tokyo it did not go unnoticed that while these missiles are currently deployed for an assault on Taiwan, many are mobile and could swiftly be moved to threaten Japanese or American interests.

The Chinese missiles played a significant part in polarizing voter opinion during the 2004 campaign. For supporters or those inclined toward the Pan Blue Alliance of Lien Chan and James Soong, the missiles were a vivid indication of President Chen's failure to manage the China file. Instead of maintaining the status quo, Chen's persistent push toward establishing Taiwan's independence appeared to be creating a situation that threatened the survival of island society. On the other side of the political divide, the missile deployment convinced those inclined toward Taiwanese nationalism that China could never be trusted. The sheer impersonality of missiles and their capacity to rain down death and destruction indiscriminately convinced many voters that Beijing's protestations of affection for its "Taiwan compatriots" were not to be believed.

Chapter Twenty

29,518 VOTES

When the polling stations closed at four o'clock on the evening of March 20, 2004, thousands of people began streaming toward the headquarters of the Democratic Progressive Party on Minsheng East Road in Taipei. By the time the first results started being reported, at least 100,000 people were thronged in front of a huge television screen and stage that had been erected across the road in front of the party headquarters. There was an atmosphere of keen anticipation tinged with uncertainty as the crowd scrambled for vantage points and spilled into the side streets where food stalls, election memorabilia hawkers, and all-night corner stores were doing a roaring trade. In an effort to generate confidence and excitement DPP organizers fired off rockets into the gathering night sky and relays of speakers up on the stage bellowed out rousing words or sang the old campaign songs of the political reform movement. But the undercurrent of uncertainty remained.

Taiwan does not permit the publication of public opinion polls in the last week of election campaigns. Political parties, academic institutions, and other interested groups carry on sampling the public mood, however. Rumors of the results spread quickly by word of mouth, the Internet, and text messages. There was a reasonable consistency in the unpublished polls done in the final days of the presidential campaign before the attempted killing of Chen Shui-bian during the parade the day before voting. They all showed a marginal victory of between 200,000 and 300,000 votes for Pan Blue presidential candidate Lien Chan of the Kuomintang and his running mate, vice president James Soong of the People First Party. The outcome was in the hands of undecided voters and those who might not bother to vote. What was entirely unpredictable at that point was the effect the attempted assassination would have on voter intentions.

A few miles across Taipei in the heart of the capital's administrative and ceremonial district, a similar crowd of supporters was massing outside the Kuomintang party headquarters. While the DPP election headquarters was a temporary affair in a half-completed office block whose skeletal upper floors were hidden behind huge party banners, the Kuomintang headquarters was redolent of a political organization basking in the assumption of the right to rule. The great, expensively decorated tower block sits confidently close to the vast walled gardens enclosing the national theater, the national concert hall, and the massive, glowering memorial to the father of modern Taiwan, Generalissimo Chiang Kai-shek. The Kuomintang headquarters also looks straight down Katagalan Boulevard, Taipei's main processional way, to the presidential office building at the other end. The link between the Kuomintang and power on Taiwan could not be more clearly stated. For the past four years, however, that historic chain had been broken. The tenant of the presidential office, originally built as the governor's headquarters during the half century of Japanese colonial rule, had been Chen and his coterie of vehement Taiwanese nationalists. Their political style and sentiments had been formed under the decades of Kuomintang repression. The bitterness felt in the upper echelons of the DPP for the Kuomintang and its power core of men who had come with Chiang Kai-shek to occupy Taiwan is still raw. In conversation senior DPP figures frequently divide island society into two segments, "Taiwanese" and "Chinese," the latter word usually spoken with a sneering inflection. For their part, Kuomintang disdain for the DPP and its bedrock of support among the native Taiwanese working classes is equally strong. DPP politicians are often dismissed as uncouth and "barefooted."[1] Their own Kuomintang leaders, in contrast, are respectfully referred to as "leather-shoed gentlemen."[2] There is an unhealed and suppurating wound at the heart of Taiwanese society. The Kuomintang's horror at, in their view, the rabble that had threatened Taiwan with ruin for the past four years was neatly, if unintentionally, expressed by a huge banner hanging down the front of their headquarters building. It carried a picture of Lien and Soong making the Taiwanese version of the defiant black power salute. But by some quirk of the images, Lien and Soong looked more as though they were shaking their fists down the boulevard toward Chen's office in the presidential building.

There is sometimes an unattractive element of triumphalism in the way that Chen's DPP pursues its affirmation of Taiwan's distinct identity. In this atmosphere of mutual suspicion and disdain, even efforts at reconciliation sometimes have the opposite effect. One such effort is the annual commemoration of the February 28, 1947, uprising by Taiwanese against the then newly arrived Kuomintang. In 1998 the Kuomintang president, Lee Teng-hui, designated February 28 as "Peace Day" to symbolize the healing of old wounds. "Two-Two-Eight," as it is known, has proved anything but a day for reconciliation. Instead it has become a moment when the evils of early Kuomintang rule are dug up, reexamined, and the old bitterness revived.

On February 28, 2004, just three weeks before the presidential election, Lee organized the "2–28 Hand-in-Hand Rally" with the objective of having a line of Taiwanese, hands joined, stretching the entire 249-mile length of the island. The rally was a huge success with some three million Pan Green supporters taking part. But there was very little peace and reconciliation in the atmosphere. It was far more a demonstration of the triumph of native Taiwanese over their old masters. The rally raised anger and some fear among Kuomintang supporters and their allies in the Pan Blue alliance, the People First Party. The next weekend the Pan Blue camp organized their own rallies in response and attracted at least as many people. Conversations with people in the crowds showed a high proportion of middle-class and professional people who were not usually politically active but felt the Two-Two-Eight rally was intimidating and required a firm response.

Islanders cannot be divided politically along clear "Taiwanese" and "Chinese" lines. Many people classed as native Taiwanese support the Kuomintang, as the election results showed. They do so not because of a fundamental disagreement with Chen and Lu that Taiwanese are an independent and sovereign people. Public opinion polls show a growing majority of islanders think of themselves either exclusively as Taiwanese or Taiwanese first and ethnic Chinese second. This phenomenon is neatly summed up in the local saying that there are many people with "blue skin and green bones," referring to the two main political alliances. Opposition to the DPP among native Taiwanese is rooted in fear that the Chen administration's fixation on identity blinds it to other critical issues: the economy and the overarching threat from China to invade the island. Taiwan's economy remains a great success story by most counts, but its performance on Chen's watch has not been at the high levels Taiwanese have come to expect. The economy contracted by 2.18 percent in 2001 and only just edged back into positive territory the following year. Unemployment reached 4.6 percent, a level unheard of in recent years, and private investment fell by 29.2 percent. The average Taiwanese per capita income remains one of the world's highest, at U.S. $12,876, but an air of foreboding hangs over the island. Much of that unease comes from the rush by Taiwanese industrialists to move their production facilities to China, where costs are considerably lower. Since the opening up of China's economy to market forces in the 1980s, Taiwanese businesses have invested around $100 billion in China. At least 500,000 Taiwanese businesspeople and managers spend most of their lives in China operating these transplanted operations, though some estimates put the number much higher.

One difficult social consequence of this foray into China by Taiwanese businessmen is a return flow of new wives from the mainland. These women are widely despised, not least because they are frequently the cause of the breakup of previous marriages on Taiwan. Some Taiwanese even voice the extreme view that these women are a Beijing fifth column who are trained and able to disrupt the defenses of the island when China is ready to invade.

Of less emotional and more thoughtful concern is how to manage the increasingly intertwined economic relationship between China and Taiwan. The exodus of assets and investments has raised the specter of Taiwan's economy being hollowed out and its factory workers facing a bleak future. Many of these industrial workers are DPP supporters. President Chen's administration remains undecided about whether to embrace the opportunity of China's booming economy or to continue to deter business between the island and the mainland. The remaining deterrents, such as the ban on direct air and sea links for travelers and goods, are more an irritant than a restriction on commercial intercourse. It is an emotional issue for many Taiwanese, who fear that if economic integration is allowed to continue at its current pace, no invasion by China's forces may be necessary. One day Taiwanese will wake up to discover they have become so economically dependent on China that they will have no option but to agree to accept Beijing's sovereignty.

It is on the broad aspects of the China file that Chen and Lu have raised the most disquiet, not only at home but also abroad and especially in Washington. What diehard DPP supporters see as Chen's courageous championing of Taiwan's de facto independence and refusal to bow to Beijing's blackmail, others see as a cavalier disregard for the island's long-term security interests and for the sensitivities of its allies.

Taiwan may be a young democracy, but its Central Elections Commission is highly efficient. Within two hours of the polls closing on March 20, results began tumbling out of the vote counting centers and onto television screens. Outside the DPP headquarters party cheerleaders kept the spirits of the crowd buoyed up, but the story unfolding on the television screen behind them was not so optimistic. The early results came inevitably from the island's northern cities, the managerial and entrepreneurial centers with the heaviest populations of people of mainland descent and of native Taiwanese who had benefited most from the Kuomintang's successful economic management. These people saw Lien and Soong as steady hands on the tiller; uninspiring perhaps, but men who could be relied upon not to rock the boat or to enrage China by indulging in dangerous displays of Taiwanese nationalism. So the early results showed the Pan Blue's Lien and Soong taking an early lead of around the 200,000 votes that the unpublished polls had predicted. As the evening progressed the voices of the DPP activists on the stage became more hoarse and the volleys of fireworks rockets more persistent, as though volume alone could drown out what was unfolding on the screen. But then the tallies started coming in from the rural areas and the blue-collar industrial south of the island. The Pan Blue lead quickly eroded. Then, for about an hour, the lead switched back and forth between Lien and Chen, seemingly with each polling station that reported. After this topsy-turvy hour a pattern settled in. Chen and Lu stayed just ahead, but only just. Sometimes their margin was only a few hundred votes. At other times it was a respectable tens of thousands. The underlying theme, though, was a lead by Chen and Lu of between 20,000 and 30,000 votes.

It was at this point, with the result still far from certain but with the trend running against them, that Lien and Soong made a desperate effort to stave off defeat. They got up in front of their assembled supporters and a seething press corps to announce they wanted the election annulled and all the ballot boxes sealed for a vote recount. "The overall impression among the public is that this election is an unfair election," Lien told his supporters.[3] The shooting the previous day of Chen Shui-bian and Annette Lu had swayed the election outcome in a "direct and complete" way. "If we remain silent at this time, how are we supposed to give history, the 23 million people [of Taiwan] and our offspring an answer?" he said. James Soong, always a more visceral politician than the aristocratic Lien, was more blunt. The presidential campaign "had been manipulated from beginning to end" by Chen, he said.[4] "It has been an unfair campaign full of mysteries. What is at stake here is Taiwan's democracy. It is our most effective weapon against China, and what kind of self-defence will we have if we destroy the weapon ourselves?" Soong asked.

This outburst by Lien and Soong, calling for the annulment of the election, was doubly strange and brimming with irony because they had taken the opposite position the previous afternoon just after the shooting. At that point Lien expressed fears that Chen, fearful of losing the election, might use the shooting as a pretext to postpone the vote. Lien had been adamant that the election must go ahead regardless of how seriously injured the president was. Indeed, in taking this position Lien was following Taiwan's law, which says the election can be called off only if one of the candidates dies or is killed during the campaign. The difference between the Pan Blue view of the world on Friday afternoon and Saturday evening was that immediately after the shooting, they believed their lead in the polls would be enough to them to carry them to victory. By Saturday evening they knew it was not enough.

Lien and Soong undoubtedly did genuinely believe Chen and Lu had stolen a march on them. But it is also true that the timing of their outburst was self-serving. One facet of democracy that Taiwan has enthusiastically adopted is the doctrine of political accountability. It is perhaps more accurate to say Taiwan has adapted the old Chinese idealized notions of the responsibility and accountability carried by those in power. At any rate, Taiwanese politicians and officials readily take the blame for failure by resigning. Lien and Soong were, however, trying to avoid their own political demise. Once the vote counting was complete and their defeat, which seemed at that stage of the evening increasingly certain, was announced, Lien and Soong would have been dutybound to tender their resignations from the Pan Blue leadership. By disputing the fairness of the election before defeat was confirmed they salvaged some hope of political survival. The reasons for their quarrel with the conduct of the election were not convincing, however. If they believed the shooting had distorted the election result, why had they not pressed on Friday afternoon, immediately after the assassination attempt, for a postponement of the vote rather than waiting until the last few minutes of the ballot counting?

When the final tally came in of the 12,914,422 valid votes cast, Chen and Lu had won by a mere 29,518 votes, a margin of victory of just one-tenth of one percent. The turnout at the polling stations was 80.2 percent of the 16,507,179 registered voters. This was appreciably higher than the 2000 presidential election, when the turnout was 77.6 percent, and the island's first free presidential elections in 1996, when the turnout was 76.9 percent. Chen and Lu took the bullish view that a victory was a victory no matter how slim the margin. The president marched onto the stage looking robust and in his usual hyperactive mode despite his near-death experience the previous day. Lu followed, walking firmly with the aid of a crutch to join Chen behind a bulletproof glass screen. The crowd was overjoyed. Chen's words, however, were prosaic, and even the most supportive newspapers found it hard to find something to quote for the following day's editions. Chen called the result a victory for democracy and said he believed the election marked the opening of a new era of opportunity for peace across the Taiwan Strait. This, he said, was not only what Taiwanese and Chinese wanted, but also the United States and Japan, Taipei's closest allies.

What almost got lost in the closeness of the election result and the angry rejection by the Pan Blue camp of the entire process was that voters had not only been asked to vote on the presidency on March 20. Chen and his DPP organizers had also offered Taiwanese a chance to vote on two referendum questions for the first time in the island's history. This was perhaps the most contentious aspect of Chen's election campaign. The linking of the referenda questions to the presidential ballot was a crass piece of politicking, though Chen dressed it up as an essential element in his campaign theme of affirming and enhancing Taiwanese identity. Taiwan's constitution, a relic of Chiang Kai-shek's rule of mainland China in the 1940s, did not allow for referenda. Late in 2003 Chen proposed legislation to permit plebiscites on matters of key public concern. A framework for referenda would be, Chen said, a significant step in furthering Taiwan's democratic reform. The opposition, Beijing, and even Taiwan's allies in the United States, Europe, and Asia saw it differently. The inclusion of referenda in the toolbox of Taiwan's democratic instruments could, at some point, enable Chen to call for a public decision on the island's legal status. Few doubted that with a carefully crafted question and a skillful political campaign Chen could get a majority of Taiwanese to opt for internationally recognized independence for the island.

On December 9, 2003, White House reporters were called into the Oval Office after a 40-minute private meeting between President George W. Bush and the Chinese prime minister, Wen Jiabao. Uppermost in reporters' minds was Taiwan and the plans by Chen Shui-bian to hold a two-question referendum in tandem with the presidential election. Only the previous day American government officials, briefing the White House press corps in advance of the Bush-Wen meeting, had given a strong warning to Taiwan from the administration not to hold a referendum that could provoke China by fueling the island's independence movement. When Bush was asked whether he wanted Chen to cancel the referendum, he didn't directly answer the question. But, with his tone and expression showing clear irritation, Bush said "the comments and actions made by the leader of Taiwan indicate that he may be willing to make decisions unilaterally to change the *status quo,* which we oppose."[5]

The rebuke to the Taiwanese president was compounded when the Chinese premier Wen told reporters that during the Oval Office meeting Bush had expressed his "opposition to Taiwan independence." Bush did not try to correct his guest, perhaps for reasons of inattention. For 30 years U.S. policy had been carefully worded as "not supporting Taiwan independence," a significant difference. But the impression left by the brief press conference was that Bush, who soon after he assumed the presidency said he would "do whatever it takes" to defend Taiwan against attack by Beijing's forces, had sharply turned American policy in favor of China.

Just as Taiwanese leaders have become skilled at avoiding China's red lines of unacceptable provocation, so they are adept at playing off the centers of power in Washington. In framing his response to the Oval Office meeting, Chen and his advisers took a calculated risk that American congressional and public opinion support for democratic Taiwan would be enough to allow him to politely stand his ground in the face of the Bush criticism. Chen was right.

Within hours of the White House rebuke Chen made a statement affirming his view that it was entirely appropriate to hold a referendum on how Taiwanese wished to confront the nearly five hundred missiles China had aimed at the island. The referendum, he said, didn't involve seeking to establish formal independence from China. "A defensive referendum is for avoiding war and to help keep the Taiwanese people free of fear. It is also for preserving the status quo," he said.[6]

Meanwhile in Washington there were predictable reactions to Bush's comments, and they came from within his own ideological cathedral of hard right-wing Republicans. Bush was accused of "appeasement of dictatorship" by a troika of influential conservative commentators for whom Communist China remained the last bastion of the Great Satan. At the Heritage Foundation, a conservative think tank, the China expert John Tkacik sounded as though he had been stunned into near incoherence by the president's apparent cozying up to China. "He's lost his bearings," Tkacik said of Bush. "It just boggles the mind. I'm just appalled. Clinton never would have gone this far."[7]

Anonymous official spin doctors began telling reporters that despite Bush's comments, America's policy toward Taiwan had not changed. Washington's loyalty to Taiwan remained firm, and the United States was not about to sell out the island democracy to China. The job of publicly calming the situation went to Secretary of State Colin Powell, the courteous voice of reason in the first Bush administration. A few weeks after the Bush-Wen meeting Powell appeared before the House International Relations Committee and restated the U.S. commitment to Taiwan, including to the island's security. As a democracy, Powell said, Taiwan has every right to hold a referendum if it wants to. "Taiwan is a democratic place, and if they choose to have a referenda [*sic*], they can have a referenda [*sic*]."[8] He did add, though, "We don't really see a need for these referenda. We don't believe any action should be taken in the region that would unilaterally change the situation," a reaffirmation of Washington's established position that it did not want either Taipei or Beijing to do anything to change the cross-strait status quo.

Despite this backpedaling and reinterpretation of what had been said, Chen had evidently irritated Bush. This emboldened the Pan Blue camp, which in the autumn of 2003 determined to use its majority in parliament to deny Chen the ability to hold referenda except under the most extreme and limited circumstances. When the legislation came up for votes, the opposition amended it so that referenda could only be called at times of national emergency. Chen and his advisers were undaunted by the restrictions placed on calling referenda and by the opposition to the move in Washington, Japan, South Korea, and Europe. They announced that as China had nearly five hundred missiles aimed at Taiwan, the island clearly faced a national emergency and a referendum was appropriate. That was never a convincing argument for angering allies and goading China. The altruistic bunting in which the referendum was draped could not disguise its reality as an opportunistic hunt for votes. Simply holding a referendum would indeed embellish Taiwan's democratic reform, but it would also be a signal moment that further emphasized the island's separateness from China. Of major concern to Chen's campaign strategists was that the president's supporters might not come out to vote in sufficient numbers on March 20 for him to retain office. They hoped to use the democratic novelty of attaching referendum questions to the presidential vote to encourage wayward DPP supporters to go to the polls. Having determined his course, President Chen was not going to back down on the question of holding a referendum in tandem with the presidential ballot. However, when he announced the wording of the referendum questions on February 3, 2004, they showed a good deal of recognition of the criticism he had received. The first question asked:

> The People of Taiwan demand that the Taiwan Strait issue be resolved through peaceful means. Should Mainland China refuse to withdraw the missiles it has targeted at Taiwan and to openly renounce the use of force against us, would you agree that the Government should acquire more advanced anti-missile weapons to strengthen Taiwan's self-defence capabilities?[9]

The second question asked:

> Would you agree that our government should engage in negotiation with Mainland China on the establishment of a "peace and stability" framework for cross-strait interactions in order to build consensus and for the welfare of the peoples on both sides?[10]

Both questions were largely meaningless. The acquisition of sophisticated anti-missile systems was already written into Taiwan's defense budget. Talks with China had been stalled for over four years on the critical point of Taiwan's refusal to accept the "one China principle" as a precondition.

Chen's plans to use the referendum as a vote catcher were further undermined by a ruling by the Central Election Commission. The Pan Blue camp held that the referendum was illegal. It urged the commission to set up separate booths for the presidential and referendum questions so voters could decide whether to participate in one or both of the ballots. After much dithering the commission went along with the Pan Blue request. The results on March 20 showed voters were just as divided on the referendum question as they were on the presidency. Almost all the DPP voters also voted on the referendum and approved both propositions while Pan Blue supporters boycotted the referendum questions en masse. The outcome was that the questions failed to attract votes either pro or con from over half the 16 million registered voters and hence were not valid. Chen claimed a moral victory on the basis that 95 percent of the people who did vote in the referendum supported his propositions. But it is hard to escape the view that the exercise debased the currency of the referendum as an instrument in Taiwanese politics.

The cracks in Taiwan society levered open by the election spawned weeks of demonstrations, some of them violent, by Pan Blue supporters in the center of the capital, Taipei. On several occasions riot police were used to quell the outbursts. These protests presented a delicate problem for the mayor of Taipei, Ma Ying-jeou, a senior member of the Kuomintang and one of its campaign managers. As mayor of the capital it was his responsibility to control the demonstrations and to maintain law and order. But he was also being cajoled by his fellow party members to clearly show his support for the protests and his opposition to the election and its results. It would have been an easier path for Ma to navigate if he had not had his own political ambitions. The young, urbane, and photogenic mayor is a leading candidate to be the Kuomintang contender for the presidency in 2008. Indeed, early in 2005 he announced his intention to seek the Kuomintang leadership. He needed to strike a balance between fulfilling his obligations as mayor and maintaining his position within the Kuomintang. Ma veered toward meeting his responsibilities as mayor, clearly believing that most Taiwanese, whatever their feelings about the election, oppose violent demonstrations. He and other party officials also had to keep in mind that parliamentary elections to the Legislative Yuan, where the Kuomintang held marginal control, were due in December 2004. Being tainted by a history of violent protest would not help the Kuomintang win seats in December. Ma appeared to have struck the right note. Within a few days of the first mass demonstrations after the elections, protesters camped out close to the Presidential Palace had dwindled to a few hundred hard-liners, many apparently from James Soong's People First Party, which harbors some of the strongest supporters of rapid and unilateral unification with China.

Beijing had, when the demonstrations started in the days after the election, given encouragement to the estimated one percent of islanders who were in favor of unification with the mainland. On March 26, six days after the election, China's Taiwan Affairs Office issued a statement saying Beijing would not "look on unconcerned" if the postelection situation on the island led to "social turmoil, endangering lives and property of Taiwan compatriots and affecting stability across the Taiwan Strait." To Taiwanese that message spoke to the third of Beijing's list of situations that would prompt it to invade the island: the collapse of civil order. The reaction among most members of the Kuomintang was to moderate their protests. Giving China an excuse to invade was too heavy a price to pay for the satisfaction of venting their anger and suspicions over the election outcome. The number of people attending the Pan Blue demonstrations dwindled fast. Within a few days it was only hard-core supporters of unification who were still protesting on the streets.

After much partisan squabbling back and forth it was agreed that there should be a recount, with the result announced on May 10, shortly before the May 20 inauguration. That didn't happen. The review commission labored mightily to examine some 300,000 votes from polling stations the Pan Blue alliance labeled as problem areas. The commission identified only 30,000 ballots as problematic and worthy of further examination. As about 80 percent of those votes were for Chen and Lu, it was statistically impossible that when the recount was completed it would alter the election result announced on the night of March 20 and certified by the Central Election Commission a week later. At the most, Chen and Lu's victory might have been shaved by 3,000 votes. But they would still be the winners.

The Pan Blue alliance didn't fare any better in the courts. Lawyers for the alliance went to the Taiwan High Court and presented four arguments for the election to be overturned or declared invalid. First, it claimed the DPP used the referendum as propaganda for campaign purposes. Second, Pan Blue claimed that the heightened state of security after the March 19 assassination attempt meant that tens of thousands of military and police personnel—enough to change the election result—were not able to vote. Most security force members, the suit contended, would have voted Pan Blue. Third, Pan Blue blamed the Central Election Commission for failing to postpone the election after Chen and Lu were shot. Fourth, the suit claimed the election commission did not properly separate voters participating in the referendum. The presiding judge, Cheng Ya-ping, was not impressed by the claims and gave Pan Blue two weeks to come up with more substantial reasons for questioning the election's validity. "According to the vague indictments you presented, obviously you did not try your best," she said. "Please reconstruct and resubmit your indictment." The Pan Blue lawyers did go away and attempt to build a stronger case. But their efforts were in vain, and subsequent court hearings produced no more compelling evidence justifying nullification of the election and a new ballot. Late in 2004 the Pan Blue case was finally thrown out of court for lack of substance. By that time, however, the country and the world had already accepted the reality of Chen as president for a second term.

No reliable analysis was done in the months immediately after the election to determine what role the assassination attempt played in the narrow Chen-Lu victory. Two samplings of public opinion claimed to find that the shooting did arouse a strong sympathy vote that overrode the previous lead of Lien Chan and James Soong. But as one of those polls was done by a television station that strongly supports the Pan Blue camp and the other was done by Lien's own think tank of policy advisers, neither can be counted credible. Other factors in the campaign were just as important. Lien and Soong did not work well together. The Lien-Soong alliance was a political marriage of convenience without any love or affection in the arrangement. It was, after all, Soong who had foiled Lien's run for the presidency in 2000, allowing Chen to win with only 39 percent of the vote. The alliance was never a convincing union, and the two were unable to produce a policy program to attract voters. They kept the loyalty of most Kuomintang diehard voters by offering an air of uninspiring basic competence and some assurance that they would not goad China into invasion or other retaliatory measures. But even this was turned effectively against the Pan Blue candidates by Chen and Lu. The incumbents portrayed Lien and Soong, both born on the mainland, as puppets of Beijing and collaborators with the foreign Chinese Communists. Lien was born in 1936 at Xian in Shaanxi province and Soong was born in Hunan province in 1942. Portraying the Pan Blue contenders as alien interlopers was especially effective with new, younger voters who could easily take pride in the DPP emphasis on promoting and enhancing "Taiwan identity." For these voters, too, the older divisions in Taiwanese society had less meaning than they did for their parents' generation. The DPP's campaign line that there was something intrinsically untrustworthy about the loyalty to Taiwan of Lien and Soong because of their mainland heritage was very effective. This effectiveness was dramatically demonstrated a week before the election when at a Pan Blue rally Lien and Soong felt compelled to prostrate themselves on the ground and kiss the Taiwanese soil to demonstrate their love for the island. All they ended up doing, however, was to provide newspapers with vivid pictures of the essential weakness of their campaign.

In his speech at the inauguration ceremony two months later, on May 20, 2004, Chen could not ignore the sharp social divisions exposed by the vehemence of the election campaign and the narrowness of his own victory. Without taking any personal responsibility for these divisions, Chen talked about the need for "candid self-reflection" and called for greater tolerance and understanding among Taiwan's various ethnic and cultural groups.[11] Taiwanese must, Chen said, "scale the wall of antagonism" and find "ways to reconcile the deep divide caused by distrust."

> No matter what year they arrived, regardless of their ancestral origins and their mother tongues, even in spite of their different hopes and dreams, all are our forefathers; all have settled down here and together face a common destiny. Whether indigenous peoples or "new settlers," expatriates living abroad, foreign spouses or immigrant workers who labour under Taiwan's blazing sun—all have made a unique contribution to this land and each has become an indispensable member of our "New Taiwan" family.[12]

To underline his intention of being president of all Taiwanese now that the rigors of the election campaign were past, Chen indicated in his speech several modifications to his party platform. One platform promise was to write a new constitution for Taiwan to replace the cumbersome and ponderous affair brought to the island by Chiang Kai-shek in 1949. During the campaign Chen said he wanted a new constitution agreed upon by 2006 and functioning in time for the next presidential elections, in 2008. This aim attracted opposition at home and abroad, and for similar reasons. Among many Taiwanese as well as in the capitals of the island's allies it seemed impossible to rewrite the constitution without severing the few remaining legal ties to mainland China, in effect declaring independence and stirring Beijing to military action. In his inauguration speech Chen significantly modified his position, specifically excluded the question of independence from the constitution project, and even held out the prospect that the process might be accomplished by amendment to the existing document rather than the more trouble-prone rewriting.

In his remarks aimed at China, and by association to Washington as the guarantor of Taiwanese independence, Chen was more fulsome in his flowery words calling for peace and mutual understanding than he was in content. He emphasized, as he had to for his followers, that Taiwan is a free, independent, and democratic nation. So long as Beijing recognizes those facts, there is a foundation for new and productive relations across the Taiwan Strait, he said. "We would not exclude any possibility, so long as there is the consent of the 23 million people of Taiwan."[13] Chen said he understood the historical factors that have led Beijing to claim ownership of Taiwan and its attempts to diplomatically isolate the island under the "one China principle."

> By the same token, the Beijing authorities must understand the deep conviction held by the people of Taiwan to strive for democracy, to love peace, to pursue their dreams free from threat and to embrace progress. But if the other side is unable to comprehend that this honest and simple wish represents the aspiration of Taiwan's 23 million people, if it continues to threaten Taiwan with military force, if it persists in isolating Taiwan diplomatically, if it keeps up irrational efforts to blockade Taiwan's rightful participation in the international arena, this will only serve to drive the hearts of the Taiwanese people further away and widen the divide in the Strait.[14]

Chen's agenda for constitutional reform and accelerated Taiwanization faced a serious political hurdle. His DPP and its allies held only a minority of seats in the 225-seat Legislative Yuan. The Pan Blue alliance was in the majority and able to block, divert, or derail the administration's plans. Chen hoped this impediment would be removed if the DPP could win a majority in parliamentary elections at the beginning of December 2004. That objective appeared to be within Chen's grasp in the final days of the campaign. Polls showed the DPP would likely win a slim but working majority in parliament, but it didn't turn out that way. There was a low voter turnout, especially among DPP supporters. About two million people who had supported Chen in the presidential race in March didn't go to the polls to vote for their local DPP candidate in December. As a result the Kuomintang and the People First Party were able to hang on to 114 seats, a parliamentary majority.

Chen's campaign strategy for the parliamentary election was flawed. He saw this vote as an extension of the presidential race eight months before and campaigned as though he wanted a clear popular mandate denied him in March. The DPP's campaign themes remained the issues of Taiwanese nationalism. Chen suggested the island's overseas representative offices should include "Taiwan" in their names rather than "Republic of China" in order to avoid confusion with the mainland. For the same reason he suggested Taiwanese state-owned companies, such as the China Petroleum Corp. and China

Airlines, should also change their names. Since the election DPP strategists have said this approach was adopted to stave off a challenge by Lee Teng-hui's vehemently pro-independence Taiwan Solidarity Union, which appeared set to gain a significant number of seats. This explanation is not very convincing and smacks of making excuses for a misjudged strategy.

Democracy may be still a fresh element in island life, but Taiwanese have absorbed the culture. Many voters distinguished between issues they considered appropriate for a presidential campaign and those they wanted debated in the parliamentary election. In December, matters such as the economy and social services were uppermost in the minds of many voters. Chen's continued emphasis on the large issues of the island's future were not what voters wanted to hear. So many, especially DPP supporters more enamored of the party's left-of-center policies than Chen's personality, stayed home.

The DPP election strategists also mismanaged their assault on Taiwan's multicandidate constituency system. The system assigns, say, ten seats to a region, and winning candidates are chosen in order of the percentage of the vote they win. This style of selection requires careful management by party organizers. A highly popular candidate, for example, can siphon off votes from other candidates from the same party, who may then end up too far down the list to get elected. The lesser candidates would, however, have a good chance of getting elected if they ran in constituencies without star attractions. Several DPP candidates fell foul of this kind of lack of attention to managerial detail. Chen took personal responsibility for the failure to win a parliamentary majority by resigning the DPP party leadership, but he did not, of course, relinquish the presidency.

Chen's political deflation was more symbolic than real. Taiwan's political balance after the Legislative Yuan elections was almost exactly the same as it had been before. The DPP managed to significantly advance its Taiwanization program in the first four years of Chen's presidency and in the face of Pan Blue opposition. There was little cause to think the setback in parliamentary representation would do more than give Chen and his advisers pause for thought to readjust their timetable and strategy.

The results of the Legislative Yuan election did not revive the political career of Kuomintang leader Lien Chan. His retention of the party's parliamentary majority did, though, allow him to retire from politics with honor. A few days after the election Lien announced he would step down from the leadership in 2005. A big loser in the elections was James Soong and his People First Party. It lost 12 seats and over 560,000 votes compared with its support in the Legislative Yuan elections three years before. Soong continued to be evasive when asked about any permanent alliance with the Kuomintang. There is no good reason to imagine that a new generation of Kuomintang leaders would see much long-term advantage in courting the People First Party, which exists largely to provide a carriage for Soong's ambitions.

In Beijing the first reaction to the parliamentary election results was to think that attempting to intimidate Taiwan's voters had worked. Analysts in the Chinese capital leaned toward the view that the DPP's failure to win a parliamentary majority showed that China's policy of threatening the islanders with invasion was correct and productive. "Really there are even fewer reasons to try to reach an agreement with Chen now," Shi Yinhong, a foreign policy specialist at Beijing's Qinghua University, told *The New York Times.*[15] Yan Xuetong, a former adviser to the Chinese government on Taiwan policy, said, "If the conclusion of the leadership is that the hard-line stance it has taken against Chen Shui-bian had good results, then they will also conclude that the basic policy should not change."[16] But, Yan added, "China still has work to do to eliminate any doubt it is ready to attack." That hard-line approach has continued since the coming to complete power of President Hu Jintao's so-called fourth generation of Communist Party leaders.

The transfer of power was completed late in 2004 when Jiang Zemin retired from the chairmanship of the party's powerful military commission. Jiang and his Shanghai clique had infected the new leaders with dogmatic views on a number of issues, but they withdrew from power reasonably gracefully, leaving the field to the new men. Hu and his premier, Wen Jiabao, were free to confront the task of changing the internal mentality of the Communist Party from that of a revolutionary movement to a true governing party without the constant worry of serious ideological schisms. Beyond the party bulwarks China was exhibiting an air of self-confidence not seen since the start of European incursions in the mid-nineteenth century. Predictions abounded that China would soon overtake Japan as the world's second-largest economy. The world began to perceive in reality what had been long imagined, as China's demand for resources began to shape international markets and global business. The priority for the Fourth Generation leaders is maintaining China's economic growth and its reemergence as a world power. Taiwan's de facto independence remains an issue of great symbolic and emotional significance in Beijing, but the leaders in the Zhongnanhai compound believe that time is on their side. At some point the islanders will be forced to recognize that their continued existence outside the grasp of Mother China is futile and makes no sense. The islanders got a stark foretaste of the future in the weeks just before the December 2004 parliamentary elections. In mid-November

China signed a free trade agreement with the ten countries in the Association of Southeast Asian Nations. That agreement was a prelude to the inclusion of Japan and South Korea in the commercial group. The future of Taiwan looks very lonely in the middle of that trade powerhouse.

The next month, December 2004, the Hu and Wen administration further emphasized that the change of leaders did not mean any change in Beijing's determination to possess Taiwan. The National People's Congress, China's ersatz parliament, was instructed to pass an antisecession law. The legislation, which was finally approved by the congress in March 2005, makes it illegal to promote the separation of any part of what China considers its territory, including Taiwan. The sting in the tail of the legislation is that it gives the state council, the equivalent of the cabinet in western governments, the authority to use force if it feels the territorial integrity of China is being compromised. The wording of the legislation left it an open question of what that force might be. It appears to cover everything from a full invasion, targeted killing of Taiwan's leaders, to an economic embargo. "If possibilities for a peaceful reunification should be completely exhausted, the state shall employ non-peaceful means and other necessary measures to protect China's sovereignty and territorial integrity," Wang Zhaoguo, a senior legislator, explained to the members of the National People's Congress.[17]

In real terms, the antisecession legislation is meaningless. Taiwan remains an independent state with its own constitution and laws. The Chinese Communist Party has never exercised any authority over the island. But the law does decorate China's claim with embroidery of legality that Beijing may present in the future to try to justify its actions in the court of world opinion.

There were massive protest marches on Taiwan condemning China's antisecession law, but the most significant response came in February 2005 while the National People's Congress was still deliberating. The United States and Japan renegotiated their security alliance for the first time since 1960. In a joint communiqué Washington and Tokyo expressed disquiet at the threats to their own and international security in the Far East. The statement named China's threat to Taiwan as a major concern. This was the first time Tokyo put its name to a document indicating that it considers the future of Taiwan to be of direct strategic interest to Japan. The statement raised the possibility that, in the event of a Chinese invasion of Taiwan, Japan would intervene on the island's side. Tension between Japan and China was already rising with the growing economic and regional political rivalry of the old enemies. Japan's open indication of its support for Taiwan sparked a wave of government-inspired protests in China during the spring of 2005. There was also alarm in

South Korea, where anti-Japanese sentiments remain strong, that Japan might be entering an era of renewed militarism.

On Taiwan President Chen Shui-bian sees a narrowing window of opportunity to transform the island's de facto independence into de jure statehood within the next decade or so, before China's power becomes so overwhelming as to be irresistible. He is counting on America's deep-seated suspicions about China's rising power. If push comes to shove, Chen believes, Washington and the American political establishment will come down on the side of "one Taiwan, one China," rather than just "one China." That is a risky judgment. Like most countries and all superpowers, the United States will only follow its national interest. Washington will go along with Taiwanese independence so long as it can be achieved without threatening American interests. The Bush administration is preoccupied with the war in Iraq, global terror, the challenges of trying to stop proliferation of nuclear weapons in places like North Korea and Iran, and the demands of homeland security. In the foreseeable future, it is hard to imagine a scenario in which Washington sees the prospect of a military confrontation with China over Taiwan as being necessary or of benefit to America. It is easy to understand and sympathize with the desire for recognized statehood that most Taiwanese nurse with great passion. That dream may seem to be tantalizingly closer now than it ever has been. But Taiwan will always carry the curse of geography that has placed it at the crossroads of other people's journeys.

NOTES

CHAPTER 1

1. Bloomberg News Agency, April 5, 2004
2. George H. Kerr, *Formosa: Licensed Revolution and the Home Rule Movement, 1895–1945* (Honolulu: University of Hawaii Press, 1974), p. 65.
3. Reuters News Agency, December 13, 2004.
4. Ron Gluckman, *Asiaweek* (August 2000).
5. Ibid.
6. *Time* magazine, April 24, 2000.
7. Ibid.
8. Gluckman.
9. Richard C. Kagan, *Chen Shui-bian: Building a Community and a Nation* (Taipei: Asia-Pacific Academic Exchange Foundation, 1998), p. 47.
10. State Council of the People's Republic of China, "The Taiwan Question and Reunification of China," White Paper, 1993.
11. National Policy Foundation, November 24, 2002.
12. Ibid.

CHAPTER 2

1. Richard Pflederer, "Early European Adventurers and the Opening of Japan," *www.mercatormag.com.*
2. Peng Ming-min, *A Taste of Freedom: Memoirs of a Formosan Independence Leader* (New York: Holt, Rinehart and Winston Inc., 1972).
3. *Taipei Times,* April 26, 2005.
4. Agence France Presse, August 8, 1998.
5. *New York Times,* January 8, 2002.
6. *Taiwan News,* November 28, 2003
7. Interview with the author, February 2004.
8. W. G. Goddard, *Formosa: A Study in Chinese History* (London: Macmillan and Co. Ltd., 1996), p. 13.
9. Ibid., p. 16.
10. John Keay, *India: A History* (London: HarperCollins, 2000), pp. 123–124.

CHAPTER 3

1. W. G. Goddard, *Formosa: A Study in Chinese History* (London: Macmillan and Co. Ltd., 1996), p. 19.
2. Ibid., p. 26.
3. *www.ripon.edu/academics/global/Levathes.html.*
4. Gavin Menzies, *1421: The Year China Discovered the World* (New York: William Morrow & Company, 2003).

CHAPTER 4

1. James W. Davidson, *The Island of Formosa Past and Present* (London: Macmillan and Co., 1903), p. 6.
2. Hung Chein-chao, *A History of Taiwan* (Rimini, Italy: Cerchio Iniziative Editoriali, 2000), p. 14.
3. Ibid.
4. Davidson, *Island of Formosa,* p. 5.
5. Ibid., p. 6.
6. W. G. Goddard, *Formosa: A Study in Chinese History* (London: Macmillan and Co. Ltd., 1996), p. 44.
7. Davidson, *Island of Formosa,* p. 8.
8. Goddard, *Formosa,* p. 42.
9. W. M. Campbell, *Formosa Under the Dutch: Described from Contemporary Records* (London: Kegan Paul, Trench, Trubner & Co. Ltd., 1903), p. 38.
10. Ibid.
11. Ibid., p. 39.

CHAPTER 5

1. Hung Chein-chao, *A History of Taiwan* (Rimini, Italy: Cerchio Iniziative Editoriali, 2000), p. 31.
2. W. G. Goddard, *Formosa: A Study in Chinese History* (London: Macmillan and Co. Ltd., 1996), p. 67.
3. W. M. Campbell, *Formosa Under the Dutch: Described from Contemporary Records* (London: Kegan Paul, Trench, Trubner & Co. Ltd., 1903), p. 384.
4. James W. Davidson, *The Island of Formosa Past and Present* (London: Macmillan and Co., 1903), p. 33.
5. A. Grove Day, *Pirates of the Pacific* (New York: Meredith Press, 1968), p. 35.
6. Campbell, *Formosa Under the Dutch,* p. 459.

CHAPTER 6

1. W. M. Campbell, *Formosa Under the Dutch: Described from Contemporary Records* (London: Kegan Paul, Trench, Trubner & Co. Ltd., 1903), p. 420.
2. Ibid., p. 423.

3. Ibid., p. 424.
4. Ibid., p. 433.
5. Ibid., p. 439.
6. Ibid.
7. Ibid., p. 442.
8. Ibid., p. 83.
9. Ibid., p. 327.
10. James W. Davidson, *The Island of Formosa Past and Present* (London: Macmillan and Co., 1903), p. 41.
11. Campbell, *Formosa Under the Dutch,* p. 85.
12. Ibid., p. 445.

CHAPTER 7

1. *Xiamen City Guide Book;* also quoted by Macabe Keliher, *Far Eastern Economic Review,* September 26, 2002.
2. Ibid.
3. Wong Kwok Wah, *Asia Times,* March 14, 2002.
4. Keliher.
5. W. G. Goddard, *Formosa: A Study in Chinese History* (London: Macmillan and Co. Ltd., 1996), p. 85.
6. Keliher.
7. Ibid.
8. James W. Davidson, *The Island of Formosa Past and Present* (London: Macmillan and Co., 1903), p. 50.
9. Ibid.
10. Ibid., p. 52.
11. Ibid.
12. Ibid.
13. Ibid., p. 56.

CHAPTER 8

1. James W. Davidson, *The Island of Formosa Past and Present* (London: Macmillan and Co., 1903), p. 61.
2. Ibid., p. 62.

CHAPTER 9

1. Hung Chein-chao, *A History of Taiwan* (Rimini, Italy: Cerchio Iniziative Editoriali, 2000), p. 128.
2. Kyoshi Ito, *Taiwan: 400 Years of History and Outlook,* trans. Walter Chen, p. 25. Available on line at http://www.china-institut.org/bibliothek/geschichte%20taiwans.pdf.
3. Ibid.
4. Hung, *History of Taiwan,* p. 136.
5. Ito, *Taiwan,* p. 28.

6. W. G. Goddard, *Formosa: A Study in Chinese History* (London: Macmillan and Co. Ltd., 1996), p. 96.
7. James W. Davidson, *The Island of Formosa Past and Present* (London: Macmillan and Co., 1903), p. 69.
8. Ibid., p. 100.
9. Ibid., p. 97.
10. Ibid.

CHAPTER 10

1. James W. Davidson, *The Island of Formosa Past and Present* (London: Macmillan and Co., 1903), p. 103.
2. Ibid., p. 105.
3. Ibid., p. 129.
4. Ibid., p. 220.

CHAPTER 11

1. W. G. Goddard, *Formosa: A Study in Chinese History* (London: Macmillan and Co. Ltd., 1996), p. 139.
2. James W. Davidson, *The Island of Formosa Past and Present* (London: Macmillan and Co., 1903), p. 252.
3. Johanna Menzel Meskill, *A Chinese Pioneer Family: The Lins of Wu-feng, Taiwan, 1729–1895* (Princeton, N.J.: Princeton University Press, 1979), p. 188.
4. Davidson, *Island of Formosa,* p. 253.
5. Goddard, *Formosa,* pp. 124–139.
6. Davidson, *Island of Formosa,* p. 254.
7. Ibid.

CHAPTER 12

1. W. G. Goddard, *Formosa: A Study in Chinese History* (London: Macmillan and Co. Ltd., 1996), p. 145. Hung Chien-chao, *A History of Taiwan* (Rimini, Italy: Cerchio Iniziative Editoriali, 2000), p. 171. James W. Davidson, *The Island of Formosa Past and Present* (London: Macmillan and Co., 1903), p. 279, uses slightly different wording in the English translation.
2. Hung, *History of Taiwan,* p. 161. Goddard, *Formosa,* p. 144. Davidson, *Island of Formosa.*
3. Goddard, *Formosa,* p 149.
4. George H. Kerr, *Formosa: Licensed Revolution and the Home Rule Movement, 1895–1945* (Honolulu: University of Hawaii Press, 1974), p. 15.

CHAPTER 13

1. Kyoshi Ito, *Taiwan: 400 Years of History and Outlook,* trans. Walter Chen, p. 69. Available on line at http://www.china-institut.org/bibliothek/geschichte%20taiwans.pdf.

2. Ibid.
3. George H. Kerr, *Formosa: Licensed Revolution and the Home Rule Movement, 1895–1945* (Honolulu: University of Hawaii Press, 1974), p. 56.
4. Ibid., p. 67.
5. Ibid.
6. Ibid., pp. 189–190.
7. Hung Chein-chao, *A History of Taiwan* (Rimini, Italy: Cerchio Iniziative Editoriali, 2000), p. 235.
8. Denny Roy, *Taiwan: A Political History* (Ithaca, N.Y.: Cornell University Press, 2003), p. 53.

CHAPTER 14

1. Edgar Snow, *Red Star Over China* (New York: Grove Weidenfeld, 1968).
2. Sterling Seagrave, *The Soong Dynasty* (London: Sidgwick & Jackson Ltd., 1986), p. 403.
3. Barbara W. Tuchman, *Stilwell and the American Experience in China, 1911–45* (New York: Macmillan Company, 1970), p. 401.
4. Seagrave, *Soong Dynasty,* p. 404.
5. The Cairo Declaration, December 1, 1943. The Taiwan Document Center, http://www.taiwandocuments.org/cairo.htm

CHAPTER 15

1. Douglas Mendel, *The Politics of Formosan Nationalism* (Berkeley: University of California Press, 1970), pp. 40–41.
2. Alan D. Romberg, "Finding a Basis for Sustainable Peace Across the Taiwan Strait," conference presentation, St. Anthony's College, Oxford, May 2002, p. 2.

CHAPTER 16

1. Harry S Truman, *Memoirs of Harry S Truman, 1946–1952: Years of Trial and Hope* (New York: Smithmark Publishers, 1996).
2. President Truman's statement of policy neutralizing Formosa and declaring its legal status unsettled, *U.S. State Department Bulletin* 23, July 23, 1950, p. 5.
3. Douglas Mendel, *The Politics of Formosan Nationalism* (Berkeley: University of California Press, 1970), p. 185.
4. Jonathan Charney and J. R. V. Prescott, "Resolving Cross Strait Relations Between China and Taiwan," *American Journal of International Law* (July 2000): 8.
5. Mendel, *Politics of Formosan Nationalism,* 175.

CHAPTER 17

1. Douglas Mendel, *The Politics of Formosan Nationalism* (Berkeley: University of California Press, 1970), p. 70.
2. Jay Taylor, *The Generalissimo's Son: Chiang Ching-kuo and the Revolutions in China and Taiwan* (Cambridge, Mass.: Harvard University Press, 2000), p. 22.

3. Ibid., p. 25.
4. Ibid., p. 63.

CHAPTER 18

1. Alan D. Romberg, "Finding a Basis for Sustainable Peace Across the Taiwan Strait," conference presentation, St. Anthony's College, Oxford, May 2002, p. 5. Also, Henry Kissinger, *The White House Years* (Boston: Little, Brown and Company, 1979), p. 783.
2. David E. Kaplan, *Fires of the Dragon: Politics, Murder, and the Kuomintang* (New York: Macmillan Publishing Company, 1992), p. 225.
3. Anthony Kubek, *Ronald Reagan and Free China* (Tampa, Fla.: Hallberg Publishing Corporation, 2002), p. 49.
4. Ibid., p. 54.
5. Ibid., p. 64.
6. Ibid., pp. 106–107.
7. Ibid., p. 108.
8. Richard Fisher, "To Take Taiwan, First Kill a Carrier," China Brief, Jamestown Foundation, July 8, 2002.
9. Ibid.
10. Jim Yardley and Thom Shanker, *New York Times,* April 8, 2005.
11. Associated Press, June 4, 2005.

CHAPTER 19

1. Agence France Press, March 15, 2000.
2. *Taipei Times,* June 29, 2000
3. *New York Times,* July 16, 2004.
4. Arthur Waldron and John Tkacik, *Wall Street Journal,* August 13, 2004.

CHAPTER 20

1. Interviews with the author, February-March 2004.
2. Ibid.
3. *China Post,* March 21, 2004.
4. Ibid.
5. *Washington Post,* December 10, 2003.
6. Associated Press, December 11, 2003.
7. *Washington Post,* December 10, 2003.
8. *China Post,* February 13, 2004.
9. "Writing History with Democracy and Defending Taiwan with Referendum," Statement issued by the Office of President Chen Shui-bian, February 3, 2004.
10. Ibid.
11. "Paving the Way for a Sustainable Taiwan," Inaugural address of President Chen Shui-bian, May 20, 2004, issued by the Government Information Office.
12. Ibid.
13. Ibid.

14. Ibid.
15. Joseph Kahn, *New York Times,* December 13, 2004.
16. Ibid.
17. Edward Cody, *Washington Post,* March 8, 2005.

BIBLIOGRAPHY

Booth, Martin. *The Triads: The Chinese Criminal Fraternity.* London: HarperCollins, 1990.

Caltonhill, Mark. *Private Prayers and Public Parades: Exploring the Religious Life of Taipei.* Taipei: Department of Information, Taipei City Government, 2002.

Campbell, W. M. *Formosa Under The Dutch: Described from Contemporary Records.* London: Kegan Paul, Trench, Trubner & Co. Ltd., 1903.

Chen, C. J. *After Hong Kong: Whither Taiwan?* Taipei: Government Information Office, 1999.

_______. *Getting Real: International Media Perspectives on the Special State-to-State Relationship between the ROC and the PRC.* Taipei: Government Information Office, 1999.

Chen, Shui-bian. *The Son of Taiwan: The Life of Chen Shui-bian and His Dreams for Taiwan.* Taipei: Taiwan Publishing Co. Ltd., 2000.

Chen, Ya-ping, and Chao, Chi-fang. *Dance Studies and Taiwan: The Prospect of a New Generation.* Taipei: Ju Tzong-ching, National Chang Kai-Shek Cultural Center, 2001.

Ching, Leo T. S. *Becoming "Japanese": Colonial Taiwan and the Politics of Identity Formation.* Berkeley: University of California Press, 2001.

Copper, John F. *Taiwan: Nation-State or Province?* Boulder, Colo.: Westview Press, 1990.

Croizier, Ralph. *Koxinga and Chinese Nationalism.* Cambridge, Mass.: Harvard University Press, 1977.

Davidson, James W. *The Island of Formosa Past and Present.* London: Macmillan and Co., 1903.

Day, A. Grove. *Pirates of the Pacific.* New York: Meredith Press, 1968.

Eyton, Lawrence. *Shattering the Myths: Taiwanese Identity and the Legacy of KMT Colonialism.* Taipei: Yu Shan Press, 2004.

Fairbank, John King. *The United States and China.* Cambridge, Mass.: Harvard University Press, 1976.

Feigon, Lee. *Mao: A Reinterpretation.* Chicago: Ivan R. Dee, 2002.

Goddard, W. G. *Formosa: A Study in Chinese History.* London: Macmillan and Co. Ltd., 1996.

Hsu, Immanuel C. Y. *The Rise of Modern China.* Hong Kong: Oxford University Press, 1970.

Hung, Chein-chao. *A History of Taiwan.* Rimini, Italy: Cerchio Iniziative Editoriali, 2000.

Kagan, Richard C. *Chen Shui-bian: Building a Community and a Nation.* Taipei: Asia-Pacific Academic Exchange Foundation, 1998.

Kaplan, David E. *Fires of the Dragon: Politics, Murder, and the Kuomintang.* New York: Macmillan Publishing Company, 1992.

Keay, John. *India: A History.* London: HarperCollins, 2000.

Keliher, Macabe. *Out of China: Or Yu Yongshe's Tale of Formosa.* Taipei: SMC Publishing Inc., 2003.

Kerr, George H. *Formosa Betrayed.* London: Eyre & Spottiswoode (Publishers) Ltd., 1996.

_______. *Formosa: Licensed Revolution and the Home Rule Movement, 1895–1945.* Honolulu: University of Hawaii Press, 1974.

Kissinger, Henry. *The White House Years.* Boston: Little, Brown and Company, 1979.

Kubek, Anthony. *Ronald Reagan and Free China.* Tampa, Fla.: Hallberg Publishing Corporation, 2002.

Kwitney, Jonathan. *The Crimes of Patriots: A True Tale of Dope, Dirty Money, and the CIA.* New York: W. W. Norton & Company, 1987.
Lederer, William J. *A Nation of Sheep.* New York: W. W. Norton & Company, 1961.
Lee, Ao. *Martyrs' Shrine: The Story of the Reform Movement of 1898 in China.* Hong Kong: Oxford University Press Ltd., 2002.
Lin, April C. J., and Keating, Jerome F. *Island in the Stream: A Quick Case Study of Taiwan's Complex History.* Taipei: SMC Publishing Inc., 2000.
Lin, Mosei. *Public Education in Formosa Under the Japanese Administration: Historical and Analytical Study of the Development and the Cultural Problems.* New York: Columbia University Press, 1929.
Loh, Pichon P. Y. *The Kuomintang Debacle of 1949: Conquest or Collapse?* Boston: D. C. Heath and Company, 1965.
McCoy, Alfred W. *The Politics of Heroin in Southeast Asia.* Singapore: Harper & Row, Publishers, Inc., 1972.
Meisner, Maurice. *Mao's China and After: A History of the People's Republic.* New York: The Free Press, 1986.
Mendel, Douglas. *The Politics of Formosan Nationalism.* Berkeley: University of California Press, 1970.
Meskill, Johanna Menzel. *A Chinese Pioneer Family: The Lins of Wu-feng, Taiwan, 1729–1895.* Princeton, N.J.: Princeton University Press, 1979.
Peng, Ming-min. *A Taste of Freedom: Memoirs of a Formosan Independence Leader.* New York: Holt, Rinehart and Winston Inc., 1972.
Rankin, Karl Lott. *China Assignment.* Seattle: University of Washington Press, 1964.
Roy, Denny. *Taiwan: A Political History.* Ithaca, N.Y.: Cornell University Press, 2003.
Seagrave, Sterling. *Lords of the Rim.* London: Bantam Press, 1995.
_______. *The Soong Dynasty.* London: Sidgwick & Jackson Ltd., 1986.
Shackleton, Allan J. *Formosa Calling: An Eyewitness Account of the February 28th, 1947 Incident.* Upland, Calif.: The Taiwan Publishing Company, 1998.
Snow, Edgar. *Red Star Over China.* New York: Grove Weidenfeld, 1968.
Taylor, Jay. *The Generalissimo's Son: Chiang Ching-kuo and the Revolutions in China and Taiwan.* Cambridge, Mass.: Harvard University Press, 2000.
Tien, Hung-mao. *The Great Transition: Political and Social Change in the Republic of China.* Stanford, Calif.: Hoover Institute Press, 1989.
Treat, John Whittier. *Contemporary Japan and Popular Culture.* Honolulu: University of Hawaii Press, 1996.
Truman, Harry S. *Memoirs by Harry S. Truman: Volume Two, Years of Trial and Hope.* New York: Signet Books, 1956.
Tuchman, Barbara W. *Stilwell and the American Experience in China, 1911–45.* New York: Macmillan Company, 1970.

INDEX